Job Training Policy
in the
United States

Job Training Policy in the United States

Christopher J. O'Leary
Robert A. Straits
Stephen A. Wandner[*]
Editors

2004

W.E. Upjohn Institute for Employment Research
Kalamazoo, Michigan

Library of Congress Cataloging-in-Publication Data

Job training policy in the United States / Christopher J. O'Leary, Robert A. Straits, Stephen A. Wandner editors.

  p. cm.
 Includes bibliographical references and index.
 ISBN 0-88099-306-5 (pbk.: alk. paper)—ISBN 0-88099-307-3 (hardcover : alk. paper)
 1. Occupational training—Government policy—United States. 2. Occupational training—United States—Evaluation. I. O'Leary, Christopher J. II. Straits, Robert A. III. Wandner, Stephen A.
 HD5715.2.J626 2004
 331.25'92'0973—dc22

2004007770

W.E. Upjohn Institute for Employment Research
300 S. Westnedge Avenue
Kalamazoo, Michigan 49007–4686

The facts presented in this study and the observations and viewpoints expressed are the sole responsibility of the authors. They do not necessarily represent positions of the W.E. Upjohn Institute for Employment Research.

Cover design by J.R. Underhill.
Index prepared by Nancy Humphreys.
Printed in the United States of America.
Printed on recycled paper.

As it becomes like one of them,
we dedicate this book to our children.

Amanda, Erin, and Helen.
Erin and Tara.
Erica, Ian, Karin, and Laura.

Contents

Preface

Public job training programs funded by the U.S. Department of Labor (USDOL) are now 40 years old. Since their inception, the programs have evolved from strong federal control to significant local autonomy, from narrowly targeted to broadly available services, and from prescribed training options to significant customer choice. The evolution has been marked by four distinct stages. The 1962 Manpower Development and Training Act (MDTA) provided funding administered by regional offices of USDOL directly to job training providers delivering classroom training in local areas. The first elements of decentralized decision making were introduced by the Comprehensive Employment and Training Act (CETA), which superceded MDTA in 1973. CETA required establishment of local administrative entities, called "prime sponsors," to coordinate programs and competitively finance training providers. MDTA and CETA each targeted job training services to economically disadvantaged workers and youth. CETA was supplanted by the Job Training Partnership Act (JTPA) in 1982. JTPA continued the decentralization trend that CETA had begun by significantly reducing the federal and state role and replacing it with a well-developed performance management system. JTPA was a results-driven job training program, which added dislocated workers as an eligible client group.

The Workforce Investment Act (WIA) of 1998 replaced JTPA. WIA retained local administration but created a customer focus to programs with universal access and a greater reliance on market mechanisms. It expanded the array of job training, education, and employment services that could be accessed by customers, and mandated that one-stop centers for employment services be created in every labor market throughout the country. Universal access to programs has welcomed a wide variety of customers into the system, many of whom are served through core and intensive services. The provision of training services changed radically with the introduction of vouchers (individual training accounts) to provide training, and choices limited to training providers certified as eligible by the local WIA administrator. To inform their choice, voucher recipients have access to performance information about potential training providers—including job placement rates—through a system of consumer reports on past performance of job training participants.

WIA included a sunset provision, with funding beyond five years after enactment of the original program requiring WIA reauthorization. The Bush administration proposed a number of incremental changes to the current program, the most important of which is the consolidation of all adult programs:

disadvantaged adult, dislocated worker, and the employment service funded under the Wagner-Peyser Act. This change would incorporate the public labor exchange into the basic WIA system.

This book looks at federally funded training programs as they exist today. It reviews what job training is and how training programs have been implemented under WIA. More specifically, it examines training service providers and methods of delivering training services, including the use of individual training accounts and eligible training provider lists. Performance management under WIA is examined, as well as the effectiveness of training programs. Public training programs are compared to private training provided in the United States and to public training programs provided in other industrialized nations.

We intend for this book to serve as a ready companion to two other volumes published by the W.E. Upjohn Institute for Employment Research: *Unemployment Insurance in the United States: Analysis of Policy Issues* (1997), and *Labor Exchange Policy in the United States* (2004). Previous overviews of research on public job training programs have concentrated mainly on the cost effectiveness of programs, rather than on their operations and institutional framework.

In 2000, Burt Barnow and Christopher King edited and authored *Improving the Odds: Increasing the Effectiveness of Publicly Funded Training*, published by the Urban Institute. That book examined evidence about what works in job training for a variety of adult and youth populations. However, from the beginning of WIA implementation, questions were raised about the way publicly funded job training was being chosen, and about the nature of incentives for local administrators. Indeed, an expert panel, convened soon after WIA enactment to propose a broad five-year plan for research and evaluation, emphasized the need to learn more about the intermediaries who deliver job training and other employment services for the one-stop centers. This book supplements Barnow and King (2000) by delving into the institutional details of job training service delivery.

Draft chapters for this book were prepared for a conference jointly sponsored by the W.E. Upjohn Institute for Employment Research and USDOL, held in September 2002 at Brook Lodge in Augusta, Michigan. At the conference, authors presented overviews of their chapters, and discussants provided constructive critiques aimed at improving the coverage and exposition of chapters. Other employment program and policy experts in attendance added further suggestions from the floor. In addition to all conference participants (listed at the back of this book), we thank others who contributed to this effort, including publications and administrative staff at the Upjohn Institute: Claire Black, Allison Hewitt Colosky, Kevin Hollenbeck, and Phyllis Molhoek.

As editors, we are responsible for errors of fact or policy judgment. The authors and editors have been free to express their own opinions. Consequently, the text does not necessarily reflect the positions or viewpoints of the W.E. Upjohn Institute for Employment Research, USDOL, or other organizations with which chapter authors and the book editors are associated.

Christopher J. O'Leary
Robert A. Straits
Stephen A. Wandner

1
U.S. Job Training

Types, Participants, and History

Christopher J. O'Leary
Robert A. Straits
Stephen A. Wandner

Job training is a pervasive aspect of American life. Wage and salary employment is the single largest source of aggregate personal income in the United States. Every person holding a job has benefited from job training. Although most job training in the United States is undertaken by private employers in their normal course of doing business, each year hundreds of thousands of Americans in precarious economic conditions use publicly funded job training as a path to employment.

The focus of this book is on the government role in job training. To place this examination in perspective, the book also includes reviews of private job training efforts and an international comparison of government job training programs. The chapters review the effectiveness of major federal job training programs, examine important features of current programs, and speculate about directions for future job training programs.

This book is directed mainly to employment policymakers and practitioners at the local, state, and federal levels. The exposition is relatively concise and nontechnical. However, sufficient detail is included in footnotes and references to make the book a useful resource for students, researchers, consultants, and policy scholars.

TYPES OF JOB TRAINING

Job training involves teaching someone the skills required to do a job competently. It is distinct from general education because of the exclusive focus on preparation for employment. Job training can range from remedial training, which teaches people the skills they need to learn other skills, to very sophisticated occupation specific training, which teaches people detailed procedures to perform at a high level in a specific occupation. An overview of job training types is provided in Table 1.1.

Job training usually refers to short-term occupational skill training to increase job readiness. The popular notion of job training comes from the common experience in a school classroom. However, general occupational job skills training in an institutional classroom setting away from the workplace is only one of many types of job training which are used in a wide variety of settings.

Ideally, job training is selected to address the component of aggregate unemployment resulting from a structural mismatch between job seekers and job vacancies, so that training is targeted to occupations with local job vacancies. Classroom job training may be customized to fill the request of an employer with available job slots; such training could either be privately or publicly funded. Alternatively, choice of the training type and provider may be exercised by the participant through a publicly funded job training voucher program. When vouchers are used, choice for eligible training participants is framed by rules regarding eligible training provider quality and local occupational labor demand.

Job skill training may also be provided in an experiential private sector workplace setting through on-the-job training (OJT). Learning by watching someone else is one of the oldest types of occupational skill training. Such training may be paid for either privately or publicly, and may provide skills valued only in the context of the particular establishment or more generally in the job market. When OJT is privately financed, costs may be shared by trainees through lower wages (Barron, Berger, and Black 1997). When OJT is provided by a public agency, it is sometimes called work experience. Work experience may

Table 1.1 Types of Job Training

Occupational skill training

Provided in group setting is called institutional or classroom training and usually for occupations in general demand.

Customized is designed to suit the specific requests of an employer with available job slots or employees already on-board.

Vouchers are a vehicle to allow participants to choose among approved topics and training providers.

Skill training provided in an experiential workplace setting is referred to as on-the-job training **(OJT)**.

When OJT is provided through a public agency it is sometimes called **work experience**.

Remedial training

General training which seeks to remedy basic gaps in reading and mathematics skills to make job seekers ready for skill training.

Classroom soft skills training

Conveys knowledge about proper workplace behavior or job search skills.

Postemployment training

Combines classroom and practical activities intended to promote retention and advancement within a given career path.

Youth training programs

Basic skills training in a workplace context, support for further general education and credentials, mentoring, school-to-work and school-to-apprenticeship transition services, intensive residential education and occupation and job training.

be either volunteer or paid, and it may be either unsubsidized or publicly subsidized.

Direct job creation programs also have a training dimension in that they provide knowledge and practice in basic workplace behaviors such as punctuality, cleanliness, and cooperation. Practice in such behaviors through community service employment can be valuable to both new workforce entrants and to prevent deterioration of such established skills among the long term unemployed (Cook, Adams, and Rawlins 1985).

When job seekers possess neither the occupational skills in demand locally, nor the fundamental abilities required to acquire such skills, often remedial training is appropriate—that is, general training which seeks to remedy basic gaps in reading and mathematics skills to make job seekers ready for skill training. It is common for such training to be provided through local school districts with funding from federal, state, and local sources. However, increasingly employers have found it profitable to provide such training in classroom settings at the job site (Hollenbeck 1993).

In addition to occupational skill training, OJT, and remedial education, short-term job readiness training may include what is sometimes called "classroom soft skill training." This includes knowledge about workplace behavior skills or job search skills. Such training is often publicly funded and available through arrangement with the public employment service.

A relatively recent form of publicly funded job training is called postemployment training. It may combine classroom, laboratory, and related activities which are directly linked to continued employment and advancement in a specific job or occupational field. Such retention and advancement efforts have become more prominent as welfare policy has become focused on employment as a means of economic self sufficiency (Rangarajan, Schochet, and Chu 2002).

Publicly funded job training programs in the United States also often provide supportive services for training participants. These include help with child care, transportation, health care, and other personal matters, including counseling for domestic relations or substance abuse.

Youth programs include basic skills training with a workplace context and integrated with occupational skills testing, tutoring, and study skills training; alternative high school services; instruction leading to high school completion or the equivalent; mentoring; limited internships in the private sector; training and education combined with community and youth service opportunities in public agencies, nonprofit agencies and other appropriate agencies; entry-level employment experience; school-to-work transition services; school-to-postsecondary transition services; school-to-apprenticeship transition services; preemployment and work maturity skills training, and support services (including limited needs based cash payments).

States also provide customized training to employers for their new hires and incumbent workers. In 1999, 45 states had customized training programs, and the total spending on these programs in 1998–1999 was $593 million. Most of this training was funded from state general revenue or from state taxes that were offset from the state unemployment insurance taxes (Ducha and Graves 1999).

FEDERALLY FUNDED JOB TRAINING IN THE UNITED STATES

Federal lawmakers clearly expose ideologies when debating job training policy. Some have asserted a responsibility to assist individuals who cannot support themselves, calling government assistance an entitlement. Others contend that public assistance obliges the recipient to work in exchange for government support. In the end, laws concerning employment and training policy usually have been shaped from input across the political spectrum, even during the few times that one political party has controlled both the legislative and executive branches of federal government.

As a result of bipartisan negotiation, most federal employment and training laws include provisions for program evaluation. Furthermore, employment laws often have "sunset" provisions which terminate programs failing to demonstrate sufficient cost effectiveness.

Government action to promote employment in the United States has always been prompted by crisis. The federal–state Unemployment Insurance (UI) program was conceived in the widespread hardship experienced from job loss during the Great Depression of the 1930s.

Federal training policy also had its origin in depression era "New Deal" programs for public works. Renewed training efforts thirty years later were greatly influenced by new economic goals and the resulting political struggles fought during President Johnson's "War on Poverty." A summary of the four main postwar federal job training programs is provided in Table 1.2.

Manpower Development and Training Act

The Manpower Development and Training Act (MDTA) of 1962 was marketed to the American public as an antipoverty program. With MDTA, the federal government pursued a centralized and categorical approach to eradicating poverty. Job training was targeted to the low income and welfare recipient populations. Funds were available on a formula basis to communities based on population and estimates of the proportion below the poverty income level.

The federal government managed MDTA funding through 12 regional offices of the U.S. Department of Labor, each of which supervised activity in between four and six states. Sometimes competing agencies within localities bid against each other for federal funding by submitting separate proposals to regional offices for review. Federal grants often did not jibe with one another and occasionally were a duplication of effort. The need for high-level coordination became painfully obvious.

Sunset provisions ended the MDTA in 1969. Though some evaluations had been done by that time, evidence about job training effectiveness did not prevent reauthorization (Mangum 1968). The prime reasons for the demise of MDTA were the administrative structure whereby the authority of state and local political entities was circumvented with federal contracts going directly to local service providers, and the duplication of service delivery at the local level.

Job Corps

The Job Corps, a one-year residential program for disadvantaged youth, was established in 1964 by the Economic Opportunity Act. It provides remedial academic instruction, job training, and other support services. It has remained largely unchanged over the years.

Table 1.2 A Chronology of Federal Job Training Programs in the United States

Program	Training types	Eligibility	Intergovernmental relations
Manpower Development and Training Act (MDTA), 1962	Institutional and on-the-job training (OJT).	Low income and welfare recipients.	Federal funding granted directly from 12 regional offices to agencies in local areas. Administration and reporting structures similar.
Comprehensive Employment and Training Act (CETA), 1973	On-the-job training, classroom skill training, classroom soft skills training, work experience in public agencies, and Public Service Employment (PSE).	Training was targeted to low income persons, welfare recipients, and disadvantaged youth.	Federal funding granted to prime sponsors in substate regions which numbered about 470. Performance monitoring with results reported to the U.S. Department of Labor (USDOL).
Job Training Partnership Act (JTPA), 1982	On-the-job training, Classroom skill training, Classroom soft skills training, and Work experience in public agencies.	Low income, public assistance recipients, dislocated workers, and disadvantaged youth.	Federal funding through state governors to private industry councils (PICs) in each of 640 service delivery areas. PIC performance reports to governors who reported to USDOL.
Workforce Investment Act (WIA), 1998	On-the-job training, Customized classroom skill training, Classroom soft skills training, and Work experience in public agencies.	Access to core services like job search skills and job referral is unrestricted. Training is targeted to the most difficult to reemploy.	Like JTPA, but PICs became fewer (600) workforce investment boards (WIBs) with private sector majority membership. Monitoring is reduced relative to JTPA practice.

SOURCE: O'Leary and Straits (2004).

The first major evaluation of Job Corps was quasi-experimental (Mallar et al. 1980). It found modest positive effects on employment and weekly earnings but no impact on hourly wage rates. A recent study was done as a classically designed field experiment. That study found that Job Corps participation results in significant earnings gains for disadvantaged youth. "Furthermore, earnings gains, educational progress, and other positive changes were found across most groups of participants and are expected to persist as they get older" (Burghardt et al. 2001). Among training programs for youth, evaluation research finds that the interventions most likely to work are intensive, costly, and of relatively long duration.

Comprehensive Employment and Training Act

The 1970s brought a more comprehensive approach to addressing the problems of the economically disadvantaged. Decentralization became the employment policy theme for the decade. It involved the transfer of decision-making authority from the federal to state and local governments. Authority as defined in the legislation and regulations often included responsibility for designing, implementing, and evaluating program activities.

The Comprehensive Employment and Training Act (CETA) of 1973 introduced the concept of a local advisory board to assure that local public interest would guide program planning. The private industry council membership and role were established in the regulations, and in some localities representation was "guaranteed" for constituencies like education and labor. CETA job training was targeted to the economically disadvantaged, welfare recipients, and disadvantaged youth.

Three main findings emerged from 11 major CETA evaluations (Leigh 1990, p. 11). First, there were no measurable employment or earnings impacts for men; however, impacts for women were positive and significant. Second, OJT training is usually more effective than classroom training. Finally, the range of impact estimates was quite wide, despite the fact that all analysts used the same CLMS reporting data. However, it was journalists rather than economists who brought the end to CETA. The pubic service employment component of CETA became a target for national media criticism when careless management of funds and enrollment of program ineligibles were widely reported.

Job Training Partnership Act

The arrival of the Reagan administration in 1981 came with a "conservative challenge on the principles, policies, and programs of the liberal tradition of federal activism in economic and social affairs as it evolved in the half of the century starting with the New Deal" (Palmer 1987, p. 9). A major objective of Reagan-era legislation was to increase earnings and employment as well as decrease welfare dependency. Classroom skill training was identified as a major weakness of existing programs because it was often not the kind of training desired by local employers.

The Job Training Partnership Act (JTPA) of 1982 limited training choices to skills that were in demand by local employers. JTPA also increased the private sector share of members on the advisory committees to ensure that their interests were taken into consideration. Evaluation was an integral part of the program, which was said to be performance-driven through a system of performance standards for participant reemployment rates and earnings. Absent from JTPA was anything remotely resembling public service employment. In response to the widespread layoffs associated with economic restructuring in American business during the 1980s, JTPA job training was targeted to dislocated workers in addition to the economically disadvantaged and welfare recipients.

The performance standards system allowed governors receiving federal JTPA training grants to structure incentive systems, thereby simplifying relationships with substate areas. The performance monitoring system changed training program management and intergovernmental relations. It also complicated the net impact evaluation of programs by introducing the risk of *cream skimming* in program assignment. That is, program managers might select mainly the most able applicants for participation. The result is high observed reemployment rates, although many of the selected program participants may already possess the skills and abilities to get reemployed themselves.

To assure an objective net impact evaluation, Congress authorized a major national evaluation of JTPA based on methods of field experimentation with random assignment of subjects both to training and to comparison groups in 16 sites across the country. Orr et al. (1996, p. 109) report that training to economically disadvantaged adults resulted in 11 percent greater earnings for women and 6.7 percent greater earnings for men. For both genders the earnings gains were mainly due to increases in hours worked. There were positive net benefits to both men and women, and the net benefit to society for both genders was just over $500 per participant (Orr et al. 1996, p. 189).

An evaluation of dislocated worker programs was initiated during the 1990s but was cancelled in anticipation of substantial program changes resulting from implementation of a new dislocated worker program under the Workforce Investment Act. An evaluation of the new dislocated worker program is now needed.

Our focus on the main job training programs for economically disadvantaged and dislocated workers should not obscure the fact that the number of federal job training programs had proliferated to the point that by the early 1990s there were 163 distinct programs receiving funding (U.S. General Accounting Office 1994). While the great majority of these were small and targeted, including, for example, a variety of distinct programs for separate native American groups, the overlapping management burdens from the large number were seen as a problem. Funding streams for job training of particular target groups sometimes originated in two or more executive departments.

During 1999, which was the final year of JTPA authorization, there were 40 major employment and training programs funded by seven executive departments of the federal government (U.S. General Accounting Office 2000). Two-thirds of the total funding went to just six programs, three of which were JTPA dislocated workers, JTPA summer youth, and Job Corps.

Workforce Investment Act

By the late 1990s, economic conditions had improved to the point where full employment existed in most of the United States. The more than 30 years of searching for ways to reduce poverty through employment policy evolved into a new approach that shifts responsibility from government to the individual, and divests authority from the federal government to the states. It exchanges an emphasis on skill training as a path to economic security for an emphasis on job placement leading to self-sufficiency and a reduced dependence on public assistance payment.

Two pieces of legislation signed into law by President Clinton, the Personal Responsibility and Work Opportunity Act (PRWORA) of 1996 and then the Workforce Investment Act (WIA) of 1998, illustrate the intended change in federal human resources policy towards self sufficiency and local control.

PRWORA reformed the nation's welfare laws. A new system of block grants from the federal government to the states named Temporary Assistance for Needy Families (TANF) was created, changing the nature and provision of welfare benefits in America. A key feature of the new law was a five-year lifetime time limit on cash assistance.

WIA, signed into law on August 7, 1998, includes many of the political characteristics that are in the PRWORA. It reforms federal job training programs and creates a new comprehensive workforce investment system. The reformed system is intended to be customer focused, to help individuals access the tools they need to manage their careers through information and high-quality services, and to help employers find skilled workers.

Key innovations brought by WIA are 1) one-stop career centers where all employment and training programs are assembled in one physical location; 2) individual training accounts which act as vouchers for job seekers requiring skills improvement for labor market success; 3) universal access to core employment services with sequential, more restricted access to intensive services and training; and 4) accountability monitored through performance indicators.

JOB TRAINING EXPENDITURES AND PARTICIPANTS

While WIA offers broadened eligibility for core employment services, job training remains targeted to economically disadvantaged and dislocated workers. The mix of funding types supported during fiscal year 2001, which was the first full year of WIA operation, is summarized in Table 1.3. Expenditure estimates indicate that a total of nearly $68 billion was spent on job training during fiscal year 2001. Of this,

Table 1.3 Estimated Expenditures for Job Training Programs in the United States, Fiscal Year 2001 (thousands of dollars)

Programs	Federal funding ($)	Share of federal funding (%)	State supplemental funding ($)	State financed customized FY 1998 ($)	Employer financed 1998 ($)	Grand total of funding ($)
Adult and dislocated worker activities	2,540,040	39.6				
Youth activities	1,377,965	21.5				
Job Corps (youth)	1,399,148	21.8				
National programs	528,150	8.2				
Other programs (Non-WIA)	4,500	0.1				
TAA training	94,400	1.5				
NAFTA training	37,150	0.6				
CSE for older Americans	440,200	6.9				
Total funding	6,421,553	100.0	276,621	593,191	60,700,000	67,991,365
Percentage of grand total of funding	9.4		0.4	0.9	89.3	100.0

NOTE: WIA: Workforce Investment Act; TAA: Trade Adjustment Assistance; NAFTA: North American Free Trade Act; CSE: Community service employment.
SOURCE: Wandner, Balducchi, and Spickard (2001).

89.3 percent was privately financed by American employers, 9.4 percent by the federal government, and 1.3 percent by state governments.

International comparative statistics from the Organization for Economic Cooperation and Development (OECD) set the total federal expenditures on job training programs in the year 2000 at 0.04 percent of gross domestic product (GDP). As shown in Table 1.4 this level places the United States in the bottom 20 percent of OECD member nations in terms of government spending on job training. Among the top five spending national governments in 2000, only Germany is among the world's leading industrial nations. Public spending on job training in Japan and the United Kingdom closely matches that of the United States.

Considering spending on all active labor market programs (ALMPs) in 2000—which include the public employment service, wage subsidies, and programs for the disabled and youth—federal job training expenditures amount to 26.7 percent of spending on ALMPs in the United States. Within the broader category of expenditures on all U.S. labor market programs (LMPs)—which for the United States adds UI benefit payments to ALMPs—job training amounted to 10.5 percent of all labor market programs in 2000. So while the United States ranks low among OECD countries in public job training expenditures as a share of GDP, among government labor market programs job training is a relatively important activity in the United States compared to other countries.[1]

Among the fiscal year 2001 federal spending on job training, Table 1.3 shows that 39.6 percent went to adult disadvantaged and dislocated workers, 43.3 percent to youth programs (Job Corps and others), 6.9 percent to community service employment for older workers, and 2.1 percent to workers impacted by changing patterns of international trade.

Background characteristics for participants in the three main federally funded employment and training programs are summarized in Table 1.5. Among 113,774 adult participants (JTPA Title II-A) who received more than just assessment in program year 1999, most were female (65 percent), most had at least completed high school (78 percent), the ethnic make-up included 35 percent black and 16 percent Hispanic, disabled amounted to 7 percent, 26 percent were on public

Table 1.4 Government Expenditures on Job Training as a Percentage of GDP in OECD Countries, 2000

Country	Training	As a percentage of GDP		Training as a percentage of spending on	
		ALMPs	LMPs	ALMPs	LMPs
Denmark	0.84	1.55	4.51	54.2	18.6
Finland	0.35	1.07	3.29	32.7	10.6
Germany	0.34	1.23	3.12	27.6	10.9
Sweden	0.31	1.38	2.72	22.5	11.4
Netherlands	0.30	1.57	3.65	19.1	8.2
Portugal**	0.30	0.51	1.34	58.8	22.4
Spain	0.29	0.84	2.18	34.5	13.3
France	0.28	1.36	3.12	20.6	9.0
Belgium*	0.25	1.36	3.70	18.4	6.8
New Zealand	0.18	0.55	2.17	32.7	8.3
Austria	0.17	0.49	1.58	34.7	10.8
Canada	0.17	0.51	1.49	33.3	11.4
Greece**	0.17	0.35	0.83	48.6	20.5
Italy*	0.12	0.63	1.28	19.1	9.4
Korea	0.09	0.46	0.55	19.6	16.4
Switzerland	0.09	0.48	1.05	18.8	8.6
Norway	0.08	0.77	1.16	10.4	6.9
Hungary	0.07	0.40	0.88	17.5	8.0
United Kingdom	0.05	0.36	0.94	13.9	5.3
Mexico*	0.04	0.08	0.08	50.0	50.0
United States	0.04	0.15	0.38	26.7	10.5
Japan	0.03	0.28	0.82	10.7	3.7
Australia	0.02	0.45	1.50	4.4	1.3
Czech Republic	0.02	0.22	0.52	9.1	3.9
Poland	0.01	0.15	0.96	6.7	1.0

NOTE: *1999; **1998. Where GDP is gross domestic product, ALMP is active labor market programs, and LMP is labor market programs. No data available for OECD countries: Iceland, Ireland, Luxembourg, Slovak Republic, and Turkey.
SOURCE: OECD (2001).

Table 1.5 Characteristics and Outcomes of JTPA Training Participants, PY 1999

Characteristics	Adult Title II-A	Youth Title II-C	Dislocated workers Title III
Number of program participants	113,774	58,548	189,794
Female (%)	65	58	54
Aged 14–15 (%)		7	
Aged 16–21 (%)		93	
Aged 22–54 (%)	97		89
Over 55 (%)	3		11
Less than high school (%)	22	71	11
High school (%)	56	26	50
Post high school (%)	22	3	39
Black (%)	35	34	19
Hispanic origin (%)	16	23	13
White (%)	43	38	62
Disabled individual (%)	7	12	2
Welfare recipient (%)	26	19	2
Ex-offender (%)	18	13	5
UI recipient (%)	10	1	69
UI exhaustee (%)	3	1	5
Veteran (%)	6		11
Outcomes			
Entered employment rate (%)	68	47	69
Average hourly wage ($)	8.75	7.07	11.95

SOURCE: Social Policy Research Associates (2001).

welfare assistance, 10 percent were UI recipients, and 6 percent were military veterans.

Among 58,548 youth participants (JTPA Title II-C) who received more than just assessment in PY 1999, a majority were female (58 percent), some (7 percent) were very young workers (aged 14 to 15), most had not yet completed high school (71 percent), the ethnic make-up included 34 percent black and 23 percent Hispanic, disabled amounted to 12 percent, 19 percent were on public welfare assistance, and only 1 percent qualified to be UI recipients.

The JTPA program provided more than just assessment to 189,794 dislocated workers in PY 1999. Of these, a slight majority were female (54 percent), the great majority (89 percent) were prime-aged workers, a sizeable proportion (39 percent) had education beyond high school completion, the ethnic make-up included 19 percent black and 13 percent Hispanic, disabled amounted to 2 percent, only 2 percent were on public welfare assistance, and 69 percent were UI recipients.

The bottom of Table 1.5 provides some gross outcome information for participants in the three major JTPA-funded programs. Entered employment was 68 and 69 percent for the adult and dislocated worker programs, respectively, while it was 47 percent for the youth program. For youth, sizeable proportions also achieved an employment enhancement or competency which JTPA also regards as success. Among those entering employment at program exit, hourly earnings rates were estimated to be $8.75, $7.07, and $11.95 for adult, youth, and dislocated workers, respectively.

PROLOGUE

This introductory chapter has provided background for the examination of public job training policy in the United States. A review of evidence from evaluation studies of prior job training programs in the next two chapters completes setting the context for a consideration of current and future job training programs. The subsequent three chapters of this book address issues critical to implementation of the new job training strategy established by WIA. This is followed by an examination of the private sector role in job training which involves mainly employed, or incumbent, workers. An international comparison of public efforts in job training rounds out the exposition. We then offer speculation about future directions for public job training in the United States.

Evaluation of job training in the United States has involved both monitoring gross outcomes through performance management systems, and estimation of net program impacts through comparison group designs. In Chapter 2, "Performance Management of U.S. Job Training Programs," Burt Barnow and Jeff Smith review the development, use, and incentive effects of performance monitoring under CETA and JTPA, and they speculate on the practicality and value of the new approach being tried under WIA. They offer suggestions on ways to improve the implementation and use of performance management systems.

Chris King in Chapter 3 reviews a vast literature on evaluation of federally funded job training programs in the United States, and identifies the population groups and economic contexts where particular types of job training have been most effective.

WIA operations began in most states on the officially designated starting date of July 1, 2000. Ron D'Amico and Jeffrey Salzman provide an overview of the experience to date in Chapter 4, "Implementation Issues in Delivering Training Services to Adults under WIA."

A core theme of WIA is the market orientation of job training selection which involves disclosure by training providers on service effectiveness and informed choice among alternative training services by participants. Janet Javar and Steve Wandner examine mechanisms for screening and certifying job training institutions and other labor market intermediaries in Chapter 5, "The Use of Service Providers and Brokers/Consultants in Employment and Training Programs."

Expression of individual choice in job training selection is facilitated under WIA by the use of job training vouchers. However, the job training market is not laissez faire. Vouchers are government funded and customer choice is bounded by information on occupational job demand and job training provider quality. Using information from a classically designed field experiment, Paul Decker and Irma Perez-Johnson in Chapter 6 examine "Individual Training Accounts and Eligible Provider Lists" under WIA.

The focus of this book is on government-funded job training programs. However, American employers spend nine dollars on job training for every dollar spent by government agencies. Robert Lerman,

Signe-Mary McKernan, and Stephanie Riegg balance our investigation with Chapter 7, "The Scope of Employer-Provided Training in the United States: Who, What, Where, and How Much?" Their summary aims to identify areas where public expenditure may fruitfully supplement employer-provided job training.

In Chapter 8, "International Experience with Job Training," Lori Kletzer and William Koch view American job training policies in a broader context. They examine U.S. policy and experience compared with that in selected developed and developing nations. In the concluding chapter, we, the editors of this book, speculate on "Public Job Training: Experience and Prospects" based on the job training experience and trends in the United States and other countries.

Notes

Opinions expressed are those of neither the W.E. Upjohn Institute nor the U.S. Department of Labor, but are those of the authors. Errors and omissions are also ours.

1. These comparisons abstract from the Earned Income Tax Credit (EITC) paid to low-income workers with dependent children in the United States. In recent years the EITC, which is essentially a targeted wage subsidy, totaled about $30 billion or roughly equal to the total expenditures for LMPs listed in the text.

References

Barron, John M., Mark C. Berger, and Dan A. Black. 1997. *On-the-Job Training*. Kalamazoo, MI: W.E. Upjohn Institute for Employment Research.

Burghardt, John, Peter Z. Schochet, Sheena McConnell, Terry Johnson, R. Mark Gritz, Steven Glazerman, John Homrighausen, and Russell Jackson. 2001. "Does Job Corps Work? Summary of the National Job Corps Study." Document No. PR01-50. Princeton, NJ: Mathematica Policy Research, Inc., June.

Cook, Robert F., Charles F. Adams, and V. Lane Rawlins. 1985. *Public Service Employment: The Experience of a Decade*. Kalamazoo, MI: W.E. Upjohn Institute for Employment Research.

Ducha, Steve, and Wanda Lee Graves. 1999. "State Financed and Customized Training Programs." Research and Evaluation Report Series 99-E. Washington, DC: U.S. Department of Labor, Employment and Training Administration.

Hollenbeck, Kevin. 1993. *Classrooms in the Workplace*. Kalamazoo, MI: W.E. Upjohn Institute for Employment Research.

Leigh, Duane E. 1990. *Does Training Work for Displaced Workers?: A Survey of Existing Evidence*. Kalamazoo, MI: W.E. Upjohn Institute for Employment Research.

Mallar, Charles, Stuart Kerachsky, Craig Thornton, and David Long. 1980. "An Evaluation of the Economic Impact of the Job Corps Program." Project Report 80-60. Princeton, NJ: Mathematica Policy Research, Inc.

Mangum, Garth L. 1968. *MDTA: Foundation of Federal Manpower Policy*. Baltimore: Johns Hopkins Press.

OECD. 2001. *OECD Employment Outlook*. Paris: Organization for Economic Cooperation and Development, June.

O'Leary, Christopher J., and Robert A. Straits. 2004. "Intergovernmental Relations in Employment Policy: The United States Experience." In *Federalism and Labour Market Policy: Comparing Different Governance and Employment Strategies*, Alain Noël, ed. Montreal and Kingston: McGill-Queen's University Press, pp. 25–82.

Orr, Larry L., Howard S. Bloom, Stephen H. Bell, Fred Doolittle, Winston Lin, and George Cave. 1996. *Does Training for the Disadvantaged Work? Evidence from the National JTPA Study*. Washington, DC: The Urban Institute Press.

Palmer, John L. 1987. "The Next Decade: The Economic, Political, and Social Context of Employment and Training Policies." *Policy Studies Review* 6(4): 685–694.

Rangarajan, Anu, Peter Schochet, and Dexter Chu. 2002. "Targeting Job Retention Services for Welfare Recipients." In *Targeting Employment Services*, Randall W. Eberts, Christopher J. O'Leary, and Stephen A. Wandner, eds. Kalamazoo, MI: W.E. Upjohn Institute for Employment Research, pp. 245–268.

Social Policy Research Associates. 2001. *PY 99 SPIR Data Book*. Oakland, CA: Social Policy Research Associates.

U.S. General Accounting Office. 1994. *Multiple Employment and Training Programs: Overlapping Programs Can Add Unnecessary Costs*. GAO/HEHS-94-80. Washington, DC: U.S. Government Printing Office, January.

———. 2000. *Multiple Employment and Training Programs: Overlapping Programs Indicate Need for Closer Examination of Structure*. GAO-01-71. Washington, DC: U.S. Government Printing Office, October.

Wandner, Stephen A., David E. Balducchi, and Amanda B. Spickard. 2001. "Expenditures on Active and Passive Labor Market Policy in the United States Estimates for Fiscal Year 2001." Paper presented at the international workshop "Active Labor Market Programs: Improvement of Effectiveness," sponsored by Ministry of Labor and Social Development of the Russian Federation, World Bank, and Russian Foundation for Social Reforms, October 2–3, Moscow.

2
Performance Management of U.S. Job Training Programs

Burt S. Barnow
Jeffrey A. Smith

This chapter reviews the effects of performance management systems in federally sponsored employment and training programs. We focus on programs for the disadvantaged because they have the longest history, but the lessons generalize to other programs. We find in our survey that most of the evidence on the effects of performance systems relates to their failure to motivate behavior in the direction of increasing the mean impact of program participation, and their success at inducing cream skimming and strategic responses on the part of program operators. At the same time, little or nothing is known about the effects of performance systems on assignment to service types or on the technical efficiency of program operation. We recommend further research to fill in gaps in our knowledge as well as policy changes to reflect the knowledge we already have.

The remainder of the chapter proceeds as follows. The next section lays out the theory behind performance management systems in government programs. The third section provides the historical background on the use of performance management in U.S. employment and training programs, followed in the fourth section by a discussion of the available evidence on incentive effects in employment and training programs. The final section provides conclusions and recommendations.

THEORETICAL BACKGROUND

Here we explore why an incentive-based system might be useful in employment and training programs, and why existing performance management systems take the form they do. We draw primarily upon research on the Job Training Partnership Act (JTPA). The JTPA program was the primary federal training program for the disadvantaged from 1982 through 1998, at which time the Workforce Investment Act (WIA) program replaced it.[1]

The Purpose of Performance Management Systems

Consider the JTPA program (the same issues arise in WIA). This program involved the federal, state, and local levels of government. The federal government funded the program and set its broad outlines. Administration was partly devolved to the state level, and operation was primarily the responsibility of local entities. The key problem with such an arrangement is that the state and local governments, and their contractors, may have goals different from those of the federal government. In the language of economics, such multilevel programs involve a principal–agent problem in which the federal government (the principal) tries to get its agents (state and local governments and their contractors in JTPA and WIA) to further its program goals.[2] See Prendergast (1999) and Dixit (2002) for theoretical discussions of principal–agent problems.

A first step in solving principal–agent problems is for the principal to define its goals. As Dixit (2002) points out, ascertaining the goals of federal programs is not always a simple matter, and even when they are clear, there are often multiple, partially conflicting goals representing the aims of different stakeholders. In the case of JTPA, Section 141 of the statute states that opportunities for training are to be provided to "those who can benefit from, and are most in need of, such opportunities." Furthermore, the statute states in Section 106, which describes the program's performance management system, that training should be considered an investment and that "it is essential that criteria for measuring the return on this investment be developed and . . . the basic measures of performance for adult training programs under Title II are the increases in employment and earnings and the reductions in welfare dependency resulting from the participation in the program."

The statute clearly indicates both equity (serving the hard-to-serve) and efficiency (maximizing the net gain) goals for the program. As we discuss below, these goals may or may not conflict in practice. For the moment, take them as given and consider the question of how the federal government gets the state and local players in JTPA to further its goals. Under JTPA, the federal money for the program was first distributed to the states by formula and then further distributed to local areas known as "service delivery areas" (SDAs).[3] The SDAs then selected from one or more of the following options: 1) delivering services themselves, 2) contracting with for-profit organizations, 3) contracting with nonprofit organizations, typically community colleges or community-based organizations, and 4) making individual referrals to for-profit or nonprofit organizations.

States, SDAs, and the for-profit and nonprofit service providers under contract to the SDAs may each have goals that differ in whole or in part from those of the federal government. States may wish to promote use of their community college systems, or economic development in specific regions. Local governments may reduce the training given to each participant below the optimal amount in order to provide services to a larger number of participants (voters), or they may allocate funds to activities based on popularity with voters rather than based on the present value of the earnings gains.[4] For-profit vendors want to maximize profits, so they will follow the incentives implicit in a performance standards system, whether or not those incentives promote program goals. Nonprofit vendors may emphasize service to particular ethnic, religious, or target groups. They may also emphasize service to "hard to serve" clients.

The JTPA performance standards system sought, and the similar system under WIA seeks, to provide incentives for the lower level actors in the system to do the bidding of the federal government, instead of pursuing their own objectives. The system did so by setting out concrete performance measures related (it was hoped) to program goals, and by providing budgetary rewards to SDAs based on their measured performance.

Why Performance Systems Take the Forms They Do

A performance management system requires measures of performance, standards that indicate acceptable performance, and rewards and sanctions (which need not be monetary) for organizations that exceed or fail to meet the standards. Performance-based contracting is a system where the vendor receives some or all of its compensation based on achieving certain performance goals. Both approaches attempt to align the interests of the agents with those of the principal, and performance-based contracting may be thought of as a special case of performance management.

Ideally, and in some cases in practice, the performance incentive system directly measures and rewards the government's goals. In our context, that means measuring and rewarding earnings impacts and service to the hard-to-serve. The latter is relatively straightforward, as it requires only measuring the characteristics of program participants. The former, however, is not straightforward. As is well known, measuring earnings impacts is not a trivial task because of the difficulty of estimating what labor market outcomes participants would have experienced, had they not participated.[5] Social experiments, the preferred way to estimate impacts, are expensive and time consuming, while nonexperimental methods are controversial. Moreover, as shown in Heckman and Smith (1999), because of "Ashenfelter's (1978) dip," the observed phenomenon that the mean earnings of participants in employment and training programs decline in the period prior to participation, before-after estimates will not be a reliable guide to program impacts. Instead, a comparison group of nonparticipants must be utilized, an undertaking likely to greatly increase the cost of the system.

Furthermore, the real goal is long-run earnings impacts, but waiting around for the long run makes little sense in administrative terms. For administrative purposes, quick feedback is required, so that agents perceive a clear link between their actions and the rewards and punishments they receive under the incentive system (see Blalock and Barnow 2001).

The difficulty in measuring program impacts, and the desire for quick response, leaves the federal government with three alternatives as it tries to get states and local agencies to advance its goals for the program. First, it can use fixed-price contracts. This leaves local governments, for-profit vendors, and nonprofit vendors to use the money they receive to pursue their own agendas, subject to regulatory restrictions, such as program eligibility rules, and to professional norms. Second, the government can use cost-based reimbursement schemes. However, it is well documented in the health literature that such an approach can lead to overuse of resources, which is another way of saying that impacts net of costs will not be maximized and, therefore, the government's goals will not be served. Finally, the federal government can adopt a system of performance incentives based on short-term outcome levels, rather than on long-term program impacts. As we discuss in detail below, such a system provides training centers and service providers, regardless of type, with many perverse incentives, so that even a for-profit vendor with no agenda of its own may not end up pursuing the government's goals.

Despite these potential problems, JTPA and WIA make the third choice and reward short-term outcome levels. In the usual notation, the JTPA and WIA systems reward based on short-term values of Y_1, the labor market outcome levels achieved by participants.[6] In contrast, the program's goal is the maximization of long-term values of $\Delta = Y_1 - Y_0$, where Y_0 is the counterfactual labor market outcome participants would experience if they did not participate, and as a result, Δ is the impact of participation.

HISTORICAL BACKGROUND

Performance management in employment and training programs began during the Comprehensive Employment and Training Act (CETA) period in the 1970s. It was formally incorporated into JTPA in the early 1980s. Unlike many of the performance management systems established in the wake of the Government Performance and Results Act of 1993 (GPRA), the JTPA system was designed primarily by economists who wanted to maximize the employment and earnings gains of participants. Most of the other systems devised in response to GPRA focus on management issues rather than on program impacts.

The JTPA program included a performance management system that provided rankings of the local SDAs. There were about 620 SDAs in the program, each with a geographic monopoly. Six percent of the JTPA budget was set aside for two purposes: 1) for performance awards to SDAs that performed well relative to performance standards based on the labor market outcome levels (not impacts) achieved by their participants in a given program year, and 2) for technical assistance for SDAs that failed to meet their performance standards.[7]

The JTPA performance standards system evolved considerably over its life from 1982 to 2000, when WIA replaced JTPA.[8] The short but controversial history of the JTPA performance standards system illustrates how successive attempts to develop an effective system led to new reforms, which in turn led to new concerns.[9]

Originally, JTPA had four performance measures for Title II-A: the entered employment rate, average wage at placement, cost per entered employment, and the entered employment rate for welfare recipients.[10] Although the statute called for measures to use gains in employment and earnings from before the program, the U.S. Department of Labor (USDOL) believed (incorrectly) that virtually all participants were unemployed prior to entry, so that the postprogram outcomes would represent before-after changes. Although the statute also called for postprogram measures, it was widely believed that postprogram standards should only be implemented after data were collected for several years to allow the setting of appropriate standards.

A desire to hold local programs harmless for variations in local economic conditions and the characteristics of their participants, combined with the fact that the people responsible for developing the system were mostly economists, led to the use of regression models to adjust the level of satisfactory performance for differences in local conditions and participant characteristics.[11] To implement these models, the system included the collection of data on participant characteristics and local economic conditions.

Governors had a great deal of discretion in the JTPA system. They could use the national standards without making any adjustments, they could use the USDOL regression model for their SDAs, they could use the regression model and make further adjustments to take account of unique features in their states, and they could develop their own adjustment procedures. Governors also could decide how to weight the various measures and could (and did) add additional measures. They also determined the "award function" that mapped SDA performance into budgetary rewards. These functions varied widely among states at a point in time and over time within states; see Courty and Marschke (2003) for a detailed description.

When 13-week postprogram employment and earnings data became available, four additional standards were added in program year (PY) 1988.[12] At this point, the employment and training community felt that there were too many performance measures, so as of PY 1990 all the measures at the time of termination were dropped and effectively replaced by the four measures based on the 13-week follow-up data. Another important development for PY 1990 was that the cost standard was dropped. This was done because it was widely believed (especially by providers of expensive long-term classroom training) that the cost standard was leading SDAs to focus too much on "quick fix" job search activities.[13] Although most states used the USDOL regression model to adjust the standards for local economic conditions and the characteristics of participants, some states did not do so. To encourage them to do so, USDOL required states not using its model to use an alternative adjustment procedure that met criteria set out by USDOL.

When WIA became operational in July 2000, the performance management system was modified in several significant ways.[14] Standards are now set for states as well as local areas, and the standards are "negotiated" rather than set by a regression model.[15] No automatic adjustments are made to take account of economic conditions or participant characteristics, but states may petition to the USDOL if circumstances have changed. The lack of a regression adjustment model is not based on statutory language. Indeed, while not requiring the use of a regression model, the statute states that the state-level standards are supposed to be set "taking into account factors including differences in economic conditions, the characteristics of participants when the participants entered the program, and the services to be provided." Like JTPA, WIA called for the use of before–after earnings change performance measures, although under JTPA this requirement was ignored and the earnings performance measures were based on levels of post-program earnings.[16]

There are a total of 17 core performance measures for WIA. For adults, dislocated workers, and youth ages 19–21, the core measures are defined as

- the entered employment rate,
- retention in employment six months after entry into employment,
- the earnings change from the six months prior to entry to the six months after exit, and

- the obtained credential rate for participants who enter unsubsidized employment or, in the case of older youth, enter postsecondary education, advanced training, or unsubsidized employment.

For youth between the ages of 14 and 18, the core performance measures are

- attainment of basic skills and, as appropriate, work readiness or occupational skills,

- attainment of a high school diploma or its equivalent, and

- placement and retention in postsecondary education and training, employment, or military service.

Finally, there are customer satisfaction measures for both participants and employers.

The changes to the performance management system from JTPA to WIA were significant, so we discussed the rationale for the changes with individuals involved in the process.[17] The WIA legislation did not require dropping the model-based performance management system used under JTPA, so the switch was based on preferences rather than necessity. Indeed, a workgroup of practitioners established to advise the Employment and Training Administration (ETA) recommended that a model-based system be retained.

There were several reasons for substituting a negotiated standards system for a model-based system. First, ETA wanted to signal that WIA was going to be different from JTPA, so change was considered good in its own right. Second, the group charged with developing the performance management system felt that under JTPA, the system was "looking back," and they believed that a negotiated standards system was prospective in nature rather than retrospective. Finally, a model-based system, by definition, requires that data for the regression models be collected. States indicated to ETA that they found the JTPA data collection requirements to be onerous, and they urged that the data collection be reduced under WIA. Although this would not require abandonment of a model-based system, it would support such a decision.

EVIDENCE ON PERFORMANCE INCENTIVE EFFECTS

In this section, we examine the literature on the effects of performance incentives on the behavior of local training centers—e.g., SDAs in JTPA and workforce investment boards (WIBs) in WIA—that provide employment and training services to the disadvantaged. We divide the possible effects into five categories, and then consider the evidence from the literature on each category in turn. The five categories flow out of (in part) the theoretical model presented in Heckman, Heinrich, and Smith (2002).

The first type of response consists of changes in the set of persons served. Performance incentives may induce programs to serve persons who will increase their likelihood of doing well relative to the outcomes measured by the incentives, rather than serving, say, the hard-to-serve. The second type of response consists of changes in the types of services provided conditional on who is served. Here the incentives may lead to changes that will maximize the short-term outcomes, such as employment at termination from the program (or shortly thereafter), emphasized in incentive systems, rather than long-term earnings gains. The third type of response consists of changes in the (technical) efficiency of service provision conditional on who is served and what services they receive. We have in mind here both the effect of incentives on on-the-job leisure, as well as their effects on the effort devoted to the design of office procedures and the like. The fourth type of response pertains to subcontracting. Training programs may change the set of providers they contract with, and may pass along (perhaps in modified form) their performance incentives to their providers. The latter will, in turn, affect the actions of those providers. Finally, the fifth type of response consists of gaming, whereby training centers take actions to affect their measured performance that do not affect their actual performance, other than indirect effects due to the diversion of time and resources.

In the remainder of this section, we summarize what is known from the employment and training literature about each of these responses. Much of the available evidence comes from a major experimental evaluation of the JTPA program funded by USDOL and conducted in the late 1980s. This evaluation, called the National JTPA

Study, took place at a nonrandom sample of 16 JTPA SDAs around the United States. The evaluation included both adult programs and out-of-school youth programs. See Orr et al. (1996) for a full description of the study as well as experimental impact estimates.

Effects of Incentives on Who Gets Served

The majority of the employment and training literature on performance incentives addresses the question of their effects on who gets served. Under JTPA, SDAs had strong incentives to serve persons likely to have good labor market outcomes, regardless of whether those outcomes were due to JTPA. Similar incentives, with a minor exception in the form of the before-after performance measure, guide the WIA program. In fact, the absence of a regression model to adjust standards for serving individuals with labor market barriers should make these incentives stronger under WIA than they were under JTPA.

The literature divides this issue into two parts. First, do SDAs (WIBs under WIA) respond to these incentives by differentially serving persons likely to have good outcomes, whether or not those good outcomes result from the effects of the program? This is the literature on "cream skimming." Second, if there is cream skimming, what are its efficiency effects? Taking the best among the eligible could be efficient if the types of services offered by these programs have their largest net impacts for this group. In what follows, we review the literature on each of these two questions.

Do employment and training programs "cream skim"?

A handful of papers about the JTPA program examine whether or not program staff cream skim in response to the incentives provided to do so by the JTPA performance system. The key issue in this literature is the counterfactual: to what group of nonparticipants should the participants be compared in order to determine whether or not cream skimming has occurred? In all cases, because the performance outcome—some variant of Y_1 in our notation—cannot be observed for the nonparticipants, the studies proceed by comparing observable characteristics correlated with Y_1, such as education levels or participation in transfer programs such as Aid to Families with Dependent Children (AFDC) or Temporary Assistance for Needy Families (TANF). A finding that participants have "better" characteristics in the form of higher mean years of schooling or lower average preprogram transfer receipt is interpreted as evidence of cream skimming.

Anderson et al. (1992) and Anderson, Burkhauser, and Raymond (1993) compare the characteristics of JTPA enrollees in Tennessee in 1987 with the characteristics of a sample of JTPA eligibles in the same state constructed from the Current Population Survey. The literature suggests that less than 5 percent of the eligible population participated in JTPA in each year (see the discussion in Heckman and Smith 1999), which allows wide scope for cream skimming. Both papers find modest evidence of cream skimming. In particular, Anderson, Burkhauser, and Raymond's (1993) bivariate probit analysis of program participation and postprogram job placement suggests that if eligible persons participated at random, the placement rate would have been 61.6 percent rather than 70.7 percent, a fall of 9.1 percentage points.

The problem with the Anderson et al. (1992) and Anderson, Burkhauser, and Raymond (1993) papers is that they potentially conflate participant self-selection with cream skimming by program officials. As documented in Devine and Heckman (1996), the JTPA program eligibility rules cast a wide net. The eligible population included both many stably employed working poor persons and persons who were out of the labor force. Both groups had little reason to participate in JTPA.

Heckman and Smith (2004) address the issue of self-selection versus selection by program staff using data from the Survey of Income and Program Participation (SIPP) on JTPA eligibles combined with data from the National JTPA Study. They break the participation process for JTPA into a series of stages—eligibility, awareness, application and acceptance, and participation—and look at the observed determinants of going from each stage to the next. They find that some differences between program eligibles and participants result primarily from self-selection at stages of the participation process, such as awareness, over which program staff have little or no control. For example, for persons with fewer than 10 years of schooling, lack of awareness plays a critical role in deterring participation, although this group is differentially less likely to make all four transitions in the participation process than are persons with more years of schooling. The evidence in Heckman and Smith (forthcoming) suggests that while cream skimming may be empirically relevant, comparing the eligible population as a whole to participants likely overstates its extent, and misses a lot of substantive and policy-relevant detail.

The paper by Heckman, Smith, and Taber (1996) presents a contrasting view. They use data from the Corpus Christi, Texas SDA, the only SDA in the National JTPA Study for which reliable data on all program applicants are available for the period during the experiment. In their empirical work, they examine whether those applicants who reach random assignment (i.e., those who were selected to participate in the program) differ from those who do not in terms of both predicted outcome levels (earnings in the 18 months after random assignment) and predicted program impacts (projected into the future and discounted). Heckman, Smith, and Taber (1996) argue that it is this stage over which program staff have the greatest control, although even here applicants may wander off if they find employment elsewhere, get in trouble with the law, and so on. The authors find strong evidence of negative selection on levels combined with weak evidence for positive selection on impacts. They attribute the former to a strong "social worker mentality" toward helping the hard-to-serve among the eligible that was evident in interactions with program staff at the Corpus Christi site.

The WIA program offers an interesting contrast to JTPA because the WIA performance standards are not adjusted by a regression model and therefore do not hold programs harmless for the characteristics of their participants. Because programs now have stronger incentives to enroll individuals with few barriers to employment, we would expect to observe enrollment shift toward this group. A recent internal USDOL (2002) study finds that this is precisely what appears to be occurring, at least in the area scrutinized:

> A brief survey of States by our Chicago Regional Office indicated that WIA registrations were occurring at only half the level of enrollment achieved by JTPA. While some of this may be due to start up issues, there are indications that the reduced registration levels are due to a reluctance in local areas to officially register people in WIA because of concerns about their ability to meet performance goals, especially the "earnings gain" measure. It appears that local areas in these States are selective in whom they will be accountable for. Some local areas are basing their decisions to

register a person on the likelihood of success, rather than on an individual's need for services. (p. 9)

Overall, the literature provides modest evidence that program staff responded to the incentives provided by the JTPA performance standards system to choose participants likely to improve their measured performance whether or not they benefited from program services. At the same time, the evidence from the Corpus Christi SDA indicates that staff concerns about serving the hard-to-serve could trump the performance incentives in some contexts.[18]

What are the efficiency implications of cream skimming?

A number of studies have examined the efficiency implications of cream skimming by estimating the correlation between performance measures and program impacts. In terms of the usual notation, they estimate the relationship between Y_1, the outcome conditional on participation, and $\Delta = Y_1 - Y_0$, the impact of participation. If this relationship is positive, so that higher outcome levels predict higher impacts, then cream skimming is efficient because it implies serving those with the higher impacts. In contrast, if this relationship is negative, then cream skimming is inefficient because services are provided to those who benefit less from them than those who would be served in the absence of the incentive system.

Table 2.1 summarizes the evidence from the seven studies that comprise this literature.[19] The seven papers examine a variety of different programs, ranging from the Manpower Development and Training Act of the 1960s to the Job Corps program of today. Most rely on experimental data for their impact estimates. With one exception, Zornitsky et al. (1988), the findings are negative or mixed regarding the relationship between outcome-based performance measures of the type typically used in employment and training programs and program impacts. The Zornitsky findings refer to a program, the AFDC Homemaker Home Health Aide Demonstration, which differs from programs such as JTPA and WIA in that it provided a homogeneous treatment to a relatively homogeneous population. Taken together, the literature summarized in Table 2.1 clearly indicates that, in the context of employment and training programs, commonly used performance measures do *not* improve program efficiency by inducing service to those

Table 2.1 Evidence on the Correlation between Y_1 and Δ from Several Studies

Study	Program	Data	Measure of impact	Impact estimator	Performance measures	Findings
Gay and Borus (1980)	Manpower Development and Training Act (MDTA), Job Opportunities in the Business Sector (JOBS), Neighborhood Youth Corps Out-of-School Program(NYC/OS) and the Job Corps.	Randomly selected program participants entering programs from December 1968 to June 1970 and matched (on age, race, city, and sometimes neighborhood) comparison sample of eligible nonparticipants.	Impact on social security earnings in 1973 (from 18 months to 36 months after program exit)	Non-experimental "kitchen sink" Tobit model	Employment in quarter after program, before-after (four quarters before to one quarter after) changes in weeks worked, weeks not in the labor force, wage rate, hours worked, income, amount of unemployment insurance received and amount of public assistance received.	No measure has a consistent, positive and statistically significant relationship to estimated impact across subgroups and programs. The before-after measures, particularly weeks worked and wages, do much better than employment in the quarter after the program.

| Zornitsky et al. (1988) | AFDC Homemaker-Home Health Aid Demonstration | Volunteers in the seven states in which the demonstration projects were conducted. To be eligible, volunteers had to have been on AFDC continuously for at least 90 days. | Mean monthly earnings in the 32 months after random assignment and mean monthly combined AFDC and food stamp benefits in the 29 months after random assignment | Experimental impact estimates | Employment and wages at termination. Employment and welfare receipt three and six months after termination. Mean weekly earnings and welfare benefits in the three and six month periods after termination. These measures are examined both adjusted and not adjusted for observable factors including trainee demographics and welfare and employment histories and local labor markets. | All measures have the correct sign on their correlation with earnings impacts, whether adjusted or not. The employment and earnings measures are all statistically significant (or close to it). The welfare measures are correctly correlated with welfare impacts but the employment measures are not unless adjusted. The measures at three and six months do better than those at termination, but there is little gain from going from three to six. |

(continued)

36

Table 2.1 (continued)

Study	Program	Data	Measure of impact	Impact estimator	Performance measures	Findings
Friedlander (1988)	Mandatory welfare-to-work programs in San Diego, Baltimore, Virginia, Arkansas, and Cook County.	Applicants and recipients of AFDC (varies across programs). Data collected as part of MDRC's experimental evaluations of these programs.	Post random assignment earnings (from UI earnings records) and welfare receipt (from administrative data)	Experimental impact estimates	Employment (non-zero quarterly earnings) in quarters 2 and 3 (short-term) or quarters 4 to 6 (long term) after random assignment. Welfare receipt in quarter 3 (short-term) or quarter 6 (long-term) after random assignment.	Employment measure is positively correlated with earnings gains but not welfare savings for most programs. Welfare indicator is always positively correlated with earnings impacts, but rarely significantly so. It is not related to welfare savings. Long-term performance measures do little better (and sometimes worse) than short-term measures.

| Cragg (1997) | JTPA (1983–87) NLSY | Before-after change in participant earnings | Generalized bivariate Tobit model of preprogram and postprogram annual earnings | Fraction of time spent working since leaving school in the preprogram period. This variable is strongly correlated with postprogram employment levels. | Negative relationship between work experience and before-after earnings changes |
| Barnow (2000) | JTPA (1987–89) National JTPA Study | Earnings and hours worked in month 10 after random assignment | Experimental impact estimates | Regression-adjusted levels of earnings and hours worked in month 10 after random assignment | At best a weak relationship between performance measures and program impacts |

(continued)

Table 2.1 (continued)

Study	Program	Data	Measure of impact	Impact estimator	Performance measures	Findings
Burghardt and Schochet (2001)	Job Corps	Experimental data from the National Job Corps Study	The outcome measures include receipt of education or training, weeks of education or training, hours per week of education or training, receipt of a high school diploma or GED, receipt of a vocational certificate, earnings and being arrested. All are measured over the 48 months following random assignment.	Experimental impact estimates.	Job Corps centers divided into three groups: high-performers, medium-performers and low-performers based on their overall performance rankings in Program Years 1994, 1995 and 1996. High and low centers were in the top and bottom third nationally in all three years, respectively.	No systematic relationship between the performance groups and the experimental impact estimates.

Heckman, Heinrich and Smith (2002)	JTPA (1987–89)	National JTPA Study	Postrandom assignment earnings and employment	Experimental impact estimates	JTPA performance measures including employment at termination, employment 13 weeks after termination, wage at termination and earnings 13 weeks after termination	No relationship between performance measures and experimental impact estimates

who will benefit most. Moreover, the findings indicate that cream skimming likely has neither much of an efficiency benefit nor much of an efficiency cost.

Effects of Incentives on Services Provided

Marschke (2002) is the only paper we know of that has examined the effects of performance incentives on the types of services offered in an employment and training program, holding constant the characteristics of persons served. Marschke's novel analysis uses the variation in performance incentives facing the SDAs in the National JTPA Study to identify the effects of performance incentives on the types of services received by JTPA participants. This variation includes both time-series variation within states and cross-sectional variation across states during the period of the study. For each member of the experimental treatment group, Marschke estimates a predicted outcome on each performance measure. These are then entered into a service type choice model along with other factors, such as predicted impacts from each service type and measures of whether or not the participant is "hard to serve." Both the predicted impacts and the hard-to-serve measures are intended to capture any caseworker efforts to act in the interest of the participants (and the long-suffering taxpayer) or to follow their hearts by providing the most expensive services to the worst off.

Marschke (2002) finds evidence that changes in the performance measures employed in JTPA led SDAs to alter the mix of services provided in ways that would improve their performance relative to the altered incentives they faced. In some cases, these changes led to increases in efficiency, but in others they did not. Marschke (2002) interprets his evidence as indicating that SDAs' service choices are responsive at the margin, but that existing performance measures do a poor job of capturing program goals such as maximizing the (net) impacts of the services provided.

Effects of Incentives on the Technical Efficiency of Service Provision

Performance incentives may affect how hard training center employees work and how smart they work, conditional on their choices about whom to serve and how to serve them. Indeed, traditional incentive systems in industry such as piece rates, which are intended to increase the price of on-the-job leisure, aim to produce just such effects.

We have not been able to locate any evidence on this type of behavioral response in the literature on employment and training programs. This type of response is unlikely to get picked up by the sort of regression models employed in the studies summarized in Table 2.1. To see why, consider the following example. Suppose that establishing performance incentives leads training program workers to work harder, which in turn raises the expected impact of the program for every participant by $10. In this case, the regressions described above would see their intercepts increase by $10, but the coefficient on the performance measures would not increase at all.

In principle, cross-state variation in performance incentive intensity, such as that employed by Cragg (1997), in combination with data on outputs (number of persons served, etc.) and number of workers could be used to answer this question. In the absence of such evidence, it remains to refer to the broader economic literature on this question, which is summarized in Prendergast (1999). He reports that this "literature points to considerable effects of compensation on performance." How well his conclusion generalizes to government programs where the rewards consist of additional budgetary allocations, rather than higher earnings for individual workers, remains an open question.

Effects of Incentives on Subcontracts and Subcontractor Behavior

In many, if not most, employment and training programs that have operated in the United States, secondary providers operating under subcontracts have played an important role in service delivery. In this subsection, we consider the evidence on how performance incentives alter the subcontracts that agencies make with their subcontractors, and how performance-based contracts affect the performance of providers.

As elsewhere, the literature we survey draws primarily on the experience of the JTPA program. Performance-based contracting had an interesting history under JTPA.[20] Initially, SDAs that entered into performance-based contracts for training were able to exceed the 15 percent limit on administrative expenses in JTPA if the contract met certain provisions. By the late 1980s, a number of concerns surfaced about the use of performance-based contracting. As enumerated in Spaulding (2001), USDOL was concerned that states were not effectively monitoring their performance-based contracts (PBCs), that total costs billed under PBCs were not "reasonable," that SDAs were using PBCs for activities that contained little if any training, that contracts did not include the performance measures required by law, that payment schedules either eliminated contractor risk or built in high profit levels, and that profits were sometimes used to establish economic development loan funds, which was prohibited. The Department of Labor issued a series of guidance letters in the late 1980s intended to reduce the use of PBCs.

In a series of papers, Heinrich (1995, 1999, 2003) examines the contracting behavior of a JTPA SDA in Cook County, Illinois.[21] She finds that this site passed along its performance incentives to its service providers through performance-based contracts. These contracts often included performance levels in excess of those facing the SDA itself, apparently as a form of insurance. Even if some contractors failed to meet the (inflated) standards in their contracts, most would, and so the SDA would meet its own overall standards despite a few subcontractor failures. Heinrich (1995, 2003) found that at this SDA, which had technical resources that most other SDAs did not, caseworkers and managers were keenly aware of how they and their subcontractors were doing relative to their performance standards throughout the program year. This was particularly true of the cost-per-placement standard. Heinrich (1999) shows that subcontractor performance in one program year relative to the cost-per-placement standards in their contract affected whether or not they were awarded a contract in the next year.

Now consider the studies that examine the effects of performance based contracting on subcontractor behavior. Dickinson et al. (1988) performed some analyses looking at how the use of performance-based contracting affected the mix of participants in JTPA. They found that, contrary to their expectations, the use of performance-based contracting was associated with a statistically significant increase in services to minority groups, and had no effects on services to welfare recipients, females, older workers, or individuals with other barriers to employment. Dickinson et al. (1988) also analyzed the impact of higher wage at placement provisions on participants served, and found that they led to a reduction in services to welfare recipients; estimated effects on other hard-to-serve groups were also negative but not statistically significant.

Heinrich (2000) focuses primarily on the relationship between organizational form (for-profit or nonprofit) and performance, but she also explores the effects of having performance incentives in provider contracts. She finds, for her study of an Illinois SDA, that inclusion of performance incentives has a very strong positive effect on realized wages and employment at termination and up to four quarters following termination. Similarly, Spaulding (2001) analyzed the effect of performance-based contracting in JTPA programs on the performance of SDAs in program year 1998. Her results indicate that the use of performance-based contracting is generally associated with higher outcomes.

Overall, the literature makes two things clear. First, local training programs sometimes pass along the performance incentives they face to their subcontractors, perhaps with something added on as insurance. Second, performance-based contracts yield higher performance on the rewarded dimension.

Strategic Responses to Performance Incentives

In addition to the substantive responses to performance incentives considered above, in which training centers changed what they actually did, training centers can also attempt to change their measured performance without changing their actual performance. We refer to this as a strategic response, or as "gaming" the performance system. Regardless of their differing goals, all types of organizations have an incentive to respond strategically to performance incentives, provided the cost is low, as doing so yields additional resources to further their own goals. The literature provides clear evidence of such gaming behavior under JTPA.

One important form of strategic behavior under JTPA was the manipulation of whether or not participants were formally enrolled. Under the JTPA incentive system, only persons formally enrolled counted towards site performance. In addition, for the first decade of JTPA's existence, SDAs had substantial flexibility in regard to when someone became formally enrolled. Clever SDAs improved their performance by basing enrollments on job placements rather than the initiation of services. For example, some SDAs boosted performance by providing job search assistance without formally enrolling those receiving it in the program. Then, if an individual found a job, the person would be enrolled, counted as a placement, and terminated, all in quick succession. Similarly, SDAs would send potential trainees to employers to see if the employer would approve them for an on-the-job training slot; enrollment would not take place until a willing employer was found.

There are two pieces of evidence regarding the empirical importance of this phenomenon. The first is indirect, and consists of the fact that USDOL found it enough of a problem to change the regulations. Specifically, in 1992 USDOL required that individuals become enrolled once they received objective assessment and that they count as a participant for performance standards purposes once they received any substantive service, including job search assistance.[22]

The other evidence comes from the National JTPA Study. As part of their process analysis of the treatments provided at the 16 SDAs in the study, Kemple, Doolittle, and Wallace (1993) conducted interviews of nonenrolled members of the experimental treatment group at 12 of the 16 sites. These results, reported in their Table 3.2, show that 53 percent of nonenrolled treatment group members received services, most often referrals to employers for possible on-the-job training (36 percent of all nonenrollees) and job search assistance (20 percent of all nonenrollees). They report that ". . . most of the study sites enrolled individuals in classroom training when they attended their first class or in OJT when they worked their first day . . ."

The flexibility of JTPA also allowed strategic manipulation of the termination decision. Because performance standards in JTPA were based on terminees, SDAs had no incentive to terminate individuals from the program that were not successfully placed in a job. By keeping them on the rolls, the person's lack of success would never be recognized and used against the SDA in measuring its performance. As USDOL explains in one of its guidance letters, "Without some policy on termination, performance standards create strong incentives for local programs to avoid terminating failures even when individuals no longer have any contact with the program."[23]

Problems with local programs retaining participants on the rolls long after they stopped receiving services go back to the days of JTPA's predecessor, the Comprehensive Employment and Training Act (CETA). In one of their guidance letters, USDOL observed that "monitors and auditors found that some participants continued to be carried in an 'active' or 'inactive' status for two or three years after last contact with these programs."[24] For Title II-A of JTPA, USDOL limited the period of inactivity to 90 days, although some commentators suggested periods of 180 days or more.

Courty and Marschke (1996, 1997, 2004) provide additional evidence on the strategic manipulation of termination dates using data from the National JTPA Study. The first type of evidence consists of the timing of termination relative to the end of services as a function of the employment status of the trainee as of the end of services. Assuming that the timing of termination responds mainly to the employment at termination standard in place during the time their data were collected (rather than the wage rate or cost standards, which would be more difficult to game), they argue that sites should immediately terminate participants who are employed when their services end. In contrast, they should not terminate participants who are not employed at the end of their services; instead, they should wait and see if they later become employed, at which point they should then terminate them from the program. Not surprisingly, Courty and Marschke (1996, 1997, 2004) find that the sites in the National JTPA Study did exactly this with, for example, Courty and Marschke (1997, Figure 1), revealing a spike in terminations at the end of services for employed participants, and a spike in terminations at the end of the mandatory 90 days after the end of services for participants not employed at the end of services. Their analysis likely understates the full extent of sites' strategic behavior, as it takes the date of the end of services as given, when in fact sites had some control over this as well. For example, a participant without a job at the end of classroom training could be assigned to a job club in the hopes that employment would soon follow.

Courty and Marschke (1997) interviewed 11 of the 16 sites in the National JTPA Study regarding their responses to the switch from measuring employment at termination to measuring it 90 days after termination. They report that

> [m]ost administrators indicated that . . . case managers began tracking terminees until the follow-up period expired. To

increase the chances that an employment match lasted until the
third month, some SDAs reported that they offered special services between termination and follow-up, such as child-care,
transportation and clothing allowances. Case managers also
attempted to influence employers to keep their clients until the
third month. (p. 387)

Moreover, "training administrators reported that after the third month,
they did not contact the client again." While these follow-up services
may add value, their sudden termination at 90 days, and their sudden
use after the change in performance standards, suggests motives other
than impact maximization.

The second type of evidence from the National JTPA Study
reported in Courty and Marschke (1996, 1997, 2004) concerns the timing of terminations relative to the end of the program year. In JTPA,
performance was measured over the program year from July 1 to June
30. For SDAs in states where there were no marginal rewards for performance above the standard, this leads to an incentive to wait on termination until the end of the program year when possible, and then to
strategically terminate each participant in the program year in which
his or her marginal value is highest. Consider a site that comes into
June well above its performance standard. It should then terminate
nonemployed participants who have finished their services until its
measured performance is just above the standard. It thereby gets its
reward in the current year, while starting the next year with as small a
stock of poorly performing enrollees as possible.

Courty and Marschke (2004) builds on the analyses of Courty and
Marschke (1996, 1997) by embedding them in an econometric framework, and by examining whether the manipulation of the termination
dates is merely an accounting phenomenon or whether it has efficiency
costs. To do this, they look at nonexperimental differences in mean
impacts between persons terminated at training centers that appear to
engage in more gaming (based on measures of the average waiting
time to termination after the conclusion of training), at differences in
mean impacts for trainees terminated in June (at the end of the program
year) relative to other trainees, and at whether or not trainees are more
likely to have their training truncated at the end of the program year.
The impacts at the end of the training year are also interacted with how
close the center is to its performance standards for the year. All of their

analyses indicate an apparent (and surprisingly large) efficiency cost to the gaming behavior.

CONCLUSIONS AND RECOMMENDATIONS

The literature on the behavioral effects of performance management systems in employment and training programs is a small one. From it, we draw the following conclusions. First, there is modest evidence of cream skimming in JTPA, which had such a system. Because the performance management system in WIA does not adjust the standards for sites that serve more disadvantaged groups, WIA provides even stronger incentives to cream skim than did JTPA. There is no evidence, however, that cream skimming behavior would not have occurred even in the absence of the federal performance standards system, perhaps in response to local political incentives. Second, there is fairly strong evidence in the literature that the performance measures typically used in these systems, which focus on short-term outcome levels of participants, have little or no relationship to long-run impacts on employment or earnings. As such, to the extent that program administrators devote time and effort to including persons in the program who will do well on the performance measures, they are not promoting efficiency. Third, there is not much empirical evidence about the effect of performance standards systems on the types of services provided. The single paper that exists suggests that SDAs under JTPA allocated services to increase their measured performance; effects on efficiency are mixed.

Fourth, there is essentially no evidence on the important question of the effects of performance management on the technical efficiency of service delivery. Fifth, performance management at the level of the SDA or WIB leads to changes in the relationship between the two and their subcontractors in some instances. The nature of the contracts changes as local programs seek to insure their aggregate (across contractors) performance, and contractors respond by changing their own behavior to please the local program. Sixth, and finally, there is strong evidence that local programs devote time and resources to gaming performance management systems by increasing their measured performance in ways that do not affect their actual performance. These strategic responses represent a cost of having a performance management system.

In light of these findings, we make two main recommendations. The first is that USDOL commission additional research on the effectiveness of and incentive structure created by performance management systems and that it devote resources to providing the data necessary to support such research. USDOL has spent large sums evaluating its employment and training programs, but much less on evaluating its performance management systems. It is clear to us that marginal returns have not been equated on these two lines of research.

Several types of research would serve to improve our understanding and use of performance management systems. These include, but are not limited to, the following:

- The search should continue for short-term outcome measures that are reliably correlated with long-run program impacts and cannot be gamed by local programs.

- Additional research on the effects of performance management on the types of services offered, on the match between participant characteristics and service type, and on the technical efficiency of service provision would provide a fuller understanding of what the current types of standards actually do.

- Research on the effects of other types of performance measures sometimes adopted at the state level, such as measures designed to encourage service to particular subgroups among the eligible, would inform decisions about whether or not to introduce such measures at the national level.

- Finally, research on the response of WIBs to alternative reward functions at the state level would provide useful information about how to design such functions in the future. Key aspects here include the extent of competition among WIBs, as in tournament systems, variation in the number of standards a WIB must pass to receive any budgetary reward, and the effects of marginal incentives for performance above the standard.

The data required to support the proposed research effort include a panel data set, with the WIB as the unit of observation, containing for each program year the negotiated standards for each WIB, the actual performance of the WIB, characteristics of the economic environment and eligible and participant populations for the WIB, and the details of the relevant state policies, including any additional standards and related outcomes, and the reward function linking WIB outcomes to budgetary rewards. Had such data been collected under JTPA, the knowledge base for redesigning the WIA system would be much more solid. Even the limited information for the National JTPA Study experimental sites described in Courty and Marschke (2003) yielded useful insights. These data should be collected, maintained, and distributed to the research community, presumably by a private research firm under contract to USDOL.

Our second recommendation is that USDOL take advantage of the WIA reauthorization process to redesign the WIA performance management system to reflect the current base of evidence on the performance of these systems. As we show in this paper, the systemic changes from the JTPA performance management system to the WIA system ignored the literature and, overall, took the system farther away from the evidence than it was before. In the absence of a redesign along the lines suggested here, we view the present system as a step backward that should either be scrapped or have its effects reduced by limiting the amount of incentive payments based upon it, pending further research.

We envision four possible scenarios for such a redesign effort, which we list in order of what we see as their desirability. The first redesign scenario represents adoption of an "ideal" performance system. In an ideal system, randomization would be directly incorporated in the normal operations of the WIA program. Such randomization need not exclude persons from any services, but only assign a modest fraction to low-intensity services, e.g., the core services under WIA. It could be incorporated directly into a system similar in spirit to the Frontline Decision Support System (if that system is used to assign individuals to services) and so made invisible to line workers Eberts and O'Leary 2002). The randomization would then be used, in conjunction with outcome data already collected, to produce experimental impact estimates that would serve as the performance measures. For sample size reasons, randomization might be viable in practice only for state-level performance incentives or only when applied to performance measures consisting of moving averages over several program years.

The second reform scenario takes a different direction. It acknowledges that short-term outcome levels have little or no correlation with program impacts and so changes the system to focus on the program's goals other than efficiency. Such a system could focus, for example, on measures related to who gets served and measures of customer (participants and employers) satisfaction. The customer satisfaction measures would focus on aspects of the program such as waiting times and courtesy of staff, about which the customer is the best judge, and not on value-added, of which the customer is likely to be a poor evaluator (as shown empirically for JTPA in Heckman and Smith, 1998). Somewhat surprisingly, the present system does not do a very good job of guiding behavior along these dimensions, though it easily could. The timeliness standards employed in the Unemployment Insurance system provide an example of a successful system along these lines (see the discussion in West and Hildebrand 1997).

The third reform scenario downplays or scraps the current system until additional research identifies measures based on short-term outcomes that correlate with long-term program impacts, or provides convincing evidence that the current system has beneficial effects on dimensions, such as the efficiency of time use by program staff, for which little or no evidence presently exists. In this scenario, the negotiated performance standards could be taken over at the national level and used in a systematic manner to generate knowledge about WIB responses to particular performance measures and to the general toughness of the standards.

The fourth and final reform scenario simply modifies the WIA system to look more like the JTPA system. In practice, this scenario might represent a baseline to which elements of the other scenarios could be added. The heart of this scenario consists of replacing the negotiated standards with a model-based system similar to that in JTPA. Within the context of such a model-based system, a number of suggestions for marginal changes become relevant. First, the model should not be reestimated every year using a single year's data. Doing so caused a lot of volatility in the standards, and in the effects of particular variables, but did not produce any corresponding benefit. Barnow (1996) discusses how this variability applied to persons with disabilities. Second, given the current focus on return on investment within WIA, a cost standard might be reintroduced, designed in a way to get around problems with WIBs that mix funds from a variety of sources, but that encourages local programs to focus more on the return on investment. Third, the literature surveyed here has some lessons for the optimal length of the follow-up period for the outcome-based performance measures. In particular, the literature suggests that longer is not always better in terms of correlation with program impacts, above and beyond the problem that longer follow-up periods interfere with the system's ability to provide reasonably quick feedback.

Notes

We thank Richard West and participants at the "Job Training and Labor Exchange" conference in September 2002 for helpful comments.

1. See D'Amico et al. (2002) and D'Amico (2002) for more information on the implementation of WIA and its relationship to JTPA.
2. A principal–agent problem is not a necessary condition for a performance management system. An individual or firm might adopt such a system as a way of quantifying and rewarding progress toward distant or difficult to measure goals.
3. In some instances, the state government assumed responsibility for some or all of the service delivery in the state.
4. See Barnow (1979) for illustrative models of this type of behavior.
5. See, for example, the discussion in Heckman, LaLonde, and Smith (1999).
6. WIA also includes measures of the change in earnings from the pretraining period to the posttraining period.
7. See Blalock and Barnow (2001) and Barnow (2000) for discussions about the origins of the performance management system in JTPA.
8. WIA became law in 1998 but was not implemented until 2000.
9. We have more to say about this back-and-forth pattern in a later section.
10. For a description of the performance management system in the early days of JTPA, see Barnow and Constantine (1988).
11. It might make more sense to hold constant the characteristics of the eligible population, which the sites do not choose, rather than of program participants, which they do.
12. JTPA operated on a program year rather than a fiscal year basis. PY1990 began July 1, 1990, and ran through June 30, 1991.
13. See the discussion in Dickinson et al. (1988).
14. See Section 136 of the WIA statute for a description of the law's performance management requirements.

15. States we have spoken with indicated that the negotiations are largely one sided, with USDOL establishing the standards.
16. See USDOL (2000a,b) for more details on the WIA performance standards system.
17. Our discussion of the motivation for the WIA changes draws on discussions with several staff who participated in the development of the WIA performance management system. As some of our informants requested anonymity, we simply thank all of them for sharing their views without mentioning their names.
18. This is consistent with the findings from the earlier study by Dickinson et al. (1988).
19. This table is a modified version of Table 3 in Heckman, Heinrich, and Smith (2002). See that paper for a more detailed survey of these results.
20. This section is based on Spaulding (2001).
21. This section draws on Heckman, Heinrich, and Smith (2002).
22. See Training and Employment Notice (TEIN) 31-92 for the formal description of requirements on when a person must be enrolled in the program. http://wdr.doleta.gov/directives/corr_doc.asp?DOCN=299.
23. See TEIN 5-93. http://wdr.doleta.gov/directives/corr_doc.asp?DOCN=770.
24. See TEIN 3-92. http://wdr.doleta.gov/directives/corr_doc.asp?DOCN=282.

References

Anderson, Kathryn, Richard Burkhauser, and Jennie Raymond. 1993. "The Effect of Creaming on Placement Rates under the Job Training Partnership Act." *Industrial and Labor Relations Review* 46(4): 613–624.

Anderson, Kathryn, Richard Burkhauser, Jennie Raymond, and Clifford Russell. 1992. "Mixed Signals in the Job Training Partnership Act." *Growth and Change* 22(3): 32–48.

Ashenfelter, Orley. 1978. "Estimating the Effect of Training Programs on Earnings." *Review of Economics and Statistics* 6(1): 47–57.

Barnow, Burt. 1979. "Theoretical Issues in the Estimation of Production Functions in Manpower Programs." In *Research in Labor Economics, Supplement 1*, Farrell Bloch, ed. Greenwich, CT: JAI Press, pp. 295–338.

———. 1996. "Policies for People with Disabilities in U.S. Employment and Training Programs." In *Disability, Work and Cash Benefits*, Jerry Mashaw, Virginia Reno, Richard Burkhauser, and Monroe Berkowitz, eds. Kalamazoo, MI: W.E. Upjohn Institute for Employment Research, pp. 297–328.

———. 2000. "Exploring the Relationship between Performance Management and Program Impact: A Case Study of the Job Training Partnership Act." *Journal of Policy Analysis and Management* 19(1): 118–141.

Barnow, Burt, and Jill Constantine. 1988. *Using Performance Management to Encourage Services to Hard-to-Serve Individuals in JTPA.* National Commission for Employment Policy Research Report 88-04. Washington, DC: National Commission for Employment Policy.

Blalock, Ann, and Burt Barnow. 2001. "Is the New Obsession with 'Performance Management' Masking the Truth About Social Programs?" In *Quicker, Better, Cheaper: Managing Performance in American Government,* Dall Forsythe, ed. Albany, NY: Rockefeller Institute Press, pp. 485–517.

Burghardt, John, and Peter Schochet. 2001. *National Job Corps Study: Impacts by Center Characteristics.* Princeton, NJ: Mathematica Policy Research.

Courty, Pascal, and Gerald Marschke. 1996. "Moral Hazard under Incentive Systems: The Case of a Federal Bureaucracy." In *Advances in the Study of Entrepreneurship, Innovation and Economic Growth, Volume 7,* Gary Libecap, ed. Greenwich, CT: JAI Press, pp. 157–190.

———. 1997. "Measuring Government Performance: Lessons from a Federal Job-Training Program." *American Economic Review* 87(2): 383–388.

———. 2003. Unpublished manuscript. State University of New York at Albany.

———. 2004. "An Empirical Investigation of Gaming Responses to Explicit Performance Incentives." *Journal of Labor Economics* 22(1).

Cragg, Michael. 1997. "Performance Incentives in the Public Sector: Evidence from the Job Training Partnership Act." *Journal of Law, Economics and Organization* 13(1): 147–168.

D'Amico, Ronald. 2002. "Training Services for Adults and Dislocated Workers under the Workforce Investment Act." Unpublished manuscript. Social Policy Research Associates, Oakland, CA.

D'Amico, Ronald, Alexandria Martinez, Jeffrey Salzman, and Robin Wagner. 2002. *An Evaluation of the Individual Training Account/Eligible Training Provider Demonstration: Interim Report.* Report prepared by Social Policy Research Associates under contract to Mathematica Policy Research and the U.S. Department of Labor.

Devine, Theresa, and James Heckman. 1996. "The Structure and Consequences of Eligibility Rules for a Social Program." In *Research in Labor Economics, Volume 15,* Solomon Polachek, ed. Greenwich, CT: JAI Press, pp. 111–170.

Dickinson, Katherine, Richard West, Deborah Kogan, David Drury, Marlene Franks, Laura Schlichtmann, and Mary Vencill. 1988. *Evaluation of the Effects of JTPA Performance Standards on Clients, Services and Costs.*

National Commission for Employment Policy Research Report 88-16. Washington, DC: National Commission for Employment Policy.

Dixit, Avinash. 2002. "Incentives and Organizations in the Public Sector: An Interpretive Review." *Journal of Human Resources* 37(4): 696–727.

Eberts, Randall W., and Christopher J. O'Leary. 2002. "A Frontline Decision Support System for Georgia Career Centers." Working paper 02-84. Kalamazoo, MI: W.E. Upjohn Institute for Employment Research.

Friedlander, Daniel. 1988. *Subgroup Impacts and Performance Indicators for Selected Welfare Employment Programs.* New York: Manpower Demonstration Research Corporation.

Gay, Robert, and Michael Borus. 1980. "Validating Performance Indicators for Employment and Training Programs." *Journal of Human Resources* 15(1): 29–48.

Heckman, James, Carolyn Heinrich, and Jeffrey Smith. 2002. "The Performance of Performance Standards." *Journal of Human Resources* 37(4): 778–811.

Heckman, James, Robert LaLonde, and Jeffrey Smith. 1999. "The Economics and Econometrics of Active Labor Market Programs." In *Handbook of Labor Economics, Volume 3A*, Orley Ashenfelter and David Cards, eds. Amsterdam: North-Holland, pp. 1865–2097.

Heckman, James, and Jeffrey Smith. 1998. "Evaluating the Welfare State." In Econometrics and Economic Theory in the 20th Century: The Ragnar Frisch Centennial, Steiner Strom, ed., New York: Cambridge University Press for Econometric Society Monograph Series, pp. 241–318.

———. 1999. "The Pre-Programme Dip and the Determinants of Participation in a Social Programme: Implications for Simple Programme Evaluation Strategies." *Economic Journal* 109(457): 313–348.

———. 2004. "The Determinants of Participation in a Social Program: Evidence from JTPA." *Journal of Labor Economics* 22(2).

Heckman, James, Jeffrey Smith, and Christopher Taber. 1996. "What Do Bureaucrats Do? The Effects of Performance Standards and Bureaucratic Preferences on Acceptance into the JTPA Program." In *Advances in the Study of Entrepreneurship, Innovation and Economic Growth, Volume 7*, Gary Libecap, ed. Greenwich, CT: JAI Press, pp. 191–218.

Heinrich, Carolyn. 1995. *Public Policy and Methodological Issues in the Design and Evaluation of Employment and Training Programs at the Service Delivery Area Level.* Ph.D. dissertation, Irving B. Harris Graduate School of Public Policy Studies, University of Chicago.

———. 1999. "Do Bureaucrats Make Effective Use of Performance Management Information?" *Journal of Public Administration Research and Theory* 9(3): 363–393.

————. 2000. "Organizational Form and Performance: An Empirical Investigation of Nonprofit and For-Profit Job Training Service Providers." *Journal of Policy Analysis and Management* 19(2): 233–261.

————. 2003. "The Role of Performance Standards in JTPA Program Administration and Service Delivery at the Local Level. Unpublished manuscript. University of Wisconsin.

Kemple, James, Fred Doolittle, and John Wallace. 1993. *The National JTPA Study: Site Characteristics and Participation Patterns.* New York: Manpower Demonstration Research Corporation.

Marschke, Gerald. 2002. "Performance Incentives and Bureaucratic Behavior: Evidence from a Federal Bureaucracy." Working paper, Albany, NY: Department of Economics, SUNY Albany.

Orr, Larry, Howard Bloom, Stephen Bell, Fred Doolittle, Winston Lin, and George Cave. 1996. *Does Training for the Disadvantaged Work? Evidence from the National JTPA Study.* Washington, DC: Urban Institute Press.

Prendergast, Canice. 1999. "The Provision of Incentives in Firms." *Journal of Economic Literature* 37(1): 7–63.

Spaulding, Shayne. 2001. *Performance-Based Contracting under the Job Training Partnership Act.* Master's Thesis, Johns Hopkins University, Baltimore, MD.

U.S. Department of Labor (USDOL). 2000a. "Core and Customer Satisfaction Performance Measures for the Workforce Investment System." Training and Employment Guidance Letter No. 7-99. Washington, DC: Employment and Training Administration.

————. 2000b. "Negotiating Performance Goals; and Incentives and Sanctions Process under Title I of the Workforce Investment Act." Training and Employment Guidance Letter No. 8-99. Washington, DC: Employment and Training Administration.

————. 2002. *Summary Report on WIA Implementation.* Washington, DC: Employment and Training Administration.

West, Thomas, and Gerard Hildebrand. 1997. "Federal-State Relations." In *Unemployment Insurance in the United States*, Christopher J. O'Leary and Stephen Wandner, eds. Kalamazoo, MI: W.E. Upjohn Institute for Employment Research, pp. 545–598.

Zornitsky, Jeffrey, Mary Rubin, Stephen Bell, and William Martin. 1988. *Establishing a Performance Management System for Targeted Welfare Programs.* National Commission for Employment Policy Research Report 88-14. Washington, DC: National Commission for Employment Policy.

3

The Effectiveness of Publicly Financed Training in the United States

Implications for WIA and Related Programs

Christopher T. King

The principal focus of this chapter is publicly financed, subbacca-laureate education and training in the United States. I first discuss the context within which training is provided in the United States. I then examine the nature of publicly financed training and review the evidence on the effectiveness of various types of training for key target populations of interest, emphasizing the results from experimental evaluations. I conclude with a series of observations, implications, and lessons for U.S. training policies and programs, with emphasis on the Workforce Investment Act (WIA) of 1998 that is expected to be reauthorized by Congress.

TRAINING IN CONTEXT

Training comes in many different shapes and forms and is provided in many different ways. Gary Becker (1975) made the important distinction between general and firm-specific training. General training provides the trainee with skills that apply to many employers in the labor market, while specific training mainly offers skills that have value within a given firm or for a given employer. The presumption is that individuals (or government) should finance more of the former, while employers should support more of the latter, since they are its principal beneficiaries.

Many of the offerings at educational institutions, especially community and technical colleges, can be considered training, although much of it may be intended for other purposes. The late George Kozmetsky, founder and chair emeritus of the University of Texas at Austin's IC^2 Institute, made the further distinction between education as knowledge for understanding and training as knowledge for value in the market.

We can categorize training by its primary objective, as follows:

- *Qualifying training* that is intended to prepare and qualify individuals for jobs.

- *Skills maintenance and upgrading training* that is intended to maintain or improve workers' performance on the job, assist them in building new skills for retention and career advancement, and generally enhance their earnings potential in existing or new jobs.

Human capital investment in the United States tends to be focused disproportionately on qualifying training—initial preparation for work (Ganzglass et al. 2000). On a macro level, investing in training can also be viewed as part of a larger strategy to bolster national economic competitiveness (see, for example, Commission on the Skills of the American Workforce 1990; Marshall and Tucker 1992; Secretary of Labor's Commission on Workforce Quality and Labor Market Efficiency 1989).

Training can take many different forms. It can be *formal* and highly structured. Alternatively, it can be *informal* and very unstructured, occurring as part of the regular ongoing workplace processes. Institutional or classroom training is one of the more typical mechanisms for providing formal training and is often contrasted with on-the-job training (OJT), under which employers may receive a public subsidy to offset the costs of providing structured training to workers. OJT is a relatively structured form of learning by doing. In the early days of manpower training, public offerings under the Manpower Demonstration and Training Act of 1962 supported institutional training and OJT, as well as training that combined them in varying mixes. Apprenticeship training is one of the older and more intense forms of training under which workers receive both formal and informal training in conjunction with unions. In the past few decades, there has been growing emphasis on what is referred to as customized training, publicly financed training designed and offered in close collaboration with and for employers (Isbell, Trutko, and Barnow 2000).

We can also classify training by skill level. In the 1990s, training began to focus more on basic skills—e.g., reading, math, teamwork, learning-to-learn—as well as occupational skills. This trend toward basic skills training was in response to growing recognition that employers were seeking workers who were ready to be trained more so than workers with particular skill sets (Secretary of Labor's Commission on Achieving Necessary Skills 1990).

And, workers secure training from many sources. Surveys of employers and employees indicate that employers expend considerable time and resources on training, both formal and informal, for their workers (Frazis et al. 1998). In fact, the amount of training provided by employers dwarfs that provided with public support: expenditures on training by employers, public and private, may approach $80 billion or more annually by some estimates (American Society for Training and Development 2002). According to the recent review by Lerman, McKernan, and Riegg (2004), employer-provided training has been increasing in all of the surveys that measure such activity. For example, data from the Survey of Income and Program Participation (SIPP) indicate that the share of workers 18–64 years of age reporting receipt of employer-provided training rose from only 6 percent in 1984 to 20 percent in 1996. Note that the range of estimates tends to be wide and is sensitive to the definition of employer training and the sample: Lerman, McKernan, and Riegg (2003, p. 11) offer a lower-bound estimate of 26 percent from SIPP that asks most workers about most recent training of an hour or more, and an upper-bound estimate of 70 percent from the Survey of Employer-Provided Training (SEPT) that asks workers in large establishments about the receipt of short (five minutes or more) formal training.

Finally, the incidence of formal training tends to be higher in larger establishments that have lower rates of employee turnover and offer more extensive employee benefit packages. The 1995 SEPT was restricted to private establishments with 50 or more employees. Citing U.S. Bureau of Labor Statistics figures, Lynch (1994a) states that only 11 percent of workers in small establishments reported receiving training, compared to 26 percent in large establishments. In addition, data from the National Household Survey of Education indicate that young workers (aged 17–35 years) not currently enrolled in school have been participating in part-time training at an increasing rate and are more likely to do so the higher their level of formal education (Hight 1998). This is an important general phenomenon: compared with lower-skilled workers, higher-skilled workers tend to have greater access to training and have higher rates of training participation than lower-skilled workers (see, for example., Carnevale and Desrochers 2000; Mangum 2000), as do workers with higher levels of general skills and education, white workers, and male workers (Lerman, McKernan, and Riegg 2003). The incidence of training in the United States is low compared to other developed countries (Lynch 1994b).

RECENT TRENDS IN TRAINING EXPENDITURES, PRIVATE AND PUBLIC

Depending on which source we rely on, it appears that expenditures on training have been either rising or falling of late. On the one hand, Lerman, McKernan, and Riegg (2003) report that employers have been training an increasing share of employees in the past two decades and are spending more than the one percent of payroll on training that was recommended over a decade ago by the Commission on the Skills of the American Workforce (1990). According to Lynch and Black (1998), the majority (57 percent) of firms report increasing the amount of training offered in the early 1990s. In addition, the American Society for Training and Development (ASTD) reports that employers have been expending increasing amounts on training (ASTD 2002) through the 1990s and into the early 2000s. Its *2002 State of the Industry Report* states that total training expenditures increased both on a per-employee basis (to $704 in 2000) and as a percentage of annual payroll (to 2.0 percent in 2000). Training expenditures were projected to increase in both 2001 and 2002. However, ASTD relies on member surveys for such data, and its membership is comprised of larger employers that are more favorably disposed to training than the universe of U.S. employers.

On the other hand, other researchers report that aggregate *real* expenditures on training by employers and government programs have been declining. King, McPherson, and Long (2000, pp. 276–277) state that "[s]ince 1960, federal expenditures on all forms of workforce development have never exceeded 0.85 percent of gross domestic product or 2.4 percent of federal budget outlays."[1] Real federal training and employment expenditures peaked at more than $22 billion in 1980 (including large sums for public service employment), but fell to just under $8.2 billion by 1985 and have remained in the $7–$8.5 billion range since, or about the same as 1970's $7.3 billion figure (all expressed in 2001 dollars). However, workforce spending per labor force member peaked in the late 1970s and early 1980s at less than $250 and has hovered near $50 in the last few years, a level roughly one-quarter of that two decades earlier in the face of an increasingly dynamic and uncertain labor market (King et al. 2000).

Some forms of public support for education and training have increased noticeably in recent years. Pell Grants and other student aid, especially in the form of loans to students and their families, have risen sharply. "Pell Grants and other student assistance from the federal and state governments account for a growing share of the total resources devoted to work-related education and training, as well as higher education" (King 1999, p. 64). Real federal expenditures on training and employment programs and all forms of student aid (grants and loans) were approximately the same in 1970 at around $7.3 billion, and each had risen to more than $22 billion by 1980. But, by 1985, real student aid expenditures had increased to three times those on training programs ($24 billion versus $8 billion) and by 2000, real student aid expenditures were more than five times federal workforce program spending (nearly $37 billion v. almost $7 billion). This is part of a large and significant shift from place-based to people-based funding for training.

TRAINING: A "HOT-BUTTON" POLICY ISSUE

In the past 10 years, training has become a "hot-button" policy issue at all levels. Early impact findings from welfare employment programs in California (e.g., Riverside Greater Avenues for Independence, or GAIN) suggested that less costly strategies emphasizing work over training—so-called "work-first" approaches stressing labor force attachment (LFA)—were more effective than those stressing more traditional human capital development (HCD). The debate over whether to stress LFA versus HCD spilled over from the welfare reform arena into workforce development generally with the passage of WIA in 1998. Some of the larger states, including Florida, Michigan, and Texas, had already begun reorienting their workforce development strategies toward a work-first model well before the passage of WIA, some as early as 1995 (Grubb et al. 1999).

WIA mandates a sequence-of-services model in which training can be viewed as the "service-of-last-resort" by states and localities. Adults and dislocated workers participating in WIA generally are expected to proceed through core and intensive services before becoming eligible to receive training. Only job seekers who are still unable to secure jobs that allow them to become economically self-sufficient with the assistance of less costly core and intensive services are supposed to gain access to training. Early emphasis by the U.S. Department of Labor (USDOL) and many states and localities on less sophisticated variants of work-first appears to have given way more recently to mixed LFA/HCD strategies and discussion of worker access to support services on the job, including training, as well as child care and other services (e.g., Martinson and Strawn 2002).

PUBLICLY FINANCED TRAINING IN THE UNITED STATES

Major changes have taken place in publicly funded training programs. The main program administered by USDOL has evolved from the Comprehensive Employment and Training Act (1973–1982) and the Job Training Partnership Act (1983–1998) programs to the Workforce Investment Act (1999–present). Each has had a different orientation and stressed different service strategies for different target groups. Each also has placed primary responsibility for workforce policy-making and service delivery with a different level of government. WIA emphasizes a stronger state role in policymaking and encourages privatization of services that have traditionally been the domain of local governments (see, for example, O'Shea and King 2001).

Other important training programs include: TANF work-related programs serving welfare recipients; the Food Stamp Employment and Training (FSE&T) program; Adult Education and Literacy programs; secondary and postsecondary Vocational Education; Vocational Rehabilitation; the Employment Service providing labor exchange services for all jobseekers under the Wagner-Peyser Act; and, until 2003, the H1-B training program offered training for U.S. residents that are in selected occupations that are the object of employers' H1-B visa applications that fund the program. Table 3.1 provides funding and related information for the major federal employment and training programs.

In addition, 42 states have state-financed training programs (Duscha and Graves 1999), supported by either diverted Unemployment Insurance (UI) taxes—California's Employment and Training Panel (ETP) is the oldest and largest of these—or state general revenue, e.g., the Texas Skill Development Fund. State training funds tend to support training provided directly by employers or through community and technical colleges. These funds extended to more states and grew in size in the 1980s and 1990s but encountered hard times in the 2000–2001 recession, when state UI trust funds fell to levels at which dollars flowing into training funds dried up. Few rigorous evaluations have been conducted to demonstrate the effectiveness of training conducted under them.[2]

These programs—many of which now are either administered by workforce boards and other entities but co-located in one-stop centers or administered directly through the auspices of the local boards—can offer jobseekers a broad array of activities and services; the tendency since the late 1990s, however, has been to provide mainly low-intensity, LFA services, e.g., job search assistance. One typical, medium-sized workforce board in Texas, a state with relatively integrated state and local workforce services ranging from WIA and TANF to Food Stamp E&T and even child care, exhibited the following training shares for participants under its major funding sources in fiscal year (FY) 2001: WIA, 30 percent training; TANF, 7 percent training; and Food Stamp E&T, 0 percent training.[3] Ron D'Amico, in Chapter 4 of this volume, reports similar national figures for WIA adults and dislocated worker participants exiting in program year 2000: 32.3 percent

Table 3.1 Major Federal Training and Employment Programs

Program	Appropriations (FY 2002)	Target groups	Major activities and services
WIA	$5.7 billion (including $1.46 billion for Job Corps)	Adults, dislocated workers, and youth	Core, intensive and training services with training often as a 'last-resort' for adults and dislocated workers
TANF Work Programs	State discretion within the $16.5 billion TANF Block Grant	Welfare recipients and their families	Job search and related services, some training
Food Stamp E&T Program	$110 million	Food Stamp recipients and their families, esp. able-bodied adults without dependents (ABAWDs)	Limited services, mainly labor exchange, job search, very limited training
TAA, NAFTA-TAA	$416 million	Trade-affected workers	Financial assistance and training
H1-B Training	$140 million	U.S. workers pursuing fields experiencing high visa applications	Skills training in high-demand occupations
Adult Education & Literacy	$613 million	Adults with basic skills deficiencies	Basic reading, math and literacy services
Vocational Education	$1.3 billion	Secondary and postsecondary students	Career and technical education, including Tech Prep
Vocational Rehabilitation	$2.9 billion	Individuals with disabilities needing assistance to secure and retain work	Financial assistance, rehabilitation, education and training services
ES/One-Stop Grants	$987 million	Employers and jobseekers, including UI recipients	Labor exchange, LMI, counseling and related services

NOTE: WIA = Workforce Investment Act of 1998; TANF = Temporary Assistance for Needy Families, work-related program under the Personal Responsibility Act of 1996; FSE&T = Food Stamp Employment and Training program, under the Food Security Act; TAA, NAFTA-TAA = Trade Adjustment Assistance and North American Free Trade Agreement TAA serving trade-affected workers; ES = Employment Services under the Wagner-Peyser Act of 1933.

WIA adults in training, and 39.6 percent WIA dislocated workers in training, while comparable figures for JTPA carry-over participants in WIA were 73.6 percent and 65.8 percent, respectively.[4]

It should be noted that there are many shortcomings in the new WIA data collection and reporting systems, i.e., the WIA Standard Reporting and Data (WIASRD) system, that will make it very difficult to know with any degree of certainty just what is actually being provided under the program, for whom and with what success.[5] WIASRD allows states and localities wide discretion in terms of when to register or enroll participants in activities and also creates perverse incentives for doing so by only having participants count toward performance accountability if they are registered. Many local boards are delaying the point of enrollment to ensure that their participants will be recorded as "successful." In addition, workforce boards in states such as Michigan, Texas, and Utah that have authority and responsibility for a broad array of funding streams may not show up in WIASRD as having received WIA "core" (e.g., job search assistance) services, since these might be funded under Wagner-Peyser or TANF. Real differences among areas may be difficult to determine.

HOW EFFECTIVE IS TRAINING?

A number of researchers have summarized the literature on training, producing syntheses of what we do (and do not) know about the provision and effectiveness of publicly financed training. USDOL even conducted its own review (USDOL, Office of the Chief Economist 1995). Barnow (1987) critically reviewed the evidence on CETA program impacts on employment and earnings, pointing out that the quasi- or nonexperimental evaluation methods that were employed in assessing CETA had created serious ambiguities.[6] He concluded that, while the programs appeared to raise earnings by $200 to $600 (in 1987 dollars)[7] for all participants, there was wide variation across the studies, including several that produced negative results for subgroups (e.g., youth and males). He found that estimated earnings impacts also varied widely by training activity, with the highest impacts generally associated with participation in Public Service Employment (PSE)[8] and

OJT—with impacts exceeding $1,500 in 1987 dollars (or more than $2,330 in 2001 dollars)—and the lowest with Work Experience, an activity that was generally reserved for the most disadvantaged participants (Barnow 1987, Table 1, pp. 160–161).

This discussion focuses only upon experimental evaluations of training for several key groups that have been the object of attention by federal and state government efforts for decades: disadvantaged adults and youth; dislocated workers; and welfare recipients. It both draws upon earlier evaluation syntheses as well as distills findings from recently completed experimental evaluations. It stresses *per-participant earnings impacts* as the primary outcome of interest, with all impacts and associated costs (where available) converted into current (2001) dollars.

The rationale for relying exclusively on experimental evaluations is straightforward. Despite enhancements in quasi-experimental methods for evaluating training programs in recent years (e.g., Heckman, LaLonde, and Smith 1999; Hollenbeck 2002), the most reliable and credible evidence of the impacts of training comes from well-designed and structured experiments relying on randomly assigned treatment and control groups. This was recognized by the 1985 Job Training Longitudinal Survey Research Advisory Committee, which was chaired by Ernst Stromsdorfer (1985), who was instrumental in shaping approaches to evaluating education and training programs in the United States starting in the 1960s. The committee recommended that USDOL redirect its resources to conducting experimental training evaluations, resulting in the National JTPA Study that ran from 1985–1993 (Bloom et al. 1997; Orr et al. 1996). A number of studies—Barnow (1987), Fraker and Maynard (1987), LaLonde (1995), and Friedlander, Greenberg, and Robins (1997, 2000)—all reached essentially the same conclusion. Thus, findings reported here are based primarily on evidence derived from evaluations based on experimental rather than quasi- or nonexperimental designs.

Presentation of per-participant rather than per-assignee impacts is a matter of discussion among evaluation researchers. The issue arises because, despite the use of random assignment to treatment and control status, not all of those assigned to a given treatment—for example, classroom training or OJT/Job Search Assistance (JSA) in the National JTPA Study—actually received it. Not surprisingly, per-assignee impacts are generally lower than per-participant or per-enrollee ones. The results presented here are per-participant impacts, where possible, emphasizing earnings impacts for those actually receiving services rather than those merely assigned to them.

The final issue to be addressed before turning to training impacts is the appropriate basis for comparison, termed the counterfactual. In many evaluations of training and related social interventions, the standard counterfactual is that control group members receive no services, while treatment group members do. In fact, the more realistic counterfactual, is that control group members may receive whatever education, employment, and training services are generally available to the community, just not those specifically funded by the program being evaluated. This is the stance adopted for the National JTPA Study, the Job Corps evaluation and a number of other major evaluations conducted since the mid-1980s. That is, what is being estimated is the *incremental* impact of training over and above the effects of services that are readily available in the community.[9]

Disadvantaged Adults and Youth

LaLonde (1995) reviewed experimental as well as quasi-experimental evaluations, focusing on CETA, JTPA, and other federal training programs, including those for welfare recipients. He began by establishing realistic expectations for the impact of training on earnings:

> Given that existing public sector sponsored employment and training programs usually are less intensive and expensive than an additional year of schooling, it would be surprising if they generated larger earnings increases. Instead, we should expect that most JTPA programs, which usually cost several hundred to a few thousand dollars per participant, would generate annual earnings gains of perhaps several hundred dollars. (p. 156)

A year of education was associated with an 8 percent earnings gain, or around $2,200 per year (in 2001 dollars). He summarizes the consensus on earnings impacts of training for adults and youth as follows (LaLonde 1995, pp. 158–161):

- Various services raise the postprogram earnings of disadvantaged adult women, but have mixed or no effects on those of adult men or youth. Moreover, earnings gains for women tend to be "modest in size, persist for several years, arise from a variety of training strategies, and are sometimes achieved at remarkably little expense."

- There is less evidence on the value of classroom training (CT) and OJT, and the evidence that does exist is mixed.

- The results for adult males are less than encouraging.

- The National JTPA Study offers no evidence that relatively less disadvantaged youths participating benefited from the low-cost training provided.

Friedlander, Greenberg, and Robins (1997) expand upon LaLonde's conclusions based on their extensive review of both quasi-experimental and experimental evaluations of programs that they sort into services that are voluntary and mandatory for participants. Table 3.2 provides updated impact estimates (all expressed in 2001 dollars) for many of the evaluations they reviewed. Their major conclusions on the effects of voluntary training programs include the following:

- "Consistently strong evidence has accumulated that government training programs have been effective for adult women. The experimental estimates of JTPA's effects on earnings are positive and statistically significant, and the rate of return on cost in JTPA is large even in the short run . . . Nevertheless, . . . such earnings effects are not large enough to lift most families out of poverty" (p. 1833).

- Average earnings effects for adult men in JTPA were as large as those for women and also produced high rates of return even in the short run. "The JTPA finding for men, therefore, represents a significant break with the results of past evaluations" (p. 1834).

- "Evidence has been accumulating for a number of years that training programs have been ineffective in producing lasting earnings effects for youth . . . The experimental estimates from the JTPA evaluation ... are small and bracket zero . . . Moreover, no significant positive earnings effects were found for either male or female youth in any of the three program activity clusters or 39 subgroups examined by the JTPA evaluators" (pp. 1833–1834).

- "Skills development is often implicitly associated with the intensity and cost of an activity, with greater skills development seen as requiring greater effort by participants and greater costs to programs . . . In our view, the evidence is mixed. A link between increased cost and intensity of training and greater earnings effects has not been firmly established" (p. 1834).

- "The absence of long-term follow-up in most studies is a critical problem in assessing the effectiveness of lengthy and costly skills development activities. The limited evidence available (e.g., Couch [1992], U.S. General Accounting Office [1996]) suggests that earnings effects may persist" (p. 1836).

- "At present, the most important unresolved issue concerning voluntary training programs for adults is the efficacy of various policy tools intended to increase program scale by increasing the number of participants and the intensity and expense of the activities provided to them" (p. 1837).

With respect to mandatory training programs, Friedlander et al. (1997) conclude that the evaluation evidence is strong and consistent, including the following findings:

- Most of the earnings effects for mandatory programs are positive and are larger for women than for men (p. 1839).

- The evidence in favor of more intensive and expensive skills development to increase skills and near- and longer-term earnings is mixed (p. 1840).

We now have long-term results available for JTPA from USDOL/ETA and the Job Corps evaluation findings, both of which significantly bolster our understanding of training impacts for disadvantaged adults and youth.

Long-Term JTPA Impacts

Orr et al. (1996) and Bloom et al. (1997) published the findings from the National JTPA Study that ran from 1986 to 1993. These were augmented with additional follow-up data collected by USDOL in a report published by the U.S. General Accounting Office (1996). USDOL has now collected and tabulated additional follow-up data for National JTPA Study participants as well, including up to seven years of postrandom assignment Social Security Administration earnings records across all 16 of the original service delivery areas.[10]

USDOL estimated annual per-assignee earnings impacts for seven years following random assignment for adult men, adult women, youth, and welfare recipients by recommended service strategy. The three JTPA service strategies were: CT, the primary service recommended; OJT/JSA, where either OJT or job search assistance were the primary services recommended; and Other, which was a catch-all strategy where neither CT or OJT/JSA were the primary recommended strategies. Impacts were also disaggregated for those with and without significant prior work experience. Selected *per-enrollee* impact results for disadvantaged adults and youth include:[11]

- Adult women exhibited positive earnings impacts in all seven years for which data are available, with a per-enrollee impact for the entire seven-year period of $3,206 (5 percent); impacts were statistically significant in the first four years. Impacts were concentrated among women enrolled in OJT/JSA and Other, with impacts of $4,933 (7 percent) and $6,031 (9 percent), respectively.

- Adult men did not fare as well. Overall per-enrollee earnings impacts for adult men were positive for the seven-year period ($1,268, or 1 percent) but not statistically significant. This was true for all service streams as well.

- Female youth had positive but insignificant earnings impacts in each year of the period, with an overall per-enrollee earnings impact of $1,640, or 3 percent.

- Male youth experienced negative but insignificant earnings impacts in each year, with an overall per-enrollee earnings impact of –$3,167, or 4 percent. This continues the pattern reported in earlier JTPA analyses by Orr et al. (1996) and Bloom et al. (1997).

Figure 3.1 shows these longer-term per-enrollee earnings impacts by service strategy for adult males and females.

National Job Corps Program

Job Corps, the most stable and intensive program serving extremely disadvantaged youth, has been operating since 1964 and has sites spread all across the country. In 2001, Mathematica Policy Research completed an exhaustive experimental evaluation of the national Job Corps program for USDOL based on an experimental design (see Burghardt and Schochet 2001; Burghardt et al. 2001; Gritz and Johnson 2001; McConnell and Glazerman 2001; and Schochet, Burghardt, and Glazerman 2001).[12] Of the 80,883 youth who applied and were found eligible for Job Corps between November 1994 and February 1996, 9,409 were randomly assigned to the treatment group and 5,977 to the control group. The treatment group included some eligible youth who did not enroll in or receive Job Corps services.[13] Control group members were not permitted to enroll in Job Corps but could access similar services available in their communities.

Demographic data for all study participants were obtained from program records as well as baseline interviews that were conducted shortly after random assignment. Follow-up interviews were conducted with participants by telephone after 12, 30 and 48 months to determine participants' employment-related experiences. Long-term analysis was based on information from the 6,828 program and 4,485 control group members who completed the 48-month interview.

Among the key findings from the Job Corps evaluation are the following (see Table 3.3):

- Job Corps dramatically increased both participation in and near-term outcomes from education and training programs across a variety of measures, with the exception of attaining high school diplomas.

- Impacts on employment rates, hours worked, and earnings per week were significantly negative after the first five quarters, then leveled off and became positive after the second year.

- Program group members earned an average of $16 per week more than those in the control group during the fourth year. Gains resulted from a combination of increased hours of work and higher wages.

Figure 3.1 Long-Term, Per-Enrollee JTPA Earnings Impacts for Adult Males and Females, by Recommended Service Strategy

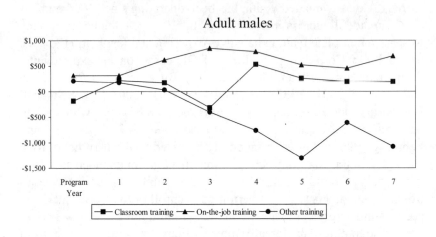

Adult males

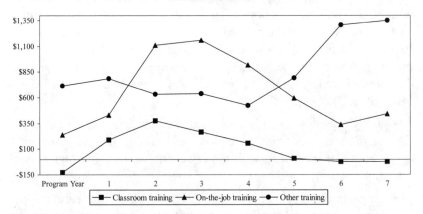

Adult females

SOURCE: Ray Marshall Center computations based on long-term follow-up data collected and tabulated by USDOL/ETA and activity enrollment rates provided in Orr et al. (1996).

Table 3.3 Selected Per-Participant Job Corps Impacts

Outcome	Per-participant impacts
Education/Training	
Ever enrolled in educational program (%)	28.9***
Ever attended academic classes (%)	32.9***
Ever received vocational training (%)	63.4***
Received GED certificate (%)	20.9***
Received high school diploma (%)	−3.1***
Employment/Earnings	
% employed at 48 months	4.2***
% of weeks employed, Year 1	−14.2***
% of weeks employed, Year 2	−2.9
% of weeks employed, Year 3	2.4***
% of weeks employed, Year 4	4.1***
Hours/week employed, Year 1	−5.8***
Hours/week employed, Year 2	−1.2
Hours/week employed, Year 3	1.4***
Hours/week employed, Year 4	1.9***
Earnings/week, Year 1	−$35.7***
Earnings/week, Year 2	−$1.7
Earnings/week, Year 3	$21.6***
Earnings/week, Year 4	$25.7***

NOTE: ***Statistically significant at the 1% level. Earnings expressed in 2001 dollars.
SOURCE: Burghardt et al. (2001).

- Impacts on employment rates and earnings were greater for program group members aged 20–24 years than for younger participants, but were similar across gender, residential, and behavioral subgroups. Impacts were significantly lower among Hispanics than other ethnic groups. Low impacts for Hispanics did not appear to be due to the heavy concentration of Hispanics in specific regions or the fact that English was the primary language for less than half of Hispanic participants.

- Significantly more program than control group members received employer-sponsored health insurance, paid sick leave, child care assistance, retirement benefits, dental coverage, and reimbursement for tuition or training.

Finally, note that Job Corps benefits were estimated to exceed costs by nearly $17,000 per participant if the positive fourth-year earnings impacts on earnings are assumed to continue over their working lifetimes.[14] Barnow and Gubits (2002) suggest that, while we might question the assumption that Job Corps earnings impacts will persist undiminished beyond the fourth year, the justification given by Mathematica researchers is sensible for several reasons. First, measured earnings impacts persisted over the entire period of study. Second, the additional education and training that Job Corps participants received was about the equivalent of an extra school year, the benefits of which tend to persist over a person's lifetime. Finally, the types of skills that Job Corps teaches—e.g., literacy, numeracy, workplace, and social skills—are unlikely to become obsolete.

To summarize, by most accounts, it appears that training—at least as it was structured and provided in the 1980s and 1990s—was associated with modest but lasting impacts on earnings for disadvantaged adult men and women. Further, intensive training for very disadvantaged youth as in Job Corps also yields impacts that are solid and lasting. Youth training of the sort delivered under regular JTPA programs in the 1990s does not appear to have been effective. In all cases, the counterfactual is not receiving no training but rather gaining access to other education, training, and employment services available in local communities. Estimated impacts thus represent the incremental value of training secured via JTPA (now WIA), Job Corps, and other publicly funded training and employment programs.

Dislocated Workers

Duane Leigh (1990, 1995, 2000) reviews what we know about dislocated workers, the various programs and approaches that have been developed since the early 1960s to assist them, and their effects. According to Leigh, dislocated workers, probably the most advantaged group served by publicly funded training programs, are distinguished by three interrelated characteristics: 1) they have been laid off from jobs they have held for some time, 2) they have significant work experience and firm-specific skills, and 3) they have low probabilities of being recalled to their old jobs or other jobs in the same industries. Dislocation has been and continues to be a large problem, with an average of two million full-time workers permanently displaced from their jobs annually from 1984–1992. The groups displaced have changed somewhat over time, however, with older, college-educated, white-collar workers from nongoods producing industries disproportionately affected in the latter half of the 1990s.

Experimental evaluations of dislocated worker programs have been the exception, such that our understanding of their impacts is quite limited. Only two have been conducted to date: the Texas Worker Adjustment Demonstration (1984–1987),[15] and the New Jersey Reemployment Demonstration (1986–1987). The dearth of experimental evaluations for dislocated worker services probably stems in part from the nature of the programs themselves: they are often viewed as "emergency" or "rapid" responses to immediate crises in communities rather than ongoing efforts to address industrial or labor market shifts.

The Texas Worker Adjustment Demonstration tested what was termed a Tier I/Tier II service model for a range of dislocated workers in two very different labor markets in the state (i.e., Houston and El Paso) in the mid 1980s (Bloom 1990). Tier I services consisted basically of job search assistance, while Tier II—which could only be reached subsequent to participation in Tier I—consisted of occupational skills training. In essence, the Texas demonstration sought to test an early version of "work-first-plus" for dislocated workers. More than 2,200 workers were randomly assigned to Tier I, Tier I/II and control group statuses for the demonstration across all sites. UI wage records and survey-based data provided information on their outcomes. Abt

Associates conducted the evaluation. Key impact results included the following (Bloom 1990):

- Earnings impacts for displaced women were substantial and sustained over the one-year follow-up period, although these diminished over time. In 2001 dollars, women participants earned approximately $1,890 (34 percent) more due to participation (see Table 3.2).

- Impacts for males were smaller and shorter-lived. Men posted gains of only $1,108 (8 percent) in 2001 dollars.

No additional gains were found for adding Tier II services to Tier I job search (p. 137), however, problems with implementing the design may well have precluded such impacts.[16]

The New Jersey UI Reemployment Demonstration also operated in the mid 1980s and sought to test whether the UI system could be used to both identify and serve UI-eligible dislocated workers early in their unemployment spells to accelerate their return to work. Some 8,675 UI claimants were randomly assigned to three service packages for the demonstration: JSA only; JSA combined with training (some enrollees) or relocation assistance (very few); and JSA combined with a cash reemployment bonus. Incremental impacts were computed relative to outcomes for UI claimants receiving regularly available services. Claimants were served via a coordinated service approach that brought together the UI, ES, and JTPA systems in the New Jersey sites. Mathematica Policy Research conducted the evaluation. Corson and Haimson (1995) found that:

- None of the treatments had any long-term impacts on employment, earnings, or weeks worked when measured up to six years after random assignment.

- While all three treatments had positive impacts, the JSA combined with the reemployment bonus was the only service strategy that led to statistically significant, initial increases in earnings, and these increases were modest and very short-lived, i.e., just the first quarter.

- Training—in which relatively few workers participated—had no added impact on earnings in either the near- or longer-term, although this may have been an artifact of the small numbers enrolled. Reanalysis of earnings impacts for those actually enrolled in training indicated that participation in training—CT and OJT—did appear to enhance participant earnings.[17]

To date, we have not fully tested the impact of skills training or retraining for dislocated workers with a solidly implemented demonstration evaluated with an experimental design. In fact, USDOL initiated an experimental evaluation of dislocated worker services toward the end of the JTPA regime, but it was never completed.[18] Note that recent analyses by Jacobsen, LaLonde, and Sullivan (2001, 2002) using Washington State administrative data suggest that the returns to community college education for dislocated workers are significant and may endure for several years. However, their estimates of the returns to education and training are derived from statistical comparisons of "observationally similar" groups of displaced workers (Jacobsen, LaLonde, and Sullivan 2002, p. 203) and do not approach the precision of most quasi-experimental estimates. Absent well-designed and conducted experimental evaluations of these strategies for dislocated workers, we cannot be very confident of their impacts.

Welfare Recipients

Plimpton and Nightingale (2000) provide a comprehensive review of both experimental and rigorous quasi-experimental evaluations of 14 welfare-to-work programs that have operated in the United States since the mid 1970s, beginning with the intensive National Supported Work demonstration of the late 1970s and welfare employment efforts under the 1980s' Work Incentive (WIN) program and ending with an initial look at the labor force attachment (LFA) and human capital development (HCD) sites of the National Evaluation of Welfare-to-Work Strategies (or NEWWS). They summarize findings from these evaluations, some of which they have contributed to, focusing on impacts on employment, earnings, and welfare receipt. They report overall impacts as well as those by subgroup and service strategy. They summarize their findings as follows (p. 49):

- "Most welfare employment programs that offer low-cost, low intensity services (like job search assistance and short-term unpaid work experience) have positive impacts on employment and earnings and in some cases reduce welfare costs.

- More comprehensive training programs offering services like supported, paid work experience and occupational training generally have larger and longer-lasting impacts.

- Even those interventions with the greatest impacts have been unable to move individuals and families out of poverty or permanently off the welfare rolls, nor have they produced economic self-sufficiency."

Nudelman (2000) analyzed a sample drawn from the National JTPA Study, consisting of 1,862 adult women (22 years of age and older) who were receiving Aid to Families with Dependent Children (AFDC) when they applied to JTPA between November 1987 and September 1989. She presents both per-assignee and per-enrollee impacts based on both UI wage records and 30-month follow-up survey data. She examines JTPA's overall net impacts on earnings and welfare receipt, impacts attained by various subgroups of recipients, impacts of various JTPA service streams, and the relationship between impact on earnings and impact on receipt of welfare. Note that, as with the larger National JTPA Study, welfare recipients were assigned to one of three main service streams: 1) CT, 2) OJT/Job Search Assistance, and 3) Other Services (i.e., a strategy that did not feature CT or OJT as the primary intended service). Impacts represent the "incremental effect of JTPA services relative to services available elsewhere in the community" (p. 104).

Before presenting her findings, Nudelman cautions that there are noteworthy differences between this group of welfare recipients in JTPA and those that have been the focus of most welfare employment evaluations in the past as well as those enrolled in current Welfare-to-Work (WtW) and TANF programs (p. 105): welfare recipients who enrolled in JTPA in the late 1980s comprised a very small share of all recipients, were usually (but not always) volunteers who were screened for program eligibility, and were not subject to welfare time limits.

Nudelman reported that:

- More than 30 months after random assignment, JTPA participation led to a statistically significant 28 percent per-enrollee earnings increase for adult welfare recipients. During the second postprogram year, per-enrollee earnings increased by a statistically significant $889 (21 percent), or about $1,205 in 2001 dollars for adult welfare recipients.

- Earnings impacts persisted over the entire 30-month period and were statistically significant for most quarters. During the final two quarters, in fact, the magnitude of earnings impacts was growing noticeably for adult welfare recipients.

- JTPA participation also resulted in significant reductions in welfare receipt (about –$1,760 in 2001 dollars), although reliable data on welfare recipiency were only available for 6 of the 16 JTPA study sites nationwide.

- Per-enrollee earnings impacts over the 30-month period were largest (and statistically significant) for white and other women ($4,733), those with a high school diploma or GED ($2,145), longer-term recipients ($6,202 for those on 2–5 years and $3,912 for those on more than five years), and those who were not required to participate in JTPA ($3,149), all expressed in 2001 dollars.

- Per-enrollee impacts also tended to be greater (and significant) for women assigned to the OJT/JSA and Other Service streams: those assigned to the former earned nearly $3,520 more in the second postprogram year and almost $7,400 for the 30-month period; those in Other Services earned $5,661 more for the entire period (all in 2001 dollars). Nudelman suggests that lower impacts for CT might be explained by the short-term nature of the training offered (only 3–6 months).

With additional years of labor market outcome data, it is possible to round out this picture of longer-term impacts for adult welfare recipients in JTPA. The USDOL/ETA data provide detailed per-assignee impacts by service strategy (i.e., CT, OJT/JSA, Other) for seven years following random assignment for welfare recipients, sorted into two groups: those on welfare less than two years, and those on welfare two years or more prior to entry. Unfortunately, the USDOL data lack the strategy-specific enrollment rates for each of the designated welfare subgroups required to convert per-assignee to *per-enrollee* impacts.

Among other findings, unpublished USDOL data on per-assignee impacts indicate that:

- With a few exceptions, statistically significant earnings impacts were concentrated among long-term welfare recipients with prior work experience.

- Long-term welfare recipients experienced earnings gains from JTPA participation in all seven years following random assignment, with significant earnings gains in the first three years. Over the entire seven-year period, long-term welfare recipients experienced a 9 percent earnings gain from participation.

- Impacts varied widely by service strategy and welfare status. Long-term welfare recipients assigned to CT experienced modest to near-zero impacts. Long-term recipients assigned to OJT/JSA enjoyed substantial impacts in most years and a 12 percent earnings gain over the period as a whole; those on welfare less than two years at entry also gained from OJT/JSA, including a statistically significant 21 percent impact in year seven and 12 percent over the entire period. For those assigned to the Other Service stream, only long-term recipients enjoyed gains: persistent annual increases and 24 percent for the seven-year period as a whole, and statistically significant gains of 33–36 percent in the first and second years.

- Only welfare recipients with at least some prior work experience enjoyed earnings gains following assignment to JTPA services.

Michalopolous, Schwartz, and Adams-Ciardullo (2000) provide *per-assignee* impact results for 20 programs serving welfare recipients across the country as part of the large National Evaluation of WtW Strategies (NEWWS) being conducted by MDRC for the U.S. Department of Health and Human Services.[19] The 20 welfare employment programs included the Saturation Work Initiative Model (SWIM) in San Diego; California Greater Avenues for Independence (GAIN) programs, located in Alameda, Butte, Los Angeles, Riverside, San Diego, and Tulare Counties; LFA and HCD programs in Atlanta (Georgia), Grand Rapids (Michigan), and Riverside (California); education-focused Job Opportunities in the Business Sector (JOBS) programs in Detroit and Oklahoma City; traditional and integrated JOBS programs in Columbus (Ohio); an employment-focused JOBS program in Portland (Oregon); Minnesota's Family Investment Program (MFIP); and finally, the Family Transition Program (FTP) in Escambia County (Florida).

Some 71,932 single-parent welfare recipients were randomly assigned to a program or control group across the participating sites. Control group members did not receive employment-related services offered under the various programs and were not mandated to participate in the programs. Thus, the NEWWS evaluation focuses on a *voluntary* program, in sharp contrast to most earlier evaluations of welfare employment programs.

Michalopoulos, Schwartz, and Adams-Ciardullo (2000) report that:

- Programs increased earnings by roughly $500 per person on average and rose for all subgroups. Earnings increased most for new welfare applicants and least for those with high risk of depression.

- Psychological and social barriers were not strongly related to earnings impacts.

- Programs reduced welfare payments by $400 per person and food stamp payments by $100 per person on average.

- Programs did not increase or decrease overall *income* for most subgroups.

- Increases in earnings were fairly constant for all levels of disadvantage, although more disadvantaged program groups had higher reductions in welfare payments.

- Programs increased earnings substantially for low-risk participants (about $800) and moderate-risk participants (about $500) but did not significantly increase earnings for the most depressed.[20]

- Among disadvantaged subgroups, program impacts were higher for those without prior work experience than for those who had not graduated from high school.

- Employment-focused programs (Portland, Riverside GAIN, MFIP, and FTP) were more effective for more disadvantaged groups.
- Programs with a mix of activities (all GAIN sites, Portland, MFIP, and FTP) helped a wider range of individuals overall.

Freedman (2000) reports on four-year employment and earnings *per-assignee* impacts from 10 of the programs evaluated by MDRC as part of NEWWS. Four of these programs—Atlanta, Grand Rapids, and Riverside LFA and Portland—were largely employment-focused, encouraging rapid entry into the labor market. Six of the programs— Atlanta, Grand Rapids, and Riverside HCD, Columbus Integrated, Columbus Traditional, and Detroit—were education-focused, striving to increase participants' skills or credentials before they looked for employment.

Some 44,569 single parents were randomly assigned to treatment and control groups over a three-and-a-half-year period. As with all NEWWS sites, members of the control group did not receive employment-related services and were not mandated to participate. Freedman's report covers roughly half of the sample ($n = 27,105$) for whom four-year postassignment follow-up data are available. Short- and long-term employment stability and earnings growth figures were calculated using state UI wage records. Regression was used to adjust impact estimates to account for sample members' differences in prior earnings and employment, welfare benefits received, and baseline characteristics.

Freedman found that a greater percentage of program group members in the employment-focused programs were employed during the first two years and remained employed at the end of year two than control group members. However, the results were mixed. The proportions of individuals who were no longer employed after year two or who experienced unstable employment or joblessness during years three and four were also higher. Earnings findings were also mixed.

Hamilton (2002) synthesizes the overall findings from the five-year NEWWS evaluation, reporting that:

- All NEWWS programs significantly increased single parents' employment and earnings and decreased their dependence on welfare (p. 23), although earnings effects tended to diminish during the fourth and fifth follow-up years (p. 24). Only Portland—a *hybrid* employment/education program—and the Riverside LFA program produced significant earnings impacts in the fifth year.

- "Notably, only a minority of program group members experienced stable employment over the five years." Even after five years, most were still earning relatively low hourly wages, e.g., $7–$8 per hour (p. 24).

- "Employment-focused programs generally had larger effects on employment and earnings than did education-focused programs" (p. 28). LFA program impacts on earnings for the full five-year period ranged from $1,500 to $2,500, while those for HCD programs ranged from $800 to $2,000 (p. 29). In both instances, these are *per-assignee* impacts.

- Compared with LFA, the more costly HCD approach did not produce additional long-run economic benefits (p. 29), nor did it lead to greater earnings growth or increase the likelihood of employment in good jobs (p. 32). These results held for nongraduates as well as graduates.

It is important to note that HCD programs included in the NEWWS evaluation stressed basic and adult education much more than occupational skills training. During the five-year period, 40 percent of all participants in the HCD programs participated in adult education for at least one day, while only 28 percent participated in vocational training. Participation in vocational training, not surprisingly, was far higher for high school graduates than for non-graduates. HCD programs increased adult education participation by fully 20 percentage points, but only increased participation in vocational training by 5 percentage points (p. 17).

The most effective program emerging from the NEWWS evaluation was the Portland program, a hybrid employment- and education-focused model. Over five years, participants in the Portland site increased their earnings by 25 percent and their average number of employed quarters by 21 percent, and also experienced more stable employment and earnings growth than all of the other programs. Its distinctive features included the following: "an employment focus, the use of both job search and short-term education or training, and an emphasis on holding out for a good job" (p. 36).[21] Portland also limited the duration of participation in some types of adult education.

Finally, Hotz, Imbens, and Klerman (2000) make an important contribution to our understanding of the duration of impacts from welfare employment and training program participation. They reanalyze long-term impacts from the four California GAIN sites that were featured in the MDRC evaluation (i.e., Alameda, Los Angeles, Riverside, and San Diego), using nine years of postrandom assignment outcomes data—the longest time period used in any random assignment evaluation conducted to date—and accounting for county-level differences in participant populations. They conclude that "work-first" programs were more successful in producing net impacts on employment, earnings and welfare reductions than "human capital accumulation" programs in the early years, i.e., one to three years after assignment. However, the relative advantage of these less expensive "work-first" interventions disappears in later years. Based on their long-term re-analysis of GAIN program impacts, Hotz, Imbens, and Klerman (2000) conclude that:

> [S]hort-term evaluation of training programs can be misleading. The relative ranking of programs is not stable over time. Simple extrapolations of early results to later results do not appear to be possible. The relation of short-term results to long-term results appears to vary with program content in ways consistent with a priori expectations. (p. 43)

Without a doubt, we know more about the impacts of various employment and training interventions on the employment and earnings of welfare recipients than any other single group. High-quality experimental evaluations of both demonstration projects and ongoing programs have been conducted over three decades in order to estimate impacts for welfare women. Fortunately for policymakers, they have yielded reasonably consistent results. First, most welfare employment and training programs evaluated over the years have led to increased employment and earnings and reduced welfare payments for welfare recipients, especially those with more education and some work experience who were longer-term (though not necessarily longest-term) recipients and who volunteered to participate. Second, while low-intensity LFA approaches worked very well in the near term, more intensive ones tended to perform better over the long haul, especially those that stressed a mix of work and skill development. And finally, while employment and training programs have worked for all concerned—for participants, taxpayers, and society—most of the participants have remained in low-paying, relatively unstable employment. Only a small share have escaped poverty.

Before concluding, we should acknowledge just how much the context for welfare employment and training programs has changed over the time period in which these studies have been carried out. Women on welfare now encounter constrained service options (e.g., work-first) and mandates to participate under the threat of sanctions that accompany welfare time limits and personal responsibility agreements, among other important changes. They are expected to work and attain economic self-sufficiency through earnings—or possibly marriage—rather than relying on public assistance.

CONCLUSIONS, IMPLICATIONS, AND LESSONS FOR TRAINING POLICIES AND PROGRAMS

What we know about the effectiveness of training can be summarized in a few brief statements, which are based on decades of experience evaluating these programs with the most reliable method available: an experimental design with random assignment to treatment and control groups. These statements also incorporate results from major evaluations that were completed in the last two years, namely the National Job Corps Evaluation and NEWWS. In general, we know with considerable confidence that:

- Training as delivered in traditional employment and training programs produces modest incremental impacts on employment and earnings (measured relative to other services available in the community) for adult men and women. While statistically significant and often lasting for years, these impacts are insufficient to lift these individuals and their families out of poverty.

- Training as delivered in traditional programs does not result in positive employment or earnings impacts for disadvantaged youth. Training for youth that is delivered through intensive and expensive programs like Job Corps does produce modest and lasting impacts on employment and earnings as well as strong returns on investment, although not for all groups (e.g., Hispanics and younger youth).

- Employment-focused approaches tend to produce modest, significant and near-term effects on employment and earnings for welfare recipients. The models that are particularly effective for welfare recipients are those that offer a mix of LFA and skills acquisition services (and only limited adult education) and that encourage participants to be selective in their search for jobs offering good wages and benefits and career advancement opportunities.

- HCD programs produce significant long-term (up to nine-year) impacts on employment and earnings for welfare recipients that exceed those of less costly "work-first" programs.

What lessons can we draw from these evaluation findings for WIA and other workforce-related policies and programs? Several features of WIA merit our attention (see Chapter 4 of this volume). Unlike its predecessors CETA and JTPA, WIA posits training as a "service of last resort," directing local one-stop centers to put adults and dislocated workers through a sequence of core and intensive services before referring them to providers for more expensive training services. This feature was incorporated into WIA to stress a "work-first" orientation much like that in the Personal Responsibility Act of 1996 for welfare recipients. WIA also stresses individual choice through the use of individual training accounts (ITAs), voucher-like mechanisms, to fund most training for adults and dislocated workers.[22] In addition, ITAs may only be used to secure training from providers certified by the state as eligible training providers (ETPs) based on their recent record of performance. ITAs and eligible training provider lists reflect WIA's increased reliance on market-like mechanisms. WIA has also introduced a far more competitive environment for delivering workforce services, both by mandating that workforce boards contract out competitively for one-stop center operators as well as by introducing ITAs and eligible provider provisions. Finally, WIA accountability provisions allow states and local boards discretion over the point at which an individual jobseeker is officially registered for services and, thus, a person for whom the board is accountable. One-stop operators may delay registration until they feel reasonably confident the individual will be successful (e.g., entered employment, earnings gain). WIA has also dropped the use of a regression model to adjust performance expectations for local conditions and participant characteristics.

We can draw several important lessons for WIA and related policies. First, workforce policies and programs should stress combinations of work and training for many if not most participants. Not only are some of the largest and more durable earnings impacts associated with such interventions (e.g., the OJT/JSA service stream for JTPA and Portland's hybrid approach under NEWWS), but we also know that various forms of work-based learning, including apprenticeship and customized training, are valued highly by employers. Moreover, for participants, often the largest cost of education and training is their foregone earnings. So, emphasizing combinations of work and training appears to make sense from all perspectives. A corollary to this lesson is that simplistic work-first, any-job-is-a-good-job approaches that push participants into jobs without access to training should be avoided.

Second, WIA's emphasis on training-as-last-resort is a good strategy only if our main goal is producing near-term labor market impacts at low cost. More recent USDOL interpretations of WIA's sequence-of-services provisions that tell states and localities to use discretion in deciding when an individual can proceed to training represent a move in the right direction. If the goal of WIA is real employment and earnings impacts over the long-term—say, 6–9 years postenrollment—then occupational skills training in the context of an employment-focused approach is the way to go. Included in a more human capital-focused strategy would be enhanced ties to community and technical colleges—what Grubb et al. (1999) refer to as "ladders of opportunity." WIA policies are currently discouraging such connections.

Third, greater reliance on market-oriented mechanisms—consumer choice, ITAs, ETP certification lists—combined with measurement focused on short-term performance and increased competition, is likely to drive WIA even more towards immediate results, low-cost services, and participant "creaming." Research conducted on JTPA programs indicated that these issues have been problematic for a while, but the combination of these WIA provisions can be expected to make matters worse.[23] The results from the Department of Labor's ITA evaluation, now being conducted by Mathematica (See Chapter 6 in this volume), should be examined very thoroughly for insights regarding necessary policy and program adjustments to avoid undesirable effects.

Fourth, the results for Portland and related evaluation research point to a number of program features associated with longer-term labor market success. Rather than leave program design completely to market forces, WIA policy should actively disseminate these findings and encourage states and local workforce boards to adopt program designs accordingly. Key features include a strong focus on employment, combining job search and short-term education or training, and being more selective about the choice of jobs, e.g., demand occupations paying self-sufficiency wages and offering greater potential for retention and advancement.

Fifth, WIA and related programs should put more resources into postprogram services geared to promoting continued access to learning, retention and career advancement opportunities. Many of those now being served in WIA, TANF, and related workforce programs are unlikely to have the desired level of access to or participation in further education and training opportunities in the workplace without an additional push from public policy. Employers are increasing their investments in training, but training is still offered disproportionately to those at higher skill levels.

Sixth, impacts for youth are unlikely to improve under WIA unless more intensive service strategies are pursued along the lines of those found in Job Corps, which remains the only program that has yielded significant, lasting labor market impacts for youth. Job Corps is expensive, but under very reasonable assumptions, produces positive returns on investment for very disadvantaged youths. USDOL, and other responsible federal agencies (e.g., U.S. Department of Education), would do well to study the lessons from Job Corps and develop mechanisms for implementing them within the mainstream programs across the nation. While doing so, special efforts must be made to determine what works for Hispanic and younger (18–19-year-old) youth.[24]

We can also offer lessons that extend beyond WIA. One is that measuring the impacts of training, a challenge in the best of circumstances, is likely to become even more difficult in the future. Even with training producing the desired impacts on earnings, if training is poorly measured in WIA information systems, and if control group members are accessing an ever-expanding array of Internet-based education and training services, then detecting incremental impacts relative to services received in the community at large will be very challenging. Making the case for funding effective workforce services may become more difficult.

Another lesson we should take from the Job Corps experience over several decades is that serious attention to the what and how of training pays off in the labor market for even the most disadvantaged participants. Job Corps is the only workforce development program that has enjoyed relative stability over many years, while retaining a focus on real skill acquisition with the necessary support services. It may be no accident that many of the Job Corps contractors also bring to the table experiences from the military sector, a sector that has made conscious, long-term investments in curricula, learning technologies and related tools (see, for example, Fletcher and Chatelier 2000). We should pursue ways to promote greater technology transfer on training from the military into other areas of the public as well as the private sectors.

Yet a third important lesson is that training and training-related strategies are necessary but not sufficient without well designed demand-side strategies. Even the most effective employment and training programs have tended to leave most of their participants in employment that was less than stable and earning wages that were inadequate to attain economic self-sufficiency. Public policy must pay careful attention to both sides of the labor market to be effective.

The importance of training is widely recognized (see, for example, International Labour Office 1998). Mangum (2000) refers to this as the "essentiality of occupational preparation." We now compete in a global economy with shortening production cycles, growing job insecurity and instability, and rising emphasis on personal and family responsibility for all things, including career development and management ("career navigators"). The labor market places a definite premium on education and skills such that the income and earnings gap between those who have them and those who do not continues to widen. We must use the lessons learned from program evaluations to improve the delivery of training services over time. In part, this may mean communicating them in a form that individual consumers can comprehend and act upon.

Notes

This chapter was prepared with funding from the W.E. Upjohn Institute for Employment Research and the U.S. Department of Labor's Employment and Training Administration. Daniel Schroeder, Sarah Looney, Andy Redman, and Dan Starr assisted with this research. David Grubb, Carolyn Heinrich, Dan Ryan, Steve Wandner, and Bill Rogers provided helpful comments on earlier versions presented to the U.S. Department of Labor/Upjohn Institute *Conference on Job Training and Labor Exchange in the U.S.* in Augusta, Michigan, in September 2002 and the *24th Annual Research Conference of the Association for Public Policy Analysis and Management* in Dallas, Texas, in November 2002.

1. King et al. (2000) rely on figures from Function 504 in the federal budget. Friedlander et al. (1997, p. 1814) state that training expenditures "broadly defined," constituted less than 0.2 percent of GDP in 1995.
2. For example, the Texas Smart Jobs Fund, which had been second in size only to California's ETP, was eliminated in 2001, a victim both of the lack of evidence of its effectiveness and of declining Texas UI trust fund balances.
3. Ray Marshall Center tabulations based on raw 2000–2001 participation data provided by the local board.
4. These figures are based on tabulations from WIA Standard Reporting and Data System.
5. I am currently participating in two USDOL-funded projects—the Administrative Data Research and Evaluation (ADARE) Project (see Stevens 2003) and the eight-state WIA Service Delivery Study that is being directed by the Rockefeller Institute (Barnow and King 2003)—that are exploring these issues and documenting WIA data collection and reporting problems.
6. Some researchers prefer the term "nonexperimental" to "quasi-experimental," on the grounds that the prefix "quasi" lends too much credence to the resulting estimates. Yet, the point of the distinction is that evaluation methods relying on various forms of comparison groups are attempting to approximate the results of experiments, while simple gross-outcome analyses that are "nonexperimental" do not. I've chosen to use the term "quasi-experimental" for this reason.
7. Note that these would translate into impacts ranging from around $312 to $935 in current (2001) dollars.
8. PSE was dropped from the federal training toolkit in the early 1980s despite showing positive (quasi-experimental) results, especially for women. Funding for PSE was eliminated from the federal budget in FY 1981. Congress eliminated

PSE as an allowable activity when JTPA was signed into law replacing CETA in late 1982.

9. Kane and Rouse (1999, p. 74) suggest that researchers have been far too conservative in interpreting JTPA training impacts, a point also made in the recent paper by Barnow and Gubits (2002).

10. I am grateful to Dan Ryan of USDOL/ETA's Office of Evaluation for providing these data.

11. USDOL's per-assignee impacts were converted into per-enrollee impacts using the activity enrollment rates provided in Orr et al. (1996) and Nudelman (2000).

12. Mathematica researchers Mallar et al. (1982) also conducted the *quasi-experimental* evaluation of Job Corps some twenty years earlier.

13. Roughly 27 percent of the applicants never enrolled in the Job Corps.

14. McConnell and Glazerman (2001), indicate that benefits exceed costs for most participant subgroups with two troubling exceptions: Hispanics and younger (18–19-year-old) participants.

15. The author served as Assistant Director of Research, Demonstration and Evaluation for the Texas JTPA program during this period and expended considerable effort to ensure that an experimental design was the basis for the Texas demonstration. An Abt Associates team led by Howard Bloom, then at New York University, conducted the evaluation.

16. Most of the Tier II referrals to training were in the Houston site, and, unfortunately, many of these were referrals of former white-collar professionals to what was seen as blue-collar training. A more appropriate test of their Tier I/II design would have been desirable.

17. Estimated earnings effects for training participation are very high: for example, second-year, per-enrollee impacts of $1,402 (insignificant) for CT and $10,987 for OJT (significant at the 99 percent level) in 1986–1987 dollars (see Corson and Haimson 1995, p. 48). Note that these estimates are based on very small numbers and are not true experimental impacts estimates. Only 15 percent of those referred to training received it, while 19 percent of those offered the reemployment bonus received it (Corson and Haimson 1995, pp. 18–19).

18. Again, thanks to Dan Ryan of USDOL/ETA for providing this information.

19. The NEWWS evaluation reports did not provide sufficient information to compute *per-participant* impacts for all groups.

20. Risk of depression was measured for sample members in Portland, Riverside, Atlanta, and Grand Rapids using four items from the Center for Epidemiological Studies-Depression (CES-D) Scale.

21. We identified many of the same features as being important factors in producing gross outcomes in a USDOL-funded research project on JTPA "success stories" in Illinois and Texas in the mid 1990s (King et al. 2000). We utilized a combination of multivariate statistical analysis of program records linked with long-term UI wage records and in-depth field interviews with program administrators and staff.

22. OJT, customized training, and a few other exceptions are allowed.

23. See Chapter 2 for a detailed discussion of these issues.

24. WIA defines two youth subgroups: younger youth (18–19) and older youth (20–24). Job Corps (part of WIA) takes the same approach.

References

American Society for Training and Development. 2002. *2002 State of the Industry Report.* Arlington, VA: ASTD.

Barnow, Burt S. 1987. "The Impact of CETA Programs on Earnings: A Review of the Literature." *Journal of Human Resources* 22(2): 157–193.

Barnow, Burt S., and Daniel B. Gubits. 2002. "Review of Recent Pilot, Demonstration, Research, and Evaluation Initiatives to Assist in the Implementation of Programs under the Workforce Investment Act." Chapter 5 in *Strategic Plan for Pilots, Demonstrations, Research, and Evaluations, 2002—2007,* Washington, DC: U.S. Department of Labor, Employment and Training Administration.

Barnow, Burt S., and Christopher T. King. 2003. *The Workforce Investment Act in Eight States: Overview of Findings from a Field Network Study, Interim Report.* Albany, NY: The Nelson A. Rockefeller Institute, May.

Becker, Gary S. 1975. *Human Capital: A Theoretical and Empirical Analysis, with Special Reference to Education.* 2nd ed. New York: National Bureau of Economic Research, Columbia University Press.

Bloom, Howard S. 1990. *Back to Work: Testing Reemployment Services for Dislocated Workers.* Kalamazoo, MI: W.E. Upjohn Institute for Employment Research.

Bloom, Howard S., Larry L. Orr, Stephen H. Bell, George Cave, Fred Doolittle, Winston Lin, and Johannes M. Bos. 1997. "The Benefits and Costs of JTPA Title II-A Programs: Key Findings from the National Job Training Partnership Act Study." *Journal of Human Resources* 32(3): 549–576.

Burghardt, John, and Peter Z. Schochet. 2001. *National Job Corps Study: Impacts by Center Characteristics.* Princeton, NJ: Mathematica Policy Research, Inc.

Burghardt, John, Peter Z. Schochet, Sheena McConnell, Terry Johnson, R. Mark Gritz, Steven Glazerman, John Homrighausen, and Russell Jackson. 2001. *Does Job Corps Work? A Summary of the National Job Corps Study.* Princeton, NJ: Mathematica Policy Research, Inc.

Carnevale, Anthony P., and Donna M. Desrochers. 2000. "Employer Training: The High Road, the Low Road and the Muddy Middle Path." In *Back to Shared Prosperity: The Growing Inequality of Wealth and Income in America,* Ray Marshall, ed. Armonk, NY: M.E. Sharpe, pp. 300–307.

Commission on the Skills of the American Workforce. 1990. *America's Choice: High Skills or Low Wages!* New York: National Center for Education and the Economy.

Corson, Walter, and Joshua Haimson. 1995. *The New Jersey Unemployment Insurance Reemployment Demonstration Project Six-Year Follow-Up and Summary Report.* UI Occasional Paper 95-2. Washington, DC: U.S. Department of Labor, Employment and Training Administration.

Couch, Kenneth A. 1992. "New Evidence on the Long-Term Effects of Employment Training Programs." *Journal of Labor Economics* 10(4): 380–388.

Duscha, Steve, and Wanda Lee Graves. 1999. *State Financed and Customized Training Programs.* Research and Evaluation Report Series 99-E: U.S. Department of Labor, Employment and Training Administration.

Fletcher, J.D., and Paul R. Chatelier. 2000. "Training in the Military." In *Training and Retraining: A Handbook for Business, Industry, Government, and the Military,* Sigmund Tobias and J.D. Fletcher, eds. New York: Macmillan.

Fraker, Thomas, and Rebecca Maynard. 1987. "The Adequacy of Comparison Group Designs for Evaluations of Employment-Related Programs." *Journal of Human Resources* 2(Spring): 194–227.

Frazis, Harley, Maury Gittleman, Michael Horrigan, and Mary Joyce. 1998. "Results from the 1995 Survey of Employer-Provided Training." *Monthly Labor Review* 121(6): 3–13.

Freedman, Stephen. 2000. *The National Evaluation of Welfare-to-Work Strategies—Four-Year Impacts of Ten Programs on Employment Stability and Earnings Growth.* Washington, DC: U.S. Department of Health and Human Services, ACF/ASPE; U.S. Department of Education, Office of the Under Secretary/OVAE, December.

Friedlander, Daniel, David H. Greenberg, and Philip K. Robins. 1997. "Evaluating Government Training Programs for the Economically Disadvantaged." *Journal of Economic Literature* 35(4): 1809–1855.

———. 2000. "Methodologies for Determining the Effectiveness of Training Programs." In *Improving the Odds: Increasing the Effectiveness of Publicly Funded Training,* Burt S. Barnow and Christopher T. King, eds. Washington, DC: Urban Institute Press, pp. 261–292.

Ganzglass, Evelyn, Neil Ridley, Martin Simon, Christopher T. King, Betty Jane Narver, and Carl Van Horn. 2000. *Building a Next-Generation Workforce Development System.* Washington, DC: National Governors Association, September.

Gritz, R. Mark, and Terry Johnson. 2001. *National Job Corps Study: Assessing Program Effects on Earnings for Students Achieving Key Program Milestones.* Seattle, WA: Battelle Memorial Institute.

Grubb, W. Norton, Norena Badway, Denise Bell, Bernadette Chi, Christopher T. King, Julie Herr, Heath Prince, Richard Kazis, Lisa Hicks, and Judith Taylor. 1999. *Toward Order from Chaos: State Efforts to Reform Workforce Development Systems.* Berkeley, CA: National Center for Research in Vocational Education, MDS-1249.

Hamilton, Gayle. 2002. *Moving People from Welfare to Work: Lessons from the National Evaluation of Welfare-to-Work Strategies.* Washington, DC: U.S. Department of Health and Human Services, ACF/ASPE and U.S. Department of Education, Office of the Under Secretary/OVAE, July.

Heckman, James J., Robert J. LaLonde, and Jeffrey A. Smith. 1999. "The Economics and Econometrics of Active Labor Market Programs." In *Handbook of Labor Economics, Vol. 3,* Orley Ashenfelter and David Card, eds. Amsterdam: Elsevier, pp. 1886–1932.

Hight, Joseph E. 1998. "Young Worker Participation in Post-School Education and Training," *Monthly Labor Review* 121(6): 14–21.

Hollenbeck, Kevin. 2002. *Washington State Workforce Program Evaluation Design.* Kalamazoo, MI: W.E. Upjohn Institute for Employment Research.

Hotz, V. Joseph, Guido W. Imbens, and Jacob A. Klerman. 2000. "The Long-Term Gains from GAIN: A Re-Analysis of the Impacts of the California GAIN Program." Working paper. Cambridge, MA: National Bureau of Economic Research. http://nber.org/papers/w8007.

International Labour Office. 1998. *World Employment Report, 1989–1999: Employability in the Global Economy, How Training Matters.* Geneva: ILO.

Isbell, Kellie, John Trutko, and Burt S. Barnow. 2000. "Customized Training for Employers: Training People for Jobs That Exist and Employers Who Want Them." In *Improving the Odds: Increasing the Effectiveness of Publicly Funded Training,* Burt S. Barnow and Christopher T. King, eds. Washington, DC: Urban Institute Press, 209–225.

Jacobson, Louis, Robert LaLonde, and Daniel Sullivan. 2001. "The Returns from Community College Schooling for Displaced Workers." Photocopy, Rockville, MD: Westat.

———. 2002. "Measures of Program Performance and the Training Choices of Displaced Workers." In *Targeting Employment Services,* Randall W. Eberts, Christopher J. O'Leary, and Stephen A. Wandner, eds. Kalamazoo, MI: The W.E. Upjohn Institute for Employment Research, pp. 187–213.

Kane, Thomas and Cecilia Elena Rouse. 1999. "The Community College: Educating Students at the Margin Between College and Work." *Journal of Economic Perspectives* 13(1): 63–84.

King, Christopher T. 1999. "Federalism and Workforce Development Policy Reform." *Publius: The Journal of Federalism* 29(2): 53–71.

King, Christopher T., Robert E. McPherson, and Donald W. Long. 2000. "Public Labor Market Policies for the Twenty-First Century." In *Back to Shared Prosperity: The Growing Inequality of Wealth and Income in America,* Ray Marshall, ed. Armonk, New York: M.E. Sharpe, pp. 275–286.

King, Christopher T., Jerome Olson, Leslie Lawson, Charles Trott, and John Baj. 2000. "Training Success Stories for Adults and Out-of-School Youth: A Tale of Two States." In *Improving the Odds: Increasing the Effectiveness of Publicly Funded Training,* Burt S. Barnow and Christopher T. King, eds. Washington, DC: Urban Institute Press, pp. 129–184.

LaLonde, Robert J. 1995. "The Promise of Public Sector-Sponsored Training Programs." *Journal of Economic Perspectives* 9(2): 149–168.

Leigh, Duane E. 1990. *Does Training Work for Displaced Workers: A Survey of Existing Evidence.* Kalamazoo, MI: W.E. Upjohn Institute for Employment Research.

———. 1995. *Assisting Workers Displaced by Structural Change: An International Perspective.* Kalamazoo, MI: W.E. Upjohn Institute for Employment Research.

———. 2000. "Training Programs for Dislocated Workers." In *Improving the Odds: Increasing the Effectiveness of Publicly Funded Training,* Burt S. Barnow and Christopher T. King, eds. Washington, DC: Urban Institute Press, pp. 227–259.

Lerman, Robert I., Signe-Mary McKernan, and Stephanie Riegg. 2004. Chapter 7 in this volume.

Lynch, Lisa M. 1994a. "Payoffs to Alternative Training Strategies at Work." In *Working under Different Rules,* Richard B. Freeman, ed. New York: Russell Sage Foundation.

Lynch, Lisa M., ed. 1994b. *Training and the Private Sector: International Comparisons.* Chicago: University of Chicago Press for NBER.

Lynch, Lisa M., and Sandra E. Black. 1998. "Beyond the Incidence of Training." *Industrial and Labor Relations Review* 52(1): 64–81.

Mallar, Charles D., Stuart Kerachsky, Charles Thornton, and David Long. 1982. *Evaluation of the Economic Impact of the Job Corps Program: Third Follow-Up Report.* Princeton, NJ: Mathematica Policy Research Inc., September.

Mangum, Garth L. 2000. "Reflections on Training Policies and Programs." In *Improving the Odds: Increasing the Effectiveness of Publicly Funded*

Training, Burt S. Barnow and Christopher T. King, eds. Washington, DC: Urban Institute Press, pp. 293–333.

Marshall, Ray, and Marc Tucker. 1992. *Thinking for a Living: Work, Skills, and the Future of the American Economy.* New York: Basic Books.

Martinson, Karin, and Julie Strawn. 2002. *Built to Last: Why Skills Matter for Long-Run Success in Welfare Reform.* Washington, DC: Center for Law and Social Policy and the National Council of State Directors of Adult Education, May.

McConnell, Sheena, and Steven Glazerman. 2001. *National Job Corps Study: The Benefits and Costs of Job Corps.* Princeton, NJ: Mathematica Policy Research, Inc.

Michalopoulos, Charles, Christine Schwartz, and Diana Adams-Ciardullo. 2000. *National Evaluation of Welfare-to-Work Strategies—What Works Best for Whom: Impacts of 20 Welfare-to-Work Programs by Subgroup.* Washington, DC: U. S. Department of Health and Human Services, ACF/ASPE; U.S. Department of Education, Office of the Under Secretary/OVAE, August.

Nudelman, Jodi. 2000. "The Impact of Job Training Partnership Act Programs for Adult Welfare Recipients." In *Improving the Odds: Increasing the Effectiveness of Publicly Funded Training,* Burt S. Barnow and Christopher T. King, eds. Washington, DC: Urban Institute Press, pp. 101–128.

Orr, Larry L., Howard S. Bloom, Stephen H. Bell, Fred Doolittle, Winston Lin and George Cave. 1996. *Does Training for the Disadvantaged Work? Evidence from the National JTPA Study.* Washington, DC: The Urban Institute Press.

O'Shea, Daniel, and Christopher T. King. 2001. *The Workforce Investment Act of 1998: Restructuring Workforce Development Initiatives in States and Localities, Rockefeller Report No.12.* Albany, NY: The Nelson A. Rockefeller Institute of Government, April.

Plimpton, Lisa, and Demetra Smith Nightingale. 2000. "Welfare Employment Programs: Impacts and Cost Effectiveness of Employment and Training Activities." In *Improving the Odds: Increasing the Effectiveness of Publicly Funded Training,* Burt S. Barnow and Christopher T. King, eds. Washington, DC: Urban Institute Press, pp. 49–100.

Schochet, Peter Z., John Burghardt, and Steven Glazerman. 2001. *National Job Corps Study: The Impacts of Job Corps on Participants' Employment and Related Outcomes.* Princeton, NJ: Mathematica Policy Research, Inc.

Secretary of Labor's Commission on Achieving Necessary Skills. 1990. Washington, DC: U.S. Department of Labor.

Secretary of Labor's Commission on Workforce Quality and Labor Market Efficiency. 1989. *Investing in People: A Strategy to Address America's*

Workforce Crisis, Volumes I and II. Washington, DC: U.S. Department of Labor.

Stevens, David W. 2003. *Mapping One-Stop Client Flows, PY 2000 (JULY 2000-JUNE 2001), Title I-B Adults and Dislocated Workers, By Core (Registered), Intensive and Training Services.* Washington, DC: Prepared for U.S. Department of Labor, Employment and Training Administration, Administrative Data Research and Evaluation Project, Research Project No. 1, January.

Stromsdorfer, E., H. Bloom, R. Boruch, M. Borus, J. Gueron, A. Gustman, P. Rossi, F. Scheuren, M. Smith, and F. Stafford. 1985. *Recommendations of the Job Training Longitudinal Survey Research Advisory Committee.* Washington, DC: U.S. Department of Labor, Employment and Training Administration.

U.S. Department of Labor, Office of the Chief Economist. 1995. *What's Working (and What's Not): A Summary of Research on the Economic Impacts of Employment and Training Programs.* Washington, DC: U.S. Department of Labor, January.

U.S. General Accounting Office. 1996. *Job Training Partnership Act: Long-Term Earnings and Employment Outcomes.* Washington, DC: GAO/HEHS-96-40, March.

4
Implementation Issues in Delivering Training Services to Adults under WIA

Ronald D'Amico
Jeffrey Salzman

The Workforce Investment Act of 1998 (WIA) represents a potentially important reshaping of the federal government's approach to worker training as part of publicly funded workforce development services. First applied nationwide in program year (PY) 2000, a number of the act's key provisions were to some extent initially greeted with confusion and uncertainty by workforce practitioners charged with implementing them. Moreover, PY 2000 represented a period of rapid economic growth and extremely tight labor markets that limited the demand for training services among what would normally have been the program's traditional clientele. Both of these facts combined to make WIA's first full year of implementation rather tentative. Subsequently, WIA has matured substantially, as the workforce development system has gained greater confidence and comfort with implementing WIA, and changes to the economic climate have increased the demand for training services.

In this chapter, we profile this trajectory with regards to the WIA adult program.[1] We begin by delineating the legislation's key provisions regarding training services and contrast them with previous approaches. We next describe the early evolution of WIA service delivery by drawing on data collected through administrative records and interviews we conducted with workforce practitioners in nearly 50 local workforce investment areas in 23 separate states around the country. We conclude by drawing attention to the inherent tension between some of WIA's key provisions and reflect on the likely implications of WIA reauthorization for resolving them.

KEY PROVISIONS REGARDING TRAINING IN WIA

WIA replaced and repealed the Job Training Partnership Act
(JTPA) and amended the Wagner-Peyser Act in response to a variety of
concerns about how the existing public workforce development system
was designed and operated. Among these concerns, it was noted that a
multitude of employment and training programs—by some counts over
150 separate programs, including, among others, those operating under
JTPA, Vocational Rehabilitation, Vocational Education, the Trade
Adjustment Assistance Act, and the Wagner-Peyser Act—often operated without effective coordination or collaboration. The resulting system suffered from redundancies and inefficiencies and confronted
customers with a confusing maze of programs through which they
found it difficult to navigate (U.S. General Accounting Office
1994a,b,c 2000).

Second, JTPA services were limited to those who met narrowly
prescribed eligibility criteria, thereby curtailing access to potentially
valuable workforce services to the broader population in need of skills
upgrading or retraining. In JTPA's adult program, participation was
limited to those who were economically disadvantaged and (after the
JTPA Amendments of 1992) at least 65 percent needed to be identified
as hard to serve, by virtue of having at least one barrier to employment
from a list of seven that were specified in the legislation. These stipulations arguably served to target services on those who needed them the
most. However, as the U.S. workforce development system moved
toward a model of one-stop service delivery over the several years
before JTPA's repeal, these eligibility restrictions created awkward
problems regarding funding and staffing support and hampered the
ability of JTPA-supported programs to operate effectively with its partners (Kogan et al. 1997). Moreover, they hampered the ability of the
public workforce investment system to be agile in upgrading workers'
skills to meet evolving employers' needs in a rapidly changing economy.

Third, JTPA was faulted for authorizing expensive training services as a first, rather than as a last, resort. Indeed, JTPA was presump-
tively a training program. Although the requirements were somewhat
looser in the dislocated worker program, virtually all persons enrolled

in the JTPA adult program were expected to receive comprehensive services that could include basic skills training and occupational skills training, among other things. Moreover, at least 50 percent of funds for the adult program needed to be spent on direct training services, and job search assistance or preemployment skill building as stand-alone activities were discouraged.[2] Given the hard-to-serve clientele that JTPA was targeting, these restrictions might have been sensible. At the same time, they arguably handcuffed practitioners and, if results from recent welfare-to-work evaluations are an indication, might have promoted training services when less costly interventions might have been more effective in leading to employment quickly (Freedman et al. 2000; Hamilton 2002).[3]

Fourth, because of JTPA's heavy use of contract training, participants' choices among courses of study and available training providers were often limited to a preselected vendor or set of vendors with which the local workforce area had worked out prior agreements. In the worst cases, participants were sometimes assigned to a course of study by a case manager primarily because a training slot in a program for which the local area had developed a contract needed to be filled. For these reasons, JTPA was sometimes criticized for not being sufficiently customer focused (Levitan and Gallo 1988; U.S. Department of Labor 1991).

Finally, JTPA was sometimes decried as being inattentive to the needs of the business community. According to these arguments, the role that publicly funded workforce development programs should play in promoting the nation's economic competitiveness and ensuring a supply of skilled workers for emerging industry needs was too little appreciated.

WIA was enacted to address these concerns, after much anticipation and delay caused by a protracted policy debate within Congress. Building on reforms that some states and the federal government had already begun (D'Amico et al. 2001; Grubb et al. 1999), it does so by purportedly improving system integration and service coordination, providing universal access while rationing services to promote efficiency, promoting customer choice and system accountability, and bringing business to the fore as a key customer of the workforce system.

Among the ways WIA attempts to accomplish these purposes is by mandating the establishment of a one-stop service delivery structure, by which key partners involved in providing public workforce development assistance are to come together to plan and coordinate their services.[4] To the extent that doing so is consistent with their authorizing legislation, partners are to contribute to the costs and maintenance of the one-stop system in a way that should reflect benefits to their own customers.

Apart from mandating a new service delivery infrastructure, WIA also changes eligibility rules and program services in comparison to JTPA. These differences are summarized in Table 4.1. As the table shows, WIA promotes universal access by abandoning JTPA's rigid criteria regarding eligibility for services and thereby allows all adults to access WIA services without regard to income status. To this degree, the public workforce system must become equipped to meet a diverse array of needs and, in so doing, can play a critical role in promoting the efficient matching of workers with job openings and enhancing workers' careers and work skills.

At the same time, recognizing the need to husband scarce resources, WIA also promotes system efficiency by establishing a hierarchy of three service tiers, with limited access to the more expensive, higher tiers of service. At the lowest level of the hierarchy, core services consist of basic informational services, self-services, or light-touch staff-assisted services primarily designed to assist individuals in conducting job search or researching training or other services on their own. Intensive services, the next level of the hierarchy, consist of activities involving somewhat greater staff involvement, but the focus is still on providing short-term assistance—such as pre-vocational services or assessment and counseling—designed to help customers access available job opportunities given their existing occupational skills. Finally, training services, including on-the-job training and classroom occupational skills training, consist of generally longer-term skill-building activities designed to provide participants with occupationally specific skills or credentials.

Abandoning JTPA's rigid criteria regarding eligibility for services, all adults are able to access these services. However, in keeping with the notion that these three service tiers constitute a hierarchy, only those who are deemed unable to achieve their employment objectives

Table 4.1 Adult Program Side-by-Side WIA and JTPA Comparison Regarding Eligibility and Services

	WIA	JTPA (Title II-A)
Eligibility and targeting	• All adults (ages 18 and over) are eligible for core services • Intensive and training services are available to those who have had at least one service at a lower tier and are deemed unable to meet their employment goals without services at the higher tier • Priority for intensive and training services must be given to recipients of public assistance and other low-income individuals, in local areas were funds are limited	• Eligibility generally restricted to economically disadvantaged adults (ages 22 or older) • 65% must be in specified "hard-to-serve" categories (e.g., basic skills deficient, dropouts, welfare recipients, offenders, homeless, those with disabilities) • 10% need not be economically disadvantaged, but they must still be in a "hard-to-serve" category or be a displaced homemaker, veteran, or alcoholic or addict
Services	• Customers must receive at least one core service before receiving intensive services, and at least one intensive service before receiving training services • Core services consist of, among other things: • Outreach, intake, and orientation to services • Job search and placement assistance, including career counseling where appropriate • Providing labor market info (e.g., job vacancy listings, occupations and skills in demand, etc.) • Providing performance and cost info on training providers	• Services shall include an objective assessment of skill levels and service needs • Basic skills training, occupational skills training, and supportive services should be provided, either directly or through referral, where the assessment indicates they are appropriate • Authorized direct training services include, among others: • Basic skills training and GED training • On-the-job training and customized training • Assessment, counseling and case management • Work experience

(continued)

Table 4.1 (continued)

- Intensive services consist of, among other things:
  - Comprehensive and specialized assessments, to identify employment goals and barriers
  - Developing the individual employment plan
  - Group and individual counseling and career planning
  - Short-term pre-vocational services
- Training services consist of, among other things:
  - Occupational skills training
  - On-the-job training
  - Skill upgrading and retraining
  - Entrepreneurial training
  - Job readiness training
  - Adult education and literacy services provided in combination with other training services
- Training services should be provided through Individual Training Accounts, except for on-the-job training and customized training, training programs of demonstrated effectiveness for those with multiple barriers, or if there are too few eligible training providers

- Skill upgrading and retraining
- Bilingual training
- Entrepreneurial training
- Vocational exploration
- Training to develop appropriate work habits
- Preapprenticeship programs
- On-site industry-specific training
- Authorized training-related and supportive services include, among others:
  - Job search assistance and outreach
  - Supportive services and needs-based payments
- Work experience, job search assistance, job search skills training, and job club activities are to be accompanied by basic and/or occupational skills training, unless the latter services are not appropriate and the former are not available through the Employment Service
- Services to older individuals (ages 55 and older) can be separately provided as part of Section 204(d)

at a lower level of service can advance to the next higher level. Moreover, priority is to be given to public assistance and other low-income individuals, whenever funds are deemed to be scarce. Thus, the intent of these provisions taken together is to provide access to basic services to all adults, while limiting the more costly services to those whose need is demonstrable and most pressing.

Customer choice and empowerment are also key tenets of the legislation. In the first instance, this objective is achieved by allowing the universal customer free and open access to a vast array of informational tools and resources that he or she can use on a self-help basis. As well, customers undertaking training are to be provided with opportunities to choose the training program and provider that they feel best meet their needs. In this regard, although WIA still allows contract training under some circumstances, it aims to empower customers by relying heavily on Individual Training Accounts (ITAs), which can be likened to vouchers that customers are generally free to use to procure training services of their choice, subject to certain limitations. Among these limitations, local workforce agencies can place caps on the duration of training that customers can undertake and the costs that will be approved. Second, the training generally must provide skills for jobs that are deemed to be in demand in the local economy (or in another location to which the customer intends to relocate). Finally, the training program selected by the customer must have been certified by the state and local area as meeting acceptable standards of quality. The latter restriction will typically mean that the vendor has provided basic information about the training program and that previous cohorts of the program's trainees have met state standards for successful training outcomes.

By virtue of these provisions, WIA offers the basis for a substantial systemwide transformation. The extent to which it in fact achieves its objectives of greater system integration, customer empowerment, and efficiency, however, will depend on the ways its key stipulations are implemented in each of the nation's 600-plus local workforce development areas. Moreover, whether it does so without abandoning a decades-long federal commitment to improving the employment prospects of those who are economically disadvantaged by investing substantially in their occupational skills development remains very much an open question.

In the remainder of this chapter we provide a glimpse of the early WIA implementation experience, focusing specifically on training services funded to serve adults. We do so by drawing on recently available data for PY 2001 from WIA's client-level reporting system, the Workforce Investment Act Standardized Record Data (WIASRD), which records client characteristics, services, and outcomes for those who exited WIA during that program year.[5] Moreover, to provide a point of contrast with JTPA, we also use the PY 1998 Standardized Program Information Report (SPIR), the client-level reporting system analogous to the WIASRD that was used under JTPA.[6] Finally, we draw on qualitative information we collected from multi-day site visits to nearly 50 separate local workforce areas from PY 1999 through PY 2001 as part of a number of separate evaluations.[7] Because not all of these local areas were selected randomly, they cannot be construed necessarily as representative of the workforce system as a whole. Nonetheless, they provide substantial coverage across all regions of the country and 23 separate states and, as such, provide important evidence about the range of variation across the WIA workforce development system in its early years.

Among the issues we examine with these data sources are the extent to which local areas focus on training (as opposed to core and intensive services), the ways they establish customers' access to ITAs, limits they impose on the training choices that customers can make, and ways they support customers through the decision-making process.

TRAINING AS A FOCUS OF PROGRAM ACTIVITY

As the above description suggests, WIA can be construed as a dramatic shift in thinking about the role of training in serving program participants. The JTPA adult program, which WIA supersedes, was intended to be predominantly a training program, while WIA establishes a sequence of service levels that will culminate in training only if core and intensive services are deemed not to meet the customer's employment needs. To this extent, Congress recognized when enacting WIA that, given constraints of available funding, service strategies would need to rely on less costly interventions to accompany WIA's broader scope for eligibility. Moreover, Congress was to some degree demonstrating its philosophical bent toward a "work first" approach that was even more clearly reflected a few years earlier in its revamping of the nation's welfare system, through the Personal Responsibility and Work Opportunity Reconciliation Act of 1996. In this context, states and local areas need to decide the emphasis they will place on WIA training and the role they see for less costly core and intensive services. Their decisions reflect both practical considerations as well as strategic thinking about how best to invest their WIA dollars for greatest impact given the context of local labor market needs.

Emphasis on Training

Implicit in the legislation is a tension between serving the universal customer with a work-first approach on the one hand, and meeting the needs of low-income and low-skilled customers who are likely to need intensive interventions on the other (O'Shea and King 2001). Table 4.2 provides a preliminary answer to how this tension is being resolved. Using WIASRD data for PY 2001, it tabulates the percentage of WIA registrants in the adult program who exited after using only core services, intensive services but no training, or training services.[8] Data from the PY 1998 SPIR are reported for comparison.

First, among WIA registrants, about 23 percent exited after receiving only staff-assisted core services, 36 percent after intensive services, and 42 percent after training services.[9] No comparable figures are available in the PY 1998 SPIR. Nonetheless, JTPA's heavier emphasis on training can be deduced in that the incidence of basic skills instruction, on-the-job training (OJT), and other occupational training were all substantially higher in JTPA than they are in WIA. Thus, the incidence of basic skills instruction went from 18 percent to 2 percent,[10] OJT from 9 percent to 5 percent, and other occupational training from 67 percent to 33 percent.[11] Similarly, the average length of participation was longer in JTPA than in WIA, with very short spells of participation (participation of less than three months) substantially more common now than previously (26 percent in JTPA versus 34 percent in WIA), though differences are much more modest when one compares the JTPA figures with those for WIA trainees.[12] All of this is in keeping with WIA's allowance that limited-duration, nontraining services—and

Table 4.2 Services Received by Adult Exiters: WIA and JTPA

	PY 1998 JTPA exiters	PY 2001 WIA exiters			
		Total	Core only	Intensive– no training	Training
Number of cases	163,223	160,529	36,344	57,648	66,537
Highest tier of service					
Core only	NA	22.6	100	—	—
Intensive (no training)	NA	35.9	—	100	—
Training	NA	41.5	—	—	100
Service Received					
Basic skills instruction	18.1	2.1	—	0.1	5.1
On-the-job training	9.4	5.1	—	—	12.8
Other occupational training	63.1	32.9	—	—	82.1
Months of participation					
Up to 3	26.4	34.1	52.9	38.5	20.1
3–6	26.6	24.1	21.2	24.0	25.7
6–9	16.6	16.3	11.7	15.4	19.7
9–12	10.0	10.6	6.3	10.2	13.5
More than 12	20.4	14.8	7.9	12.0	21.1

NOTE: All figures (except Number of cases) are given as percentages. SPIR data represent figures for adults (Title II-A) and older workers (Section 204d) who received more than only an objective assessment. Data from the PY 2001 WIASRD are preliminary figures and exclude JTPA carry-overs. A '—' represents a percentage near zero. NA = not available.

nothing more—might be suitable for many WIA registrants. Finally, as one would expect, spells of participation in WIA are longer as one moves across the three service tiers, from staff-assisted core, to intensive services, and to training.

The table suggests, then, that WIA program operators are making full use of the three levels of service activity that WIA allows, exiting registrants in substantial numbers at all three service levels. Table 4.3 shows, however, that local workforce investment areas (LWIAs) vary greatly in the extent to which they do so. Thus, in just over one-half of the nation's local areas, about half of the WIA exiters have received training service, while much smaller numbers of local areas give more emphasis to core services or to intensive services. Clearly, then, local

Table 4.3 Service Emphasis among LWIAs (%)

High emphasis on core services	11.5
High emphasis on intensive services	18.0
High emphasis on training services	56.8
Mixed emphasis	13.7

NOTE: Figures represent the percentage of local areas. "High emphasis" is defined as having more than 50% of WIA exiters, exclusive of JTPA carry overs, exit at the service level indicated. Data are from the PY 2001 WIASRD, excluding JTPA carry overs.

areas are making very different decisions about the mix of services they will provide with WIA funds, reflecting their local priorities and the needs of their communities. To this extent, WIA's provisions designed to devolve decision making to the local level seem to be in evidence. At the same time, a heavy emphasis on training that continues policies carried out under JTPA seems quite strong.

This variability is consistent with observations we gleaned from the multi-day site visits we conducted to 48 separate local areas from PY 1999 to PY 2001. Partly these differences reflected deep-seated disagreements about how WIA should be interpreted and strategic decisions about how best to use WIA funds for greatest impact, but very practical considerations came into play as well.

Thus, some areas demonstrated a strong commitment to training at the outset and sought to continue the high levels of funding for training that they had provided under JTPA, because they believed that doing so would best meet the needs of their communities or that training was WIA's most appropriate mission. Some areas were also able to concentrate on training services with their WIA funds as a consequence of the nature of their one-stop partnerships and the funding decisions that resulted from them. For example, in some local areas nearly all core services and a substantial part of the costs of the one-stop infrastructure were funded by Wagner-Peyser, which freed up substantial amounts of WIA funds for training.

Other areas adopted a strategy of emphasizing core and intensive services, and as a consequence cut back on investments in training considerably. Some did so because they were explicitly adopting a "work-first" interpretation of WIA, and, accordingly, considered training only as a last resort. Administrators in these areas often cited policy directives they were receiving from their state officials, who in turn felt that this approach was required by WIA. This interpretation seemed much more common in WIA's first year, however, than in its second, when interest in work-first appeared to wane. Clarification that the U.S. Department of Labor issued in mid PY 2000, which encouraged a flexible approach oriented to each customer's needs, seemed important in accounting for this shift.

Local areas also seemed generally more cautious in authorizing training at the outset than they did later on, because of a perceived shortage of funds and other practical considerations. For example, although they might have been very committed to training as a service activity, some program administrators noted that they had much less money to spend on training than they did under JTPA, because of WIA's requirement that they establish a one-stop infrastructure with three separate levels of service. Others expressed a general caution in using training funds in the face of substantial uncertainty regarding for whom training could be authorized and because of other general start-up difficulties, including the need to first certify eligible training providers. Notably, fewer sites made these observations as WIA matured, suggesting that initial investments in establishing one-stop systems had accomplished their objectives, and concerns and uncertainty about the use of training dissipated to a substantial degree.

Finally, the very strong economic conditions during PY 2000 also dampened the demand for training services to some degree. During this program year, jobs were generally plentiful, job seekers wanted to find employment quickly to take advantage of available opportunities, and employers were eager for workers to fill their hiring needs. Accordingly, program administrators found themselves emphasizing relatively shorter-term interventions, because they believed that doing so best met the needs of both employer and job-seeking customers. As the economy cooled in the summer of 2001, however, program administrators foresaw an increasing demand for training services among their program participants.

These observations suggest some structural and systemic factors that gave rise to variability in training incidence rates across local areas, including philosophical predispositions on the part of local WIBs, but also the nature of emerging partnerships and the funding arrangements for one-stop services that result. They also suggest, however, that training rates might have increased in PY 2001 in comparison to PY 2000, WIA's first year of implementation, as local program administrators gained greater comfort with WIA requirements and as the demand for training services increased in a generally weaker economic climate. Although deficiencies in the PY 2000 WIASRD make comparisons with PY 2001 difficult, evidence suggests that that has indeed occurred.[13]

What Counts as Training and Who Is Providing It?

The discussion in the previous section is hampered by important limitations of measurement. To begin with, the WIA legislation and implementing regulations define the three levels of service in fairly general terms, thereby allowing states and local areas substantial discretion in what activities they classify as each. For example, the line between what counts as WIA staff-assisted core services (which requires WIA registration) and self-help or informational services (which does not) is quite blurry and is operationalized inconsistently from one local area to the next. Further, because the outcomes of WIA registrants generally count as part of a local area's official performance statistics, some areas defer the point of WIA registration as long as they can, either by classifying a range of light-touch services as self-help or by funding them through non-WIA sources (D'Amico and Salzman 2002). Thus, counts of participants, and, by implication, rates of training could vary from one area to the next solely as a function of who becomes classified as a WIA registrant, regardless of what services are actually provided.

Related to this, the distinguishing line between the service tiers is similarly vague. For example, the difference between assessment and counseling that counts as staff-assisted core services rather than intensive services is a fine one, and different local areas make different practical decisions as to where that line should be drawn. More relevant for understanding WIA training services, the distinction between intensive and training services is not a clear one. For example, work experience, thought of as a training service under JTPA, is typically classified as an intensive service under WIA.[14] Similarly, what one local area classifies as training another might call pre-vocational services, classified by the WIA legislation as an intensive service.[15] In operationalizing this latter distinction, local areas commonly take into account whether the service activity provides training for a specific occupation or not, as well as its duration. Thus, short courses of instruction that arguably provide skills useful in a broad range of occupations—such as courses in computer literacy and basic computer applications—might be classified in some local areas as a pre-vocational service (and, hence, as intensive services), on the grounds that learning the basics of a desktop computer and acquiring some minimum level of proficiency with common office software are basic requirements associated with many occupations. Given that 13 percent of PY 1998 JTPA adult exiters undertook training of between 1 and 40 hours (Social Policy Research Associates 2000), much of the types of services that were provided as training in JTPA might thus now be provided and classified as pre-vocational intensive services in WIA. In other words, whatever the incidence of training services as formally measured by the WIASRD, substantial additional skill building is doubtless being carried out as part of intensive services (and perhaps even, through self-service tutorials, as part of core services).

ESTABLISHING CUSTOMER ACCESS TO TRAINING

As we noted earlier, JTPA established a means test for the adult program and required that 65 percent of enrollees have at least one from a list of characteristics that are deemed to constitute barriers to employment. WIA abandons these provisions, allowing program services to be universally accessible. At the same time, the legislation asserts that whenever funds are limited, priority for intensive and training services in the adult program should be given to those who are low income or on public assistance. An important strategic concern for local areas is balancing the obligation to provide universal access while ensuring adequate service levels to JTPA's traditional hard-to-serve clientele.

The Characteristics of WIA Registrants and Trainees

Table 4.4 provides evidence to suggest how these objectives are being balanced. It does so by comparing the characteristics of PY 2001 WIA adult exiters—including those who received core services only, intensive services but no training, and training services—with JTPA adult exiters from PY 1998.[16]

Table 4.4 A Comparison of Recent JTPA and WIA Adult Exiters

	JTPA	PY 2001 WIA Exiters			
	Exiters PY 1998	Total[a]	Core only	Intensive– no training	Training
Number of cases	163,223	160,529	36,344	57,648	66,537
Low income					
Yes	96.0	NA	NA	73.2	70.0
No	4.0	NA	NA	26.8	30.0
Cash welfare recipient	30.7	NA	NA	19.9	14.3
TANF/AFDC	25.7	NA	NA	9.7	10.2
GA, SSI, RCA	5.8	NA	NA	9.9	4.2
Highest grade completed					
Not a high school graduate	22.4	NA	NA	22.2	18.4
High school graduate	56.1	NA	NA	51.3	60.0
Post–high school	21.6	NA	NA	26.6	21.6
Labor force					
Employed	18.2	18.3	13.8	12.4	25.9
Not employed	81.8	81.7	86.2	87.6	74.1
Additional barriers					
Disability	10.4	7.6	6.4	9.9	6.3
Limited English	6.5	NA	NA	7.3	6.0
Single parent	43.7	NA	NA	29.0	26.0

NOTE: All figures (except Number of cases) are given as percentages. PY 1998 SPIR data represent figures for adults (Title II-A) and older workers (Section 204d) who received more than only an objective assessment. Percentages are based on those with non-missing data on the item in question. WIA data exclude JTPA carry-overs.

GA = General Assistance; SSI = Supplemental Security Assistance;

RCA = Refugee Cash Assistance; NA = not available

[a] The WIASRD does not require the reporting of many of the characteristics of participants who receive only staff-assisted core services. Thus, the total column for WIA registrants cannot be computed.

The table shows some substantial differences in the characteristics of program exiters that are consistent with what one might expect. Thus, given JTPA's eligibility rules, virtually all PY 1998 JTPA adult exiters were classified as low income. This percentage dropped substantially among PY 2001 WIA exiters to about three-quarters of those who received intensive or training services. Similarly, there has been a pronounced drop in service to cash welfare recipients, with nearly one-third of exiters classified as such in PY 1998, a proportion that is quite a bit higher than the available figures for WIA.[17]

With respect to other barriers, WIA exiters are much less likely to be single parents (44 percent are single parents in JTPA versus fewer than 30 percent in WIA), but they are about as likely as those who exited under JTPA to be individuals with a disability or to be limited English speakers.[18] Curiously, among WIA registrants, those who receive training are somewhat less likely to be low income or welfare recipients, or to be high school dropouts or single parents, than are those who receive intensive services but no training, even though those with these barriers presumably are more in need of training than others.[19]

In Chapter 2 of this volume, Barnow and Smith reflect on a long-standing concern (e.g., Anderson, Burkhauser, and Raymond 1993; National Commission for Employment Policy 1988; U.S. General Accounting Office 1989) that local areas engage in "cream skimming," by serving those more able to find employment from among those eligible. One might expect this concern to be exacerbated in WIA, which purports to promote universal access and lacks the explicit adjustments for participant characteristics in setting performance standards that JTPA had. Evidence to date indeed suggests local areas' ability and willingness to serve a wider customer base than they once did. At the same time, their priority for serving those who are low income still seems clearly in evidence.

Establishing Customer Eligibility for Training

Among the tensions embedded in WIA, local areas need to balance the legislation's requirements to husband resources by sequencing services across the three tiers, while also being customer-focused and responsive to customer needs. Based on our data collection, we conclude that local areas generally seem quite flexible and are not adopting a rigid "work first" interpretation of WIA that severely limits access to training. For example, only a few areas of the dozens we studied required customers to demonstrate evidence of repeated unsuccessful job search as a condition for being approved for training.

However, although few sites imposed duration requirements of this sort, some basic steps were always required before training would be 'authorized. Thus, consistent with WIA, customers needed to undertake at least one core and one intensive service before being approved for training, which might entail registering with the state Employment Service, attending a one-stop center orientation, undertaking an assessment of occupational skills and interests, conducting labor market research, and attending one or more preemployability workshops, among other things. Thereafter, as part of their training decision, they might be expected to research eligible training providers and interview prospective employers or former trainees. To accommodate these various steps, it generally took customers several weeks to complete a core and an intensive service, make a decision to train, and then conduct research associated with selecting a training program and a vendor. The shortest typical period that any site reported was about two and a half weeks, while the longest period was about nine weeks. This variability reflected how case management appointments were sequenced, the specific job search and information gathering that different local areas required, and the extensiveness of the assessment process they used.

These requirements notwithstanding, local areas emphasized their flexible approach to dealing with customers, and pointed out that those who were demonstrably in need of intervention—adults with little work history, for example—could move from core to intensive services, and then on to training, more quickly than others. The customers' own motivation and initial preferences also seemed to be very important. Thus, customers who missed appointments or took longer to schedule them could undergo protracted periods in core and intensive services before being approved for training. By contrast, those who knew they wanted and needed training, expressed this preference early in the intake process, and were prompt in scheduling appointments and completing research or other requirements could move along quite quickly.

Helping Customers Make Training Choices

WIA requires that local areas should provide access to training in a way that "maximizes customer choice" (WIA Title I.B.134). At the same time, WIA is very performance driven and demands high levels of system accountability in achieving employment and related outcomes. In keeping with this, local areas have an interest in ensuring that customers make wise training choices, because choices that result in poor outcomes will negatively affect the local area's attainments on its core measures of performance.[20] Similarly, results from the Career Management Account demonstration suggest that case managers sometimes have difficulty relinquishing control to customers over their training decisions when they feel that customers are making poor choices (U.S. Department of Labor 1999).[21]

Through the visits we conducted to nearly 50 local areas over WIA's first several years, we concluded that local areas endeavor to ensure both customer choice and system accountability by promoting a model of "informed customer choice," wherein case managers ensure that those authorized to undertake training receive ample information and assistance, so that they are led to make prudent choices (or at least defensible choices) on their own. (This approach closely approximates the middle approach, Approach 2 in the experimental ITA evaluation described by Decker and Perez-Johnson in Chapter 6 of this volume.)

This general approach of promoting informed choice seemed to be embraced virtually everywhere we visited. However, the specific mechanisms that local areas adopted differed, as did the rigor with which they were applied. Thus, nearly all areas required customers to undertake a formal assessment of their basic skills or occupational interests, although some assessment processes were much more extensive than others. Similarly, customers everywhere were required to conduct basic research on their training choices (e.g., through labor market research and the Consumer Report System, a compendium of information about eligible training providers), but some areas went further by requiring customers to undertake field research, such as visiting prospective training programs and interviewing former trainees or employers. Similarly, all sites require customers to be able to justify their training choices, but some have instituted a formal approval process, whereby customers must make a formal presentation before an

ITA review committee, or, as in one site, participate in a two-week peer-managed workshop during which fellow ITA holders scrutinize each other's training choices. Case managers, meanwhile, play the role of facilitators, guiding customers through the assessment process and other requirements without being overly prescriptive. At the same time, the case manager's opinion clearly can carry considerable weight, especially among participants without clear training plans of their own.

In keeping with WIA's intent, then, it appears that almost everywhere customer choice is being taken very seriously, but that this choice is guided and informed by assessment, research, and other requirements that vary in their specifics. The ITA Experiment, described by Decker and Perez-Johnson in Chapter 6, will shed important light on optimal approaches to providing this guidance, at least from the standpoint of maximizing the return on job training investments.

LIMITS ON ITA TRAINING CHOICES

Notwithstanding their obvious efforts to promote customer choice, nearly all local areas implicitly limit choice by exercising their authority to set limits on the ITA dollar amount or duration, establishing procedures for certifying training programs as eligible to be considered by an ITA holder, and, potentially, by using non-ITA training alternatives in some cases. In a theme that has been recurring throughout this chapter, the decisions that local areas make reflect a balance between the sometimes competing objectives that WIA promotes.

Dollar and Time Limits

In keeping with provisions in the WIA regulations (Section 663.420), states and local boards are entitled to set dollar or time limits on the training they will support through an ITA. Of the 19 states for which we have data, each devolved this authority completely to their local areas. In turn, nearly all the 57 local areas we researched do set either dollar or time limits, or both.

These limits vary greatly, often even within the same state. Thus, as Table 4.5 shows, dollar limits range from under $2,000 per ITA holder in a small number of local areas, to a high of $7,500 or more in others, with a modal value of $5,000.

In setting their dollar caps, representatives from local workforce boards made note of conflicting considerations. On the one hand, they recognized that lower caps would serve to ensure that a greater number of customers could be served overall, given the area's overall funding allocation. Similarly, they wanted to maintain some financial discipline, both for customers who otherwise have no incentive to economize in their choices and for vendors that might price their programs at whatever cap the local board set.[22] At the same time, board members recognized that setting dollar caps too low would serve to exclude from consideration many longer-term and higher-quality training opportunities, especially those offered by private vendors, and would thereby sharply curtail customer choice. Clearly, local areas balance these considerations in very different ways, presumably after taking into account the needs of their customers, the mix of training providers in their area, and the local cost structure.

Establishing Program Eligibility

Consistent with the WIA legislation, ITAs can be redeemed only from vendors whose programs are "eligible"—certified by states and local workforce areas as meeting acceptable levels of performance. In keeping with this requirement, vendors need to seek eligibility for each

Table 4.5 Dollar Caps Imposed on ITAs

	No. of LWIAs	%
Less than $2,000	2	3.5
$2,000–$3,500	8	14.0
$3,501–$5,000	19	33.3
$5,001–$7,500	12	21.1
Greater than $7,500 (or no limit)	16	28.1

NOTE: Figures represent the number (percentage) of LWIAs that established their dollar ITA caps at various levels, of 57 local areas (in 19 separate states) for which this information was collected.

training program they wish to offer to ITA recipients; those that are approved are placed on a statewide list of eligible training providers (ETPs). To the extent that vendors decide not to apply for eligibility for their programs, or those that apply are not approved, customer choice is curtailed. On the other hand, higher certification requirements are designed to promote greater system accountability and improved program performance.

States were interested in developing a very inclusive list of eligible programs during WIA's first year or two (during the so-called "initial eligibility" period).[23] Accordingly, they actively marketed the ETP list to vendors and established requirements for initial eligibility that were quite easy for vendors to meet (D'Amico and Salzman 2002). Thereafter, "subsequent eligibility" takes hold. Following the WIA legislation [WIA Section 122(c)], subsequent eligibility should involve the application of performance requirements calculated for seven measures that are based on how well the training program's previous cohorts of students performed, either while in training (e.g., program completion rates) or in the labor market thereafter (e.g., employment, retention, and wage measures). Of these seven measures, three apply to all students in a program's prior cohort of trainees and four apply to prior cohorts who received WIA funding. These performance criteria must be met not for the training provider as a whole, but separately for each program for which the provider is seeking eligibility. The objective is not only to ensure a high level of performance among programs certified as eligible, but also to assemble vendor performance in a Consumer Report System (CRS), which customers are expected to use in making training choices.

In practice, the application of these performance measures involves thorny definitional issues (e.g., what counts as a "program" for which the provider might wish to seek eligibility, or how to define key terms such as "completion" and "enrollee"), difficulties in data management and measurement (e.g., who should gather the necessary data to measure vendors' performance and by what means), and complaints from many vendors who are wary about potentially burdensome reporting requirements. Doubtless because of these reasons, among the 13 states whose requirements we examined in detail, 2 requested a waiver from the U.S. Department of Labor to defer the more stringent rules for subsequent eligibility for at least a few more years (i.e., until

2004 or 2005), and 2 others were intending to establish requirements for subsequent eligibility but had not yet done so when we visited them in early 2002. The remaining 7 states had reached decisions about what their performance requirements for vendors' programs would be during subsequent eligibility, but only after protracted and often contentious discussion and debate.

The resulting definitions, procedures, and performance levels established for subsequent eligibility show substantial disparity (D'Amico and Salzman 2002). Thus, in most states employment outcomes are measured for vendors through unemployment insurance wage matching, but in others, vendors are required to self-report their own data. Some require separate applications for each course of study offered at every unique location, but others define a course of study offered at multiple locations (say, the various campuses of a community college) as a single program for which only one application is required. The performance thresholds that vendors' programs are required to meet also vary across states. For example, some states require vendors' programs to meet performance requirement on all seven measures, but others require that performance on just a few of the measures be met. Similarly, some states set relatively high performance thresholds on each of the measures (for example, one state established a requirement for a program completion rate of 70 percent), while others set much lower thresholds (a completion rate of 25 percent in another state).

Rationales for the decisions that states made with respect to their approaches reflected some similar themes, even if they often led to very different decisions. Among the most common considerations was the states' effort to strike a balance by establishing performance criteria that are high enough to ensure quality, but not so high that customer choice will be impaired by having many vendors excluded from eligibility.

Subsequent eligibility has only recently begun in most states, so it is too soon to be certain how these requirements will play out. However, in general, proprietary institutions seemed agreeable to the ETP requirements and felt that they would have little difficulty in meeting them. By contrast, many public institutions, which have traditionally filled an important role in providing high-quality but low-cost training under JTPA, are balking at the eligibility requirements that WIA imposes. In their view, the low volume of ITA-funded trainees that they can anticipate, compared with the large numbers of conventional students, does not warrant the time and expense they expend in complying with subsequent eligibility requirements, and, as a consequence, many are threatening to refuse to apply. Finally, many community-based institutions, an important source of contract training for hard-to-serve clients under JTPA, appear to be vulnerable under the ITA system, because their small size and low capitalization are causing many of them to have difficulty in coping with an irregular flow of ITA students.

To the extent that many public institutions refuse to apply for eligibility, as they have threatened, and community-based institutions struggle, customer choice could be severely compromised. Indeed, respondents in some states were expecting that their eligible training provider (ETP) list would shrink by 50 percent or more once subsequent eligibility began. Again, the tension that WIA establishes between customer choice and system accountability is an uneasy one whose resolution can apparently sometimes lead to unexpected and perhaps unwelcome consequences.

Moreover, given the variability in the service areas and target populations that training providers serve, it is highly questionable whether performance requirements as they have been applied are equitable or if they provide customers with a sound basis for making training choices.[24] These considerations give rise to serious concerns about whether ETP requirements are worth their price. In an effort to reduce overlapping requirements and streamline the eligibility process, ways of aligning the ETP process with other certification requirements to which training vendors are already subject should be explored.

ITA and Non-ITA Training

In an effort to promote customer choice and market-based approaches to providing workforce services, WIA suggests that ITAs should be used to provide training under most circumstances. However, local areas have the option of using other forms of training besides the ITA under certain circumstances. These options include contracts that the local area can write to fund on-the-job training or customized training provided by an employer, training programs by community-based organizations or other private organizations that are of demonstrated effectiveness in serving "special participant populations that face multiple barriers to employment," and other providers if it is deemed that there are too few providers in the local area to fulfill the intent of the ITA system.

Data from the PY 2001 WIASRD suggest that local areas are making substantial use of these non-ITA alternatives. As Table 4.6 shows, there seems to be a bifurcation between areas that use ITAs extensively and those that use them very little. Thus, about 20 percent of local areas issued an ITA for fewer than 20 percent of their trainees. At the other extreme, 40 percent of them relied on ITAs heavily and, for many of them, exclusively.

Based on the site visits we conducted, it appears that non-ITA training is used for a variety of reasons. To begin with, some local areas noted that non-ITA training typically had lower unit costs. They also cited its advantages for serving targeted customer groups. For example, one site used contracts to provide vocational training, combined with English-as-a-second-language instruction, to a group of dislocated garment workers, because it believed that the mutual support afforded through the single class would be more effective in achieving positive outcomes than would individual choices. Local areas also noted that customized training was virtually assured of leading to job placements for training participants and often provided them with an income stream while they underwent training. It could also be very effective in meeting the needs of the business customer in that it yields

Table 4.6 Percent of Local Areas with Various Incidence Rates of Using ITAs to Provide Training Services

	Adult program
Fewer than 20% of trainees	20.0
20%–39% of trainees	11.8
40%–59% of trainees	11.6
60%–79% of trainees	16.5
80% or more of trainees	40.1

NOTE: Figures represent the percentage of local workforce areas with various incidence rates of the use of the ITA among exiters who received training services (excluding JTPA carry-overs). These tabulations are based on PY 2001 WIASRD data, excluding the handful of LWIAs that provided no training.

a trained workforce geared directly to the employers' hiring needs and, more generally, can be structured to advance an area's economic development objectives.

One concern is that, in their efforts to promote customer choice, many local areas may be losing sight of the substantial advantages that contract training can have, both for customers and employers. A challenge for local areas operating within the WIA context, therefore, will be developing an appropriate balance between ITA and contract training, deciding for whom each training regimen is appropriate, and doing so in a way that still promotes customer choice.

CONCLUDING OBSERVATIONS

Since WIA was enacted in 1998, the public workforce development system has been in the midst of a difficult yet potentially profound transformation. From an emphasis on providing adult training services geared toward a narrowly targeted customer pool, as in JTPA, WIA promotes universal access within a hierarchy of service levels that aims to ration more costly interventions to those whose service needs are clearest. System accountability, efficiency, customer choice, and market-based approaches are key tenets underlying the emerging system.

As we have discussed throughout this chapter, though, these principles are sometimes in an uneasy tension. Thus, promoting accountability and high system performance can limit customer choice and result in cream skimming; providing universal access to a range of workforce services limits funds that would otherwise be available to serve priority, low-income customers; promoting the efficient use of resources by adopting a service hierarchy can undermine efforts to remain customer focused; and promoting market-based approaches through the heavy use of the ITA may sacrifice economies of scale or jeopardize the adoption of alternatives that can often be better suited to directly meeting employers' workforce needs or serving customers with special needs.

What is clear is that local areas are making unique decisions about how best to balance these competing objectives, resulting in a matrix of service design and delivery systems that looks vastly different throughout the nation. To this extent, WIA's effort to devolve control for policy decisions to the local level has clearly been realized. However, how and why these local decisions are made, and with what consequences for program impacts or broader community economic and workforce development, remain uncertain. As the syntheses by Friedlander, Greenberg, and Robins (1997) and by King (Chapter 3 in this volume) suggest, evidence is not conclusive as to what kinds of service strategies work best. Indeed, after summarizing their findings from the JTPA experimental evaluation, Bloom et al. (1997) soberly conclude that " . . . we still do not know what works best for whom" (p. 574). In some sense, then, local workforce boards are making strategic decisions about how to best invest their WIA dollars with little hard evidence to guide them.

The U.S. House of Representatives recently passed H.R. 1261, which reauthorizes and amends WIA. This legislation recognizes, without necessarily resolving, some of the tensions we have drawn attention to in this chapter. The legislation, which has recently been taken into consideration by the Senate, proposes some sweeping reforms of adult program services:

1) Funding for the WIA adult and dislocated worker programs would be consolidated with Wagner-Peyser funds to streamline program administration and, potentially, reduce inefficiency. At the same time, this provision could further dilute attention on job training, continuing a trend from JTPA that WIA has already begun.

2) The one-stop infrastructure will be supported through funds drawn from each mandatory partner program's own allocation. This provision should lessen the difficult cost negotiations that partners currently undertake and ensure the one-stop system a steady and equitable funding base.

3) The proposed legislation clarifies that case managers should be customer focused, and, to this degree, should not require customers to undertake core or intensive services if it is apparent that they need training to attain self-sufficiency.

4) In recognition that WIA and the Employment Service might be consolidated under single funding, the proposed legislation stipulates that the unemployed should receive the first priority for pro-

gram services, and only secondarily should priority be given to low-income individuals.

5) Prescribed performance measures for the ETP list have been eliminated. This provision recognizes that WIA imposes overly onerous reporting and performance requirements on vendors and, as a consequence, may have inadvertently undermined customer choice. Under the proposed bill, Governors are to establish their own criteria and procedures to certify providers as eligible.

Assuming these or similar provisions are enacted, the research community will have further work to do in examining their implications for program services and customer characteristics. Further, this legislation makes explicit the need to go beyond thinking about WIA as a silo program rather than part of an integrated, or at least coordinated, workforce system. Thus, increasingly—and whether or not H.R. 1261 is enacted—we need to understand how WIA works in concert with its major partners to promote economic and community impacts. Already, we see evidence of joint decision making and planning regarding the financial and staffing support for the one-stop system that makes clear that looking at WIA alone presents only part of the story of how the workforce system is operating and who it is serving. As further evidence of this, the concurrent participation of WIA participants appears to be much more common than it once was. As Table 4.7 shows, about

Table 4.7 Rates of Concurrent Participation among Adult Exiters: WIA and JTPA

	PY 1998 JTPA exiters	PY 2001 WIA Exiters		
		Total	Core only	Intensive– no training	Training
Concurrent participation, total (%)	14.4	22.8	14.7	22.7	27.2
Other JTPA/WIA	10.3	2.8	1.7	2.6	3.5
Non-JTPA/WIA	5.7	20.8	13.3	20.9	24.8

NOTE: All figures are given as percentages. SPIR data represent figures for adults (Title II-A) and older workers (Section 204d) who received more than only an objective assessment. Data from the PY 2001 WIASRD are preliminary figures and exclude JTPA carry-overs. When they are added together, the rates of Other JTPA/WIA and Non-JTPA/WIA concurrent participation can exceed the total rate of concurrent participation because some individuals may be a participant under both Other JTPA/WIA and Non-JTPA/WIA programs.

14 percent of JTPA adult participants were coenrolled, primarily in other JTPA programs, while, in WIA, about 23 percent are coenrolled, mostly in non-WIA programs (and, primarily, in Wagner-Peyser).[25] In other words, program partners are increasingly working to form a system, and the research agenda needs to follow suit.

As a result of reauthorization, no doubt important changes and system transformations lie ahead. WIA's first few years have been fraught with some confusions and start-up problems that are understandable in light of the legislation's intended quick pace of implementation. These years have also been a learning experience whose important lessons are only now coming to light. The next few years will be important for judging whether WIA's success in establishing a first-class workforce development system—access to an array of career tools for the universal customer, coupled with concerted efforts to meet the needs of those who need extensive training services to attain self-sufficiency—can be realized.

Notes

The authors wish to thank Kristin Wolff, Richard West of Social Policy Research Associates, reviewers at the Upjohn Institute, and participants at the Job Training and Labor Exchange Forum for their helpful comments.

1.   WIA Title I authorizes training services in the adult, dislocated worker, and youth programs, as well as in targeted national programs. This chapter focuses on adult program services only.
2.   Rapid response assistance and job search services as a stand-alone activity are encouraged in the dislocated worker program, but not in the adult program.
3.   However, the longer-term efficacy of these less costly strategies is less clear (Friedlander and Burtless 1995; Grubb 1996).
4.   Mandatory partners include WIA-funded programs, the Employment Service, and Adult Education, Post-secondary Vocational Education, Vocational Rehabilitation, Welfare-to-Work, Trade Adjustment Assistance, and NAFTA Transitional Adjustment Assistance programs, among others.
5.   In WIA, program years run from July 1 of one year to the following June 30. Program years are named on the basis of the calendar year during which the program year starts. Thus, data for PY 2000 cover those who exited WIA from July 1, 2000 through June 30, 2001.
6.   WIA was mandated to be implemented nationwide by July 2000. However, some states, the so-called early implementers, began operating under WIA guidelines

during PY 1999. Thus, PY 1998 represents the last full year in which JTPA was operating nationwide.

7. These site visits were conducted by Social Policy Research Associates primarily as part of two separate evaluation studies funded by the U.S. Department of Labor. The first is the *Evaluation of the Implementation of the Workforce Investment Act*. As part of this evaluation, team members visited 23 local areas in 14 states, including 6 early implementing states and 8 others that were randomly selected. The second study is an *Evaluation of the ITA/ETP Demonstration*, being conducted by Social Policy Research Associates, under subcontract to Mathematica Policy Research. This study involved site visits to 13 states and 28 local areas within them, each of which was selected to participate in the demonstration project. Because there is some overlap in coverage between these two studies, a total of 23 states and 48 local areas were visited in total. The earliest site visits were conducted in PY 1999 to the WIA early implementing states (that is, those that agreed to implement WIA's key provisions before the mandatory deadline of July 1, 2000). Other sites were visited in PY 2000 through the middle of PY 2001. Thus, they cover WIA in its earliest stages of implementation, through its second year of full implementation.

8. One complication in using these data is that about 7 percent of PY 2001 exiters are those who are JTPA carry-overs—that is, generally those who enrolled prior to PY 2000, and hence under JTPA's requirements. JTPA carry-overs are excluded from this tabulation.

9. These figures would be slightly more tilted toward training services if JTPA carry-overs were included in the tabulations.

10. No doubt partly accounting for the decline is WIA's stipulations that adult education and literacy activities should not be carried out with WIA funds unless in combination with another training activity, because stand-alone literacy training is viewed as the purview of the partner program, Adult Education.

11. For the SPIR, other occupational training represents the category "occupational skills training (non-OJT)" and can include job-specific competency training, customized training, apprenticeship or pre-apprenticeship program, internships, entrepreneurial training, and training that when structured like a job is designed to impart work maturity competencies. In the WIASRD, this category represents occupational skills training, skill upgrading and retraining, entrepreneurial training, job readiness training, and customized training.

12. In both programs, length of participation is calculated as time elapsed from date of registration to date of exit. Differences in the average length of participation between JTPA and WIA can partly be due to differences in events that trigger registration or exit in the two programs. The computation of average length of participation in WIA is biased downward somewhat, because of the exclusion of JTPA carry-overs, who by definition have had very long spells of participation. If the percentage of WIA exiters who had a spell of participation of less than three months were recalculated after including JTPA carry-overs, the figure would be approximately 31 percent rather than the 34 percent shown.

13. Because the WIASRD was new with PY 2000, data problems were legion, and not all states submitted data. Nonetheless, the best evidence from these data suggests that the percent of WIA exiters who received training services in PY 2000 was approximately 33 percent, in comparison to the 42 percent rate for PY 2001 that we have reported here.

14. JTPA classified as training services any of the following: basic skills training, on-the-job training (OJT), occupational skills training other than OJT, work experience and private internships, and "other employment skills training" including pre-employment and work-maturity training. Of these, WIA stipulates that basic skills instruction can only be classified as training if it is provided in conjunction with another training activity, preemployment and work-maturity are practically speaking (based on our site visits) almost always being classified as pre-vocational services (and, hence, as an intensive service), and work experience is generally classified as an intensive service (pursuant to the Code of Federal Regulations, 20 CFR 663.200).

15. According to WIA, pre-vocational services is an intensive service that consists of the " . . . development of learning skills, communication skills, interview skills, punctuality, personal maintenance skills, and professional conduct, to prepare individuals for unsubsidized employment or training" [WIA Section 134(d)(3)(C)(vi)].

16. As before, the tabulations for WIA exiters exclude JTPA carry-overs. Those for PY 1998 JTPA exiters include data for Title II-A (the adult program) and Section 204d (the older worker program); these two groups are jointly referred to as adults for purposes of this discussion. Given the constraints of available data, most of the WIA data elements shown in the table reflect the characteristics of WIA exiters who received intensive or training services, because they are not required reportable data items for WIA registrants who receive only staff-assisted core services.

17. This decline may be due to a combination of the general fall-off in welfare recipiency in the nation as a whole over these years, the use of TANF or Welfare-to-Work funds to serve welfare recipients, and changes in WIA's targeting provisions as compared with JTPA. Potentially, some part of the drop-off in both these measures represents an effect of declining poverty and welfare roles nationwide during this period (the poverty rate was 12.7 percent in 1998 and 11.3 percent in 2000, according to the U.S. Bureau of the Census [2002]; similarly, there was a substantial decline in the rates of TANF recipiency during this same period). Nonetheless, with about 175 million adults living in poverty in 2000, a shortage of customers who would meet WIA's priority guidelines is clearly not a factor. A reluctance of case managers to document low-income status when it is not absolutely necessary to do so to establish program eligibility may also account for the decline to some degree.

18. SPIR and WIASRD definitions of these items are slightly different, which could account for some of the variation in incidence rates. The SPIR defines single parents as a category of family status for those who have "sole custodial support" for one or more dependent children; the WIASRD, by contrast, speaks of those hav-

ing "primary responsibility" for children under age 18. With respect to limited-English speakers, in JTPA this term would refer to those who native language is not English with an inability to communicate in English, resulting in a barrier to employment; the WIA definition seems somewhat broader, including those with a limited ability to speak, read, write or understand English and whose native language is not English or who live in a family or community where English is not dominant.

19. Potentially those who are low income are less able to support themselves through training than others, or those with barriers might be deemed by the local area to lack the foundation skills to benefit from training. Additionally, welfare recipients might be accessing training through other funding sources, such as TANF.

20. In keeping with WIA, states and, in turn, local areas are held accountable for attaining negotiated levels of performance on the so-called WIA core measures, which relate to customers' outcomes after they receive services. These core measures include postprogram employment rates, six-month retention rates, and earnings gains, and the rate at which customers are awarded degrees or credentials, among other things. States that fail to meet their negotiated levels are not eligible for incentive awards and may be subject to sanctions.

21. The Career Management Account Demonstration operated in 1995 through 1997 (hence, before WIA was enacted) in 13 grantee sites, and was designed to test ITA-like approaches for delivering training services to dislocated workers.

22. In fact, there is some evidence that training vendors were aware of a local area's ITA caps and set their prices with this in mind.

23. According to WIA, initial eligibility lasts for 12–18 months, though a 6-month extension can be granted. During this period, degree-granting post-secondary institutions and apprenticeship programs are granted automatic eligibility, so long as they apply; other providers may need to meet performance levels established by the state, at the state's discretion. During subsequent eligibility, by contrast, no provider is considered automatically eligible.

24. The WIA legislation suggests that service area and customer characteristics should be taken into account in setting performance requirements for vendors, but in actuality this rarely occurs (D'Amico and Salzman, 2002).

25. We caution, though, that these differences could be partly an artifact of measurement. On the one hand, states' data management systems have recently been striving for greater integration across partner programs, so that information about instances of concurrent participation will be readily at hand; thus, the WIASRD might be more likely to capture the incidence of concurrent participation when it occurs than the SPIR did. On the other hand, the incidence of concurrent participation was a required data field in the SPIR, while it is an optional field in the WIASRD; for this reason, the extent of concurrent participation might have been more likely to be captured by the SPIR than the WIASRD. Note, too, that, in calculating rates of concurrent participation from the WIASRD, we excluded instances where the individual was coded as having participated in the Food Stamps Employment and Training Program; the rather high incidence of partici-

pation in this program that is recorded in the WIASRD (about 4 percent of all adult WIA registrants) leads us to suspect that participation in Food Stamps was being mistakenly captured here.

References

Anderson, Kathryn, Richard Burkhauser, and Jennie Raymond. 1993. "The Effect of Creaming on Placement Rates under the Job Training Partnership Act." *Industrial and Labor Relations Review* 46(July): 613–624.

Bloom, Howard S., Larry L. Orr, Stephen H. Bell, George Cave, Fred Doolittle, Winston Lin, and Johannes M. Bos. 1997. "The Benefits and Costs of JTPA Title II-A Programs: Key Findings from the National Job Training Partnership Act Study." *Journal of Human Resources* 32(Summer): 549–576.

D'Amico, Ronald, Deborah Kogan, Suzanne Kreutzer, Andrew Wiegand, Alberta Baker, Gardner Carrick, and Carole McCarthy. 2001. *A Report on Early State and Local Progress Towards WIA Implementation.* Report prepared by Social Policy Research Associates under contract to the U.S. Department of Labor.

D'Amico, Ronald, and Jeffrey Salzman. 2002. *An Evaluation of the Individual Training Account/Eligible Training Provider Demonstration: Final Report.* Report prepared by Social Policy Research Associates under contract to Mathematica Policy Research and the U.S. Department of Labor.

Freedman, Stephen, Jean Tansey Knab, Lisa A. Gennetian, and David Navarro. 2000. *The Los Angeles Jobs-First GAIN Evaluation: Final Report on a Work First Program in a Major Urban Center.* Report prepared by MDRC under contract to the Los Angeles Department of Public Social Services.

Friedlander, Daniel, and Gary Burtless. 1995. *Five Years After: The Long-Term Effects of Welfare-to-Work Programs.* New York: Russell Sage.

Friedlander, Daniel, David H. Greenberg, and Philip K. Robins. 1997. "Evaluating Government Training Programs for the Economically Disadvantaged." *Journal of Economic Literature* 35(December): 1809–1855.

Grubb, W. Norton. 1996. *Learning to Work: The Case for Reintegrating Job Training and Education.* New York: Russell Sage.

Grubb, W. Norton, Norena Badway, Denise Bell, Bernadette Chi, Chris King, Julie Herr, Heath Prince, Richard Kazis, Lisa Hicks, and Judith Combes Taylor. 1999. *Toward Order from Chaos: State Efforts to Reform Workforce*

Development Systems. Report prepared by the National Center for Research in Vocational Education, University of California at Berkeley.

Hamilton, Gayle. 2002. *Moving People from Welfare to Work: Lessons from the National Evaluation of Welfare to Work Strategies.* Report prepared by MDRC, with funding from the U.S. Department of Health and Human Services and the U.S. Department of Education.

Kogan, Deborah, Katherine P. Dickinson, Ruth Fedrau, Michael J. Midling, and Kristin E. Wolff. 1997. *Creating Workforce Development Systems that Work: An Evaluation of the One-Stop Implementation Experience.* Report prepared by Social Policy Research Associates under contract to the U.S. Department of Labor.

Levitan, Sar, and Frank Gallo. 1988. *A Second Chance: Training for Jobs.* Kalamazoo, MI: W.E. Upjohn Institute for Employment Research.

National Commission for Employment Policy. 1988. *Evaluation of the Effects of JTPA Performance Standards on Clients, Services, and Costs.* Research Report no. 88-16. Washington, DC: National Commission for Employment Policy.

O'Shea, Daniel, and Christopher T. King. 2001. *The Workforce Investment Act of 1998: Restructuring Workforce Development Initiatives in States and Localities.* Rockefeller Report No. 12. Albany, NY: The Nelson A. Rockefeller Institute of Government.

Social Policy Research Associates. 2000. *PY 98 SPIR Data Book.* Report prepared by Social Policy Research Associates under contract to the U.S. Department of Labor.

U.S. Bureau of the Census. 2002. *Statistical Abstract of the United States: The National Data Book,* Table no. 668. Washington, DC: U.S. Government Printing Office.

U.S. Department of Labor. 1991. *Improving the Quality of Training Under JTPA.* Research and Evaluation Report Series 91-A. Washington, DC: U.S. Department of Labor.

———. 1999. *Dislocated Worker Program Report: Findings from the Career Management Account Demonstration.* Washington, DC: U.S. Department of Labor.

U.S. General Accounting Office. 1989. *Job Training Partnership Act: Services and Outcomes for Participants with Differing Needs.* Washington, DC: U.S. General Accounting Office.

———. 1994a. *Multiple Employment Training Programs: Overlapping Programs Can Add Unnecessary Administrative Costs.* Washington, DC: U.S. General Accounting Office.

————. 1994b. *Multiple Employment Training Programs: Conflicting Requirements Hamper Delivery of Services*. Washington, DC: U.S. General Accounting Office.

————. 1994c. *Multiple Employment Training Programs: Overlap among Programs Raises Questions about Efficiency*. Washington, DC: U.S. General Accounting Office.

————. 2000. *Multiple Employment and Training Programs: Overlapping Programs Indicate Need for Closer Examination of Structure*. Washington, DC: U.S. General Accounting Office.

5

The Use of Service Providers and Brokers/Consultants in Employment and Training Programs

Janet O. Javar
Stephen A. Wandner

Both public and private intermediaries have played important roles as service providers throughout the history of publicly funded employment and training programs. The Workforce Investment Act (WIA) of 1998 expanded the role of intermediaries participating in the workforce investment system by establishing new one-stop operator roles and excluding local workforce investment boards (local boards) from being direct service providers, unless waivers have been approved.[1] At the same time, WIA introduced a voucher system and state eligible training provider list (ETPL) to the training program, which had varying effects on the availability of training providers to customers. New rules governing how services can be provided and who provides them have changed the mix of intermediaries participating in the system.

Intermediaries that provide services under WIA receive funds from local boards to provide direct employment and training services to customers, or facilitate workforce development in the one-stop environment. Intermediaries serve in a range of capacities: as one-stop operators; core, intensive, or youth service providers; training providers; and brokering or consulting organizations. This chapter identifies intermediaries as falling into four general types of organizations: 1) nonprofit organizations, such as community-based and faith-based organizations; 2) community colleges and other educational institutions; 3) public governmental agencies, such as the state Employment Service (ES); and 4) for-profit companies and proprietary schools. Recent research indicates a great deal of variation and experimentation with how local boards work with different types of intermediaries in fulfilling WIA responsibilities.

The following section provides a brief background on the history and growth of intermediaries in employment and training programs, from the 1930s through the Job Training Partnership Act of 1982. We then describe the general nature of intermediaries in the one-stop system under WIA implementation, synthesizing findings from other research about local board experiences. We also describe the early impacts of state ETPLs on the availability of different types of training providers during initial and subsequent eligibility. The next section summarizes four intermediary organizations and explores the advantages of utilizing economies of scale to compete in the one-stop system. Finally, we present a summary and conclusions in the last section.

HISTORY AND GROWTH OF INTERMEDIARIES
PRIOR TO WIA

The use of intermediaries in public employment and training programs has increased over time since the inception of the workforce investment system. The workforce investment system was introduced in the United States as a public responsibility to stabilize the U.S. economy in the wake of persistently high unemployment rates experienced in the 1930s and the implementation of similar systems in other industrialized nations. The system was created with the implementation of ES and Unemployment Insurance (UI) as federal–state programs.[2] ES and UI had experimented with using the private sector in service delivery; however, that alternative was ultimately rejected, and service delivery for these programs has since remained in the public sector.[3] It was not until the 1960s, when Congress passed the first major legislation to provide extensive job training through the Manpower Development and Training Act (MDTA), that the system would rely heavily also on the private sector to deliver publicly funded services.

The training program under MDTA was federally administered, with training providers subcontracted or contracted directly with the federal government to deliver classroom training to customers. At the onset of this new program, a range of intermediaries, such as community colleges, public schools, skill centers, and private schools, were used to deliver training (Levitan and Mangum 1969; Operations Research, Inc. 1972).[4] State ES offices continued to provide labor exchange services to customers, both job-seekers and employers, as a separate program under the Wagner-Peyser Act of 1933. Over time, while other employment and training programs became affected by decentralization efforts, ES and UI continued to function as federal–state programs.

In 1973, the Comprehensive Employment and Training Act (CETA) superseded MDTA and established state and local control in the coordination of services for most of the employment and training programs. Among the changes that were made, CETA required the creation of local "prime sponsors" to coordinate CETA programs. Unlike MDTA, this structure required service providers to compete for funding directly from prime sponsors, a requirement intended to open the market for competition of services (Franklin 1984). This movement of program control from the federal government to localities had a number of results during early implementation: 1) the number of employment and training service providers increased from about 1,440 in fiscal year (FY) 1974 to over 2,400 in FY 1975; 2) prime sponsors became new entities that delivered services, with about 60 percent of the prime sponsors delivering services; 3) prime sponsors shifted away from the state ES as a service provider and transferred contracts to themselves or other organizations; 4) prime sponsors had more flexibility in designing service delivery of the training program; and 5) community-based organizations (CBOs) had significant increases in work and funding in the system (Franklin and Ripley 1984; Snedeker and Snedeker 1978).[5]

The flexibility given to prime sponsors resulted in less utilization of ES to provide labor exchange services for the CETA programs. Unlike its role under MDTA, where ES was the accepted and presumed provider of these services, ES now needed to compete with other organizations to provide the services. Even though some localities continued to contract with ES because they believed it was important, especially in the long run, to maintain a linkage with an established agency that delivered employment services, others took advantage of their flexibility to seek other alternatives. As a result, during FY 1974–1976, ES staff positions decreased by one-quarter when contracts were awarded to other organizations.[6] On the other hand, training was delivered by many of the same types of training providers as previous years, although prime sponsors became more actively involved in determining the types of training to be offered, and funding levels differed from previous years. Training was more often delivered by public educational institutions than private institutions, with over 90 percent of CETA training funds contracted to public educational institutions.[7] Some localities also began to utilize an individual referral system in place of contracting for group training (Snedeker and Snedeker 1978). CETA changed the nature of service provision as a by-product of shifting to locally administered program operations from federal administration under MDTA.

CETA continued for nearly a decade before the Job Training Partnership Act (JTPA) replaced it in 1982, significantly reducing the federal and state role (Reville and Kerman 1996). Local decision making on employment and training programs went from CETA prime sponsors to JTPA private industry councils (PICs), which required private sector majority representation. Also, greater emphasis was placed on the job training program given the cutback in the Public Service Employment program, which was a major CETA program that focused on job creation.

PICs had the flexibility to administer their own programs, but they generally found that contracting out for the services was a more cost-effective alternative (National Commission for Employment Policy 1994). PICs also chose to contract out if they believed that their role should be strictly in a policy and administrative capacity, and that their ability to manage, monitor, and evaluate programs would be compromised if they also became the service delivery organization.

In the selection of service providers, coordination between the JTPA and ES programs was supported among a number of states and PICs. Because the ES federal budget tended to be stagnant and declining in real terms, ES had an incentive to coordinate and make use of JTPA as a source of additional funding. At the same time, some PICs found that the 15 percent administrative cap for the JTPA programs was insufficient for program management, and ES became a likely choice because they believed ES was cost-effective and well-established within the community.[8] However, a number of PICs also chose not to contract with ES, believing that they could obtain better counseling and employment assistance services elsewhere for their customers (Westat 1985).

During the 1990s, states and localities experienced shifts in the welfare programs that would later have an influence on employment and training programs. Prior to the Personal Responsibility and Work Opportunity Reconciliation Act (PRWORA) in 1996, state innovation in the welfare program was supported through state waivers of federal requirements. The use of block grants under PRWORA provided states with a greater deal of flexibility than any other previous legislation. As welfare rolls fell sharply in the late 1990s, the amount of funds available for employment and support services soared, and some of this funding was provided to localities to serve welfare recipients and low-wage workers. In 1997, similar use of grants for the Department of Labor/Employment and Training Administration (ETA) Welfare-to-Work program to assist the "harder-to-serve" welfare recipients provided more flexibility to localities in determining program operation and design than any previous ETA program (Leonard 1999).[9]

The devolved system of Welfare-to-Work—and welfare employment program under state waivers and PRWORA—provided some insight on how more mature systems under WIA might react to increased flexibility and local oversight. In 1999, an intermediary study for the TANF and Welfare-to-Work programs found that most of the intermediaries in 20 localities were nonprofits with established histories in the field. Many were either affiliates of national organizations or specialized in assisting specific populations. Although considerably fewer numbers of for-profit intermediaries served welfare recipients, for-profit intermediaries tended to serve larger numbers of welfare recipients. In fact, the study suggested that for-profit intermediaries served about 45 percent of the welfare population in the study's localities (Pavetti et al. 2000). The significant role of nonprofit and for-profit intermediaries in the Welfare-to-Work programs is similarly reflected in early program experiences under WIA.

The 1990s also gave rise to federal efforts towards developing a one-stop delivery system, with federal one-stop initiative grants awarded to 50 states for capacity building and planning of one-stops. Initiatives were also being implemented at the state level (e.g., Florida, Massachusetts, and Texas) to undertake further changes to the system. When WIA legislation passed, and local control of programs changed hands from PICs to local boards, the experiences of planning and implementing a one-stop system among states and localities were quite mixed.[10]

THE NATURE OF INTERMEDIARIES IN THE ONE-STOP SYSTEM UNDER WIA

This section relies on a small number of studies that have examined the use of intermediaries for different types of WIA services: one-stop operations, and core, intensive, youth, training, and brokering/consulting services. To better understand how the system and providers participating in the system have changed from JTPA to WIA, ETA funded a study on service provision among 16 local boards in the one-stop environment (Macro, Almandsmith, and Hague 2003).[11] Analysis in this section uses the results of the study, as well as other key studies: the Private/Public Venture study of 5 local boards (Buck 2002); a study on early WIA implementing states, with site visits to 6 states and 9 local boards within those states (D'Amico et al. 2001); and a study of the Individual Training Account/Eligible Training Provider (ITA/ETP) Demonstration, with site visits to 28 local boards (D'Amico et al. 2002; D'Amico and Salzman forthcoming).

Table 5.1 summarizes information from site visits and research conducted by Macro et al. (2003) of 16 localities within 8 states for program year (PY) 2001 (July 1, 2001–June 30, 2002). The 16 localities included a total of 84 comprehensive one-stop centers and 71 affiliate (e.g., satellite and/or specialty) centers. The local boards for each of these localities were not selected to be representative of the national one-stop system, which (as of September 2003) consisted of nearly 600 local boards, over 1,900 comprehensive one-stop centers, and over 1,600 affiliate centers. However, Table 5.1 provides useful information on the type and mix of intermediaries that were used within the one-stop system.[12]

One-Stop Operator Services

Local boards have wide discretion in defining one-stop operator responsibilities, such as the division of labor between one-stop operators and organizations providing other services. One-stop operators can be responsible for coordinating with core and intensive service providers, or can serve as the exclusive intermediary for these services. One-stop operators may also subcontract directly with other providers, serve as lead providers, or serve in other capacities designated by their local boards. Local boards make their selection either through a competitive process or various non-competitive processes. The noncompetitive processes include: 1) an agreement with the local board to operate as a consortium or entity of at least three required partners; 2) a waiver by the chief local elected official and governor for the local board to act as the one-stop operator; and 3) certifying, or "grandfathering," existing service providers as one-stop operators.

Many local boards have opted for continuity of providers without further competition by extending contracts, grandfathering existing providers, or designating consortiums. Of the local boards visited in the early WIA implementation study, half used a noncompetitive process to select consortiums of partners to serve as one-stop operators (D'Amico et al. 2001). Macro et al. (2003) found that half of the local boards in the intermediary study also used a noncompetitive process, but local boards selected consortiums of partners as well as grandfathered existing service providers. Only one local board in the intermediary study requested and received a waiver to serve as a one-stop operator. This differed from the early WIA implementation study, which found that 18.4 percent of the local boards nationwide received waivers (D'Amico et al. 2001).[13]

Risk aversion may be one reason why local boards have chosen not to compete or re-compete services. Competing for a service or changing to a new provider can give local boards new opportunities for improvement, but it can also expose local programs to risk. The period of turnover and transition can be lengthy, and consequences can include disruption of services and the perception among customers and one-stop staff of an unstable system. Services may improve or worsen, costs may increase or decline, all with effects on the number of customers served and the quality of services delivered. Extensive training

Table 5.1 Mix and Utilization of Intermediaries by 16 Local Workforce Investment Boards, PY 2001 (July 1, 2001–June 30, 2002)

Types of providers	FL Region 3		MA Region 1		NV Region 6		NJ Region 1		OR Region 6	
	Hillsborough Cty.	Pinellas Cty.	Boston	Hampden Cty.	Northern Nevada	Southern Nevada	Essex Cty.	Passaic Cty.	Lane Cty.	Region 2
One-stop operators (number of participating comprehensive one-stop centers in parentheses)										
Nonprofit	1 (4)		2 (2)[b]	2 (2)[c]				1 (2)		2 (2)
For profit										
Governmental			1 (1)[d]				1 (1)			3 (5)
Educational		1 (3)								
Consortium					1 (1)[e]	1 (1)[f]				
Local board									1 (1)	
Competitive process used	✓		✓	✓						✓
Core service providers (estimated number of participating comprehensive one-stop centers and satellite/specialty centers in parentheses)										
Nonprofit	1 (5)		6 (6)	2 (2)[j]				1 (1)		2 (3)
For profit										
Government: ES[k]	1 (5)	1 (6)	1 (6)	1 (2)	1 (8)[l]	1 (4)	1 (1)	1 (2)	1 (2)	1 (7)
Other government			1 (2)	1 (2)				1 (1)		
Educational		1 (6)							1 (1)	3 (6)
Local board								1 (1)	1 (1)	
Intensive service providers (estimated number of participating comprehensive one-stop centers and satellite/specialty centers in parentheses)										
Nonprofit			2 (2)	2 (2)	5 (8)[m]	5 (4)	1 (1)	1 (1)	1 (1)	3 (3)

For profit					1 (8)					
Government: ES			1 (1)							
Other government				1 (2)			1 (1)			
Educational	1 (5)	1 (6)			1 (8)		1 (1)		1 (2)	3 (6)
Youth service providers (total number of providers serving entire local workforce investment area)										
Nonprofit	1	2	9		5	1	1		3	
For profit								2	5	
Governmental		2			1			1		
Educational	2				1		9	3	7	
Consortium				3	1					
Training providers that received an ITA (number of ITAs issued to providers in parentheses)										
Nonprofit	1 (5)	1 (4)	16 (282)	7 (115)	2 (72)	1 (108)	3 (20)	4 (16)		1 (3)
For profit	29 (543)	7 (20)	17 (90)	14 (149)	17 (306)	27 (526)	60 (221)	51 (329)	11 (52)	3 (3)
Governmental										
Educational	10 (1,042)	4 (399)	5 (23)	4 (37)	5 (236)	4 (225)	6 (12)	14 (67)	6 (216)	5 (34)
Total training providers used	40	12	38	25	24	32	69	69	17	9
Total ITAs issued	1,590	423	395	301	614	859	253	412	268	40

(continued)

Table 5.1 (continued)

Types of providers	PA Region 2		TX Region 4		WI Region 5		Total numbers	Total percentages[a]
	Northwest PA	Three Rivers	Gulf Coast	Tarrant Cty.	Bay Area	Milwaukee Cty.		
One-stop operators (number of participating comprehensive one-stop centers in parentheses)								
Nonprofit			4 (22)			3 (6)	15 (40)	38 (48)
For profit			1 (7)			1 (1)	2 (8)	5 (10)
Governmental				1 (6)			3 (8)	8 (10)
Educational							4 (8)	10 (10)
Consortium	1 (5)[g]	1 (2)[h]			10 (10)[i]		14 (19)	36 (23)
Local board							1 (1)	3 (1)
Competitive process used	✓		✓	✓				
Core service providers (estimated number of comprehensive one-stop centers and satellite/specialty centers in parentheses)								
Nonprofit	2 (4)	8 (9)	4 (25)	1 (6)	5 (5)	1 (1)	33 (67)	48 (32)
For profit	1 (4)		1 (7)				2 (11)	3 (5)
Government: ES[k]	1 (4)	1 (2)	1 (29)	1 (6)	1 (10)	1 (8)	16 (102)	23 (49)
Other government	1 (4)	4 (2)		1 (2)	1 (1)		10 (14)	14 (7)
Educational					1 (1)		7 (15)	11 (7)
Local board							1 (1)	1 (<1)
Intensive service providers (estimated number of participating comprehensive one-stop centers and satellite/specialty centers in parentheses)								
Nonprofit	1 (4)	10 (2)	4 (25)	27 (7)	6 (5)	7 (8)	75 (74)	75 (51)

							Total	%
For profit	1(4)	1(2)	1(7)				5(22)	5(15)
Government: ES					1(3)		2(4)	2(1)
Other government		1(2)		1(6)	1(1)		7(18)	7(5)
Educational		1(2)	2(7)		1(1)		11(27)	11(8)

Youth service providers (total number of providers serving entire local workforce investment area)

							Total	%
Nonprofit	1[a]	19	4	9	5	26	91	65%
For profit	•	1	1				4	3%
Governmental					1		2	1%
Educational		6		2	2		33	24%
Consortium					2		9	6%

Training providers that received an ITA (number of ITAs issued to provider in parentheses)

							Total	%
Nonprofit	2(8)	2(2)	1(10)		1(22)	13(328)	55(995)	9(9)
For profit	32(312)	27(150)	38(1,158)	19(251)	5(20)	45(838)	402(4,968)	68(44)
Governmental			1(5)				1(5)	<1(<1)
Educational	11(43)	9(65)	13(1,372)	9(207)	18(1,080)	9(359)	132(5,417)	22(48)
Total providers used	45	38	52	29	24	68	591	
Total ITAs issued	363	217	2,540	463	1,122	1,530	11,390	

[a] Does not add up to 100% due to rounding.

[b] Boston selected organizations that were formed of a collaborative of two or more organizations with a designated lead organization. The organizations consisted of 1) Jewish Vocational Services (nonprofit lead organization), which partnered with the Economic Development and Industrial Corporation of Boston/Jobs & Community Services Department (government); and 2) Goodwill Industries (nonprofit lead organization), which partnered with Dimock Community Health Center and Women's Educational and Industrial Union (nonprofits).

[c] Hampden County selected a nonprofit organization, CareerPoint, began as a collaborative of local public agencies in 1995.

[d] Boston's other collaborative organization included the state's Department of Employment and Training as the lead organization that partnered with Action for Boston Community Development (nonprofit).

[e] The consortium included Truckee Meadows Community College (educational), Department of Training and Rehabilitation (state government), and Nevada Works (Local Board).

[f] The consortium included Nevada Business Services (nonprofit), S.T. Gregg & Associates (for-profit), Nevada Partners (nonprofit), Vocational Rehabilitation (government) and Employment Service (government).

[g] The consortium consisted of the Office of Vocational Rehabilitation (government), Bureau of Employment and Career Services (state Wagner-Peyser agency), Greater Erie Community Action Committee (nonprofit), and Northwestern Regional Technology Institute (for-profit). Each of the five one-stop centers also had an additional partner who was the leaseholder. Pennsylvania's State Department of Transportation (government), Community Action Inc. (nonprofit), Warren/Forest Counties Economic Opportunity Council (nonprofit), Meadville Area Industrial Commission (nonprofit), and the Greater Erie Community Action Committee (nonprofit).

[h] The consortium consisted of the Pittsburgh Partnership (government), Allegheny County Department of Human Services (government), Bureau of Employment and Career Services (state Wagner-Peyser agency, Office of Vocational Rehabilitation (government), and Goodwill Industries (nonprofit). Other nonprofit organizations also served as a partner.

[i] One of the consortiums for the one-stop centers consisted of ES, Job Corps, Vocational Rehabilitation, county Human Services Department, Goodwill, two nonprofits, state technical college, and two Cooperative Education Services Agencies. The other consortium consisted of ES, Vocational Rehabilitation, county Departments of Human Services and Economic Support, a nonprofit, state technical college, and school-to-work program.

[j] The government agency of the nonprofit organization delivered core services.

[k] The Employment Service (ES) is a system of public employment offices that was established under the Wagner-Peyser Act of 1933. This system has also been known by other names, such as the Job Service, the Labor Board, and the Unemployment Office.

[l] All WIA partners also helped contribute in the delivery of core services.

[m] All WIA partners also helped contribute in the delivery of intensive services.

[n] The nonprofit organization subcontracted with three regional organizations.

SOURCE: Macro, Almandsmith, and Hague. (2003).

to staff of the new organization, and the transitional costs related to changing from one organization to another, can also lead to greater expenses for local boards (Macro, Almandsmith, and Hague 2003).[14] The WIA system has had little experience with turnover, both because of the noncompetitive processes in place and because many new competitive awards have not expired. Macro et al. (2003) reported that when turnover did occur, it generally related to the organizations' inability to handle the fiscal management of operations, which was described as a greater issue for smaller organizations since a line of credit was necessary in order to operate on a cost-reimbursement contract.

Many types of intermediaries, including local boards and consortiums of intermediaries, actively participate as one-stop operators. Table 5.1 shows that a wide range of intermediaries served as one-stop operators, but with different levels of participation. For example, Macro et al. (2003) found that nonprofits were contracted to operate more one-stops than any other type of intermediary.[15] The significant role of nonprofits as one-stop operators was similar to Buck's (2002) findings that nonprofits were used more than any other type of intermediary in the study's five localities. Macro et al. (2003) also found that consortiums of public and/or private organizations were selected to operate nearly one-quarter of the one-stops, with five local boards utilizing this approach.[16] Community colleges, government agencies, and for-profits were selected in a handful of localities. The governmental agencies were generally the local employment and training agencies, and the for-profits were Maximus and Affiliated Computer Services (ACS), formerly Lockheed Martin IMS.[17]

A number of reasons can help explain the types of intermediaries that have emerged as one-stop operators under WIA. For instance, states' policies can affect the types of intermediaries that are selected, such as Nevada requiring the use of consortiums with mandatory partners; Pennsylvania requiring consortiums with public and private entities; and Wisconsin explicitly prohibiting waiver requests from local boards to deliver direct services. Local constraints or policies can also be a factor, such as the perception among the community that nonprofits are more appropriate than others to serve as one-stop operators, for example, a for-profit affiliate in Hampden County (New Jersey) became a nonprofit organization after community pressure to do so.

Unexpected situations can also occur, such as when the Lane County (Oregon) local board requested a waiver to temporarily serve as a one-stop operator after it began to have financial concerns with the non-profit organization it originally selected (Macro, Almandsmith, and Hague 2003). In Montgomery County (Maryland), the one-stop operator (a for-profit organization) declined to re-bid on the contract because it believed there was insufficient funding for operations. As a result, staff of the for-profit left the company to incorporate themselves into a new nonprofit that bid for, and was awarded, the contract (Jacobson 2002).[18] In other instances, new organizations formed when two PIC areas merged into a single WIA local area. One of the former PICs generally became the new local board, while the other often played a role in one-stop operations, for example, in Gulf Coast (Texas), the former PIC of Houston designated itself into a nonprofit organization and became the new one-stop operator; and in the Bay Area and Northwest Pennsylvania, the former PICs either became a part of or worked for the one-stop consortiums.

Another response to the one-stop operator role by some consortiums has been to incorporate themselves from two or more public and/ or private entities into single nonprofit organizations. The motivation for incorporating two or more organizations into a single organization included the benefits of hiring personnel so that a definitive line of authority among staff existed, and simplified administration and accounting. This was perceived in some areas, such as Bay Area (Wisconsin) and Hampden County (Massachusetts), as a more practical approach than having the one-stop operator use various administration and accounting systems (Macro, Almandsmith, and Hague 2003).

The one-stop operator role can be a desirable one for many organizations. Local boards have commonly assigned the responsibilities of core and/or intensive service delivery with one-stop operations for competitive solicitations (D'Amico et al. 2001, Macro, Almandsmith, and Hague 2003).

As a result, service providers used under JTPA may find it beneficial to bid as one-stop operators in order to continue delivering services under WIA. Some organizations have also noted that the one-stop operator role is beneficial in that it allows their organization to maintain a presence in the workforce investment system (Macro, Almandsmith, and Hague 2003).

Core Services

A major difference between services delivered under JTPA and WIA is the "universal access" requirement that is applied to core services. Since core services are not restricted to any special or targeted population, customers are able to access a variety of core services, which can include self-services in resource rooms (e.g., computer access to labor information, automated labor exchange and job search, resume preparation software, self-assessment tools, and fax and telephone services) or staff-assisted services (e.g., labor exchange, job search, assessment, and counseling).

ES continues to serve as a major labor exchange provider under WIA. The selection of ES as the primary provider of core services was evident in 45 percent of the one-stops in the intermediary study, with nearly three-fourths of the local boards selecting ES as the primary provider. Even when ES was not a primary provider, ES played a role in the core service delivery structure among all of the comprehensive one-stops (Macro, Almandsmith, and Hague 2003). The significance of ES, particularly as primary core service providers, was also evident among a majority of the nine local boards in the early WIA implementation study (D'Amico et al. 2001).[19] This is likely the result of the state ES having the legislative and appropriation mandate to provide Wagner-Peyser services in comprehensive one-stop centers, and local boards determining that ES would be useful intermediaries to provide—in whole or in part—these types of services as core services. Local boards can define the role of ES in the one-stop system in various ways, such as by placing core service delivery entirely with ES, as a shared responsibility between ES and other organizations, or as the sole responsibility of another organization, such as the one-stop operator. When ES was not the primary provider of core services, Macro et al. (2003) found that the one-stop operator held primary responsibility for core service delivery, and those tended to be nonprofit organizations.[20]

The important role of ES in providing core services today reflects its expanding role in providing similar "core services" to ES applicants in the years just prior to the enactment and implementation of WIA. For example, in PY 1998, of the 17.3 million total applicants, 63 percent received some reportable services, including 11 percent receiving assessment services, 36 percent receiving job search services, 2 percent referred to training, and 40 percent referred to employment. During the mid 1990s, ES experienced a large increase in providing "core services," especially job search assistance, as ES became the primary provider of reemployment services for workers served by the Worker Profiling and Reemployment Service initiative that was enacted in 1993 (USDOL 2000; Wandner 1997).

Intensive Services

Intensive services include more individualized assistance from one-stop staff to help move customers into employment, self-sufficiency, or training. Customers can receive intensive services such as assessment, career counseling, financial management, training assistance, and additional placement services. While local boards can apply for a waiver to deliver direct services, only a small proportion of localities have done so.[21] Instead, nonprofits tend to play a significant role as intensive service providers; for example, Macro et al. (2003) found that nonprofits delivered services to the majority of one-stops across the 16 local boards of the intermediary study. [22]

The extensive use of nonprofits could be explained in part by the fact that local boards often assigned intensive delivery responsibilities to the one-stop operator, who tended to be nonprofits. Many of the organizations had established histories with delivering employment and training services and assisting specific populations, e.g., the local affiliate of the AFL-CIO in Milwaukee and the community college in Lane County assisted the dislocated worker population, and the Wisconsin Correctional Service assisted the ex-offender population (Macro, Almandsmith, and Hague 2003). The lack of such established relationships or prior experience could pose some difficulty for new organizations trying to enter the local market of service delivery.

The quality of intensive services can vary across and within different types of intermediaries, with some intermediaries delivering services that may result in better outcomes. However, there has not been a great deal of research in this area. An experimental study operated by the Kalamazoo–St. Joseph County Workforce Development Board (Michigan) from 1998 to 2000 made use of three nonprofit organizations, Goodwill Industries, Behavioral Foundation, and YOU, to deliver welfare-to-work services. Each provider had a different philosophy and approach to delivering services, with some providing more intensive services than others to welfare recipients, based on local staff observations. When each organization was funded at the same level per participant, Goodwill Industries was more successful than the other two providers in having welfare recipients become employed for 90 days. Goodwill provided the most intensive services, followed by Behavioral Foundation, and then by YOU. Thus, with respect to achieving employment, Goodwill Industries in this case had an absolute advantage over the other two service providers. Goodwill could better serve welfare recipients whether they were easy, moderate, or difficult in their ability to find employment. Goodwill has a long history working with economically disadvantaged individuals and a philosophy that was highly supportive of individuals. The study found that, because of differing intensity of services provided, the three providers could be assigned participants by their difficulties in finding a job to determine the best mix of participant employment outcomes (Eberts 2002). Thus, better matching clients with the appropriate service providers and services can improve outcome results and cost-effectiveness.

Youth Services

WIA affected youth programs by combining the year-round and summer youth programs into a single program. Additionally, the new combined youth program under WIA is subject to performance standards, unlike the summer youth program under JTPA. While many localities experienced and welcomed the increase in bids for contracts by intermediaries between the first and second year of WIA implementation, some localities predicted a possible decrease of competition from providers due to additional data requirements and services expected from providers without sufficient funding (Macro, Almand-smith, and Hague 2003).

Localities use different approaches to delivering youth services. Many have used multiple types of service providers for their youth population (see Table 5.1). Services may be delivered within the one-stop center by the one-stop operator staff, within the one-stop center by co-located organizations, or in specialized youth or other affiliate centers located outside of the comprehensive one-stop by contracted organizations. Intermediaries are typically selected through a competitive process with contracts for a one-year duration.

Localities utilized consortiums and various types of single organizations to deliver youth services, but nonprofits delivered a majority of the services (D'Amico et al. 2001). Similarly, in the ETA intermediary study, the majority of youth service providers were nonprofits. Almost one-quarter of the organizations were educational institutions, such as school districts and post-secondary institutions, while governmental entities and for-profits were among the least reported types of intermediaries used (see Table 5.1).[23]

Training Services

WIA legislation affected local training programs in a significant way, by requiring the use of individual training accounts (ITAs) and state ETPLs to provide increased customer choice while holding training providers accountable to performance measures. WIA experience has shown that the mix, availability, and utilization of training providers has changed as a result of these new features. The following section identifies key issues that affect training providers under initial and subsequent eligibility periods of WIA. It also focuses on three types of training providers—educational institutions, nonprofits, and for-profits— that play important roles in the public training program.

Early WIA experiences and intermediary responses

Localities experienced and anticipated changes in the availability and usage of different types of training providers with the transition to the ITA and ETPL systems. The potential loss, rather than increase, of providers has been one of the criticisms of the changes made to the training program. Indeed, in a study of five localities during early WIA implementation, Buck (2002) observed a voluntary loss of CBOs and other nonprofits; for example, Orlando lost all of its CBOs and nonprofits, and Houston lost many of its CBOs likely due to required performance benchmarks.[24] At the same time, however, Boston and Philadelphia both experienced overall increases in providers, many of which were for-profit providers new to the system. Macro et al. (2003) similarly found that most localities experienced an overall increase in training provider choices for customers. This takes into account that many states waived some, if not most, of the reporting requirements for the initial eligibility period. Few had begun subsequent eligibility, and most localities anticipated that performance requirements would affect provider participation during subsequent eligibility once requirements were enforced.

The prospect of losing a large number of providers once subsequent eligibility began was a concern to many states, including Indiana, Maryland, Michigan, North Carolina, and Pennsylvania. D'Amico and Salzman (forthcoming) found that at least 3 of the 28 localities visited had reported that some training providers refused to participate due to the reporting requirements, and four other localities believed that reporting requirements would adversely affect training providers' participation in the system.

Performance reporting requirements have been identified as potential barriers to the continuing participation of certain types of training providers, especially community colleges and other educational institutions (D'Amico and Salzman forthcoming; Macro, Almandsmith, and Hague 2003). Placement on the state ETPL requires that training providers submit performance and cost information, e.g., completion, placement, retention, employment, and wage information. Providers must also meet WIA performance measures to remain eligible to participate. This requires many training providers to establish new systems of data collection and reporting, which many have considered onerous. Texas, an early WIA implementing state, experienced an initial decline in community colleges in response to the introduction of performance reporting requirements. The programs available to local customers decreased from 8,000 to 1,000 training programs on the ETPL once subsequent eligibility began. Texas was later able to recapture its earlier numbers after it took steps to restore participation of training providers. Other states, such as Oregon and Florida, took similar efforts to coordinate among the community colleges and the workforce investment system for continued participation in the local training programs (D'Amico and Salzman forthcoming).

Despite much of the effort invested into the development of the ETPL and Consumer Reports Systems (CRS), states have for a number of reasons requested waivers to extend their initial eligibility period, thereby delaying subsequent eligibility. As of July 2003, ETA received requests from 27 states for extensions in the initial period of provider eligibility by waiving the 18-month requirement for subsequent eligibility. Most of the states requested extensions of initial eligibility through June 2004—past the expected WIA reauthorization.[25] In order to relieve information collection by training providers, states are looking at utilizing existing data sources. Some states, such as Texas, are looking at using state Unemployment Insurance (UI) wage records, and Florida is using its database on community college enrollees (Macro, Almandsmith, and Hague 2003).

In addition to data collection, certification became another issue for some states and localities. In these instances, state policy required that training providers also be certified or licensed by the state's higher education commission (or equivalent).[26] In Connecticut, which used noncertified providers under JTPA for class-size training, localities in the state could no longer refer ITA customers to those providers until they became state-certified and approved on the ETPL. In Orlando, none of the CBOs or nonprofits applied for the state ETPL as a result of the locality requiring that providers be certified with the Florida Department of Education (Buck 2002). Georgia, which also imposed a state certification requirement, provided some initial exceptions for WIA participation to noncertified providers if they showed that they had applied for certification (D'Amico et al. 2002).

The decision of training providers not to participate in WIA was made easier by the fact that WIA provides for only a small proportion of the workforce development services and financing around the country. In Texas, the state Education Agency and the state Higher Education Coordinating Board provided at least 40 percent of the workforce development funds in 2000. Within the Texas Workforce Commission, WIA provided only one-sixth of the funding for workforce services in 2000, and relied on other sources, such as Welfare-to-Work grants, Food Stamp program, TANF work programs, and the Employment Service (O'Shea and King 2001). In Philadelphia, the first-year WIA allocation was $17 million, which was less than one-seventh of the funding for workforce services (Buck 2002).[27] With WIA funds dwarfed by other federal sources, training providers may seek to participate in publicly funded training outside the WIA system.

State and local variation in the application and eligibility process can also be perceived as more burdensome for some training providers. Some states (e.g., Georgia, Michigan, Nebraska, and Pennsylvania) require training providers to submit applications to a central state office; other states (e.g., California) have training providers submit applications to their own localities; and others (e.g., North Carolina and Texas) have providers submit applications to multiple areas for determination. Additionally, local boards can set up different local performance standards than their neighbors, so long as their policies meet or exceed their states' performance standards. In effect, an approved training provider in one locality does not necessarily translate into an approved provider for another locality, even within the same state. These local variations can be a cumbersome and confusing process for training providers, especially when they serve multiple areas. To create a more "regional" approach to the requirements, some local boards have begun work with neighboring boards to develop consistency in how providers would be used; for example, local boards in Texas have agreements to use providers approved by their neighboring local boards, and the local boards of the Detroit and Atlanta areas are also working towards more consistency in their respective regions (Macro, Almandsmith, and Hague 2003; D'Amico et al. 2002).

In an effort to encourage training providers to focus on improving customer outcomes, some local boards have experimented with alternative methods, such as "benchmarking" payments made to training providers. In Southwest Connecticut, 50 percent of the training fees was paid to a provider when the customer completed the first half of the program, 25 percent of the fees was paid when the customer completed the program, and the remaining 25 percent was paid when the customer entered in employment (D'Amico et al. 2002).[28] In Milwaukee, 10 percent was paid when a customer enrolled, 40 percent was paid when a customer completed the program, and the remaining 50 percent was paid when the customer became employed within 60 days of completing the training program, earned at least $8 per hour, and retained employment for 30 days. Essex County (New Jersey) also used employment retention as a factor for payment by providing the final 10 percent of the costs to the training provider once the customer retained employment for 60 days (Macro, Almandsmith, and Hague 2003). Different types of training providers may or may not assume this financial risk. CBOs, even if they have a track record for achieving high performance outcomes, may find this payment structure financially unstable and offer their services elsewhere, especially if these

WIA customers are a small proportion of the provider's population and source of revenue. Similarly, other nonprofits and for-profits may simply decide not to participate if they consider the payment structure to be too demanding or unfair, especially when non-WIA customers or other programs are readily available to make full payment of services.

Types of training provider participation

Educational institutions, for-profit/proprietary schools, and non-profits participate in the WIA training program nationwide, but utilization of each type can vary widely by locality. For example, the important role of community and technical colleges can be seen in Lane County (Oregon) and Pinellas County (Florida), where nearly 60 percent or more of the customers were referred into community colleges, and the Bay Area where more than 90 percent of its customers were referred into technical colleges in PY 2001.[29] On the other hand, community or technical colleges can also be seldom used, such as in Northwest (Pennsylvania), Essex County (New Jersey), and Boston (Massachusetts). Instead, Northwest and Essex counties utilized for-profits and Boston utilized nonprofits a majority of the time in PY 2001 (Macró, Almandsmith, and Hague 2003). Although localities may rely on certain types of providers over others, all three types of providers play an important role for the national workforce investment system.

Community colleges and other educational institutions. Community and technical colleges are used for a number of reasons, including the reasonable costs associated with a state-subsidized system, the ability of customers to utilize Pell Grants, strong support from some states for localities and the public educational system to work together, and the availability of a wider range of programs than what is generally offered by for-profits and nonprofits (Macro, Almandsmith, and Hague 2003; D'Amico and Salzman forthcoming). Macro, Almandsmith, and Hague (2003) found that educational institutions played an important role as training providers, receiving a larger percentage of ITAs than either for-profits or nonprofits in the intermediary study. Among all public and private educational institutions, community and technical colleges accounted for over 40 percent of the total ITAs issued by the localities. However, the certification process under WIA has had an adverse impact on the participation of community colleges. In April 2002, only 35 of more than 100 community colleges in California were participating in the WIA system.[30] In fact, based on early experiences of WIA, community colleges were expected to decrease in WIA participation due to state performance requirements for the ETPL (D'Amico et al. 2001). WIA-funded training customers are a small subset of the colleges' entire student body, but these small proportions can constitute a large proportion of the WIA training population.

Many educational institutions generally believe that they are responsible for "education, not employment," and that focusing on employment is inconsistent with the institutions' goals (Grubb 1996; D'Amico et al. 2002). However, community college perception of a conflict between "education" and "employment" is disappearing. The community college system in the 1990s placed increasing emphasis on workforce development. While continuing to maintain a role in supporting academic students who seek to transfer to four-year colleges, community colleges have aimed to gain an increasing share of the workforce development training market, whether funded by employers or publicly, and thereby provide current and future employees with education, training, competencies, and skills that employers need to maintain high performance in a competitive market environment (Forde 2002). Community colleges in some localities, such as Macomb-St. Clair (Michigan) and Metro Portland, are also tailoring their programs to WIA customers by developing shorter-term courses (D'Amico and Salzman forthcoming).

Community colleges have responded to shortages of skilled workers by providing training directly to workers who came to community colleges on their own or through JTPA and WIA programs. Community colleges also increasingly have developed alliances with firms to provide customized training for incumbent workers, seeking to be a key or principal source of training for employers. Increased emphasis on workforce development has not been in response to expected increases in JTPA/WIA funding, but rather in response to actual large increases in formal employer training occurrences that began in the 1980s and the projected continued increase in the future (Carnevale and Desrochers 1997).

Both JTPA and WIA have put a heavy emphasis on placement. Under WIA, training providers' success is documented by the Consumer Report System. Yet, one study found that the community college system does not have strong placement programs. Community colleges as large as 25,000 tend to have understaffed placement offices consisting of two or three staff. Placement offices tend to put more emphasis on temporary placement during school attendance; as a result, job openings posted by employers are mostly temporary, low-wage jobs for students. There are few openings listed for full-time jobs in areas of study. Placement offices are also perceived by employers as not following up sufficiently or making effective use of employer openings, and when they do follow up, not referring the best candidates for the job. A community college was more effective when its state set a placement goal, had effective co-op programs, and when its placement office made use of job developers to find job openings for students. Placement can also be made by occupational instructors, but few instructors were found to engage in placement activities, and placement is not normally considered part of their job (Grubb 1996).

In the past, community colleges have had limited incentives to collect postenrollment labor force outcome data or serve the disadvantaged, especially without any clear guidance from the state. Community colleges serve students with a wide variety of goals, many of which do not deal with subsequent employment. Also, transfer placement rates of students into four-year colleges has often been considered the "primary measure of success" (Alssid et al. 2002). With weak incentives, postenrollment labor force outcome data can be difficult and expensive to collect. It has also not been a high priority for community colleges because, in most cases, federal, state and local governments have not pushed colleges to collect the data. The coming of performance accountability indicators under WIA and the Carl D. Perkins Vocational and Technical Education Act has changed this situation. While the WIA Consumer Reports System requires that there be records of customer placement, employment, and earnings, the community college system generally does not collect this information. Except in states that have previously emphasized placement as an important outcome for community colleges, little information has been collected that could be used for submitting data for certification for the WIA Eligible Training Provider list. Prior to the enactment of WIA, Florida, Minnesota, and Ohio were among the few states that developed tracking systems using telephone surveys. Based on these systems, the states developed placement goals of around 70–75 percent. As a precursor to the approach of WIA, some states were testing the use of unemployment insurance wage records, but this was only in its early stages when WIA was enacted (Grubb 1996; Baj et al.1991).

The American Association of Community Colleges (AACC) has responded to the introduction of WIA performance accountability measures by asking for more flexible measures that would allow community colleges to use data they already collect or data that would be easiest for them to collect. Community colleges would like flexibility in what they measure, such as choosing whether the program completion measure was attainment of a degree/certificate, a measured skill, an individual's personal goal, or learning a defined skill. They would also like to choose the method of measurement, such as measuring earnings using unemployment insurance wage records or a wage survey (AACC 2002). This interest in easing the burden of collecting outcome data is understandable given the small incidence of WIA-funded students at community colleges, and it may provide the best available, easily collectible outcome information. However, these changes would also reduce the comparability of data and, therefore, the degree of accountability in training and education programs.

More recently, there has been close coordination of policy between the U.S. Departments of Education and Labor to coordinate the reauthorization of the Perkins Act and WIA. The goal of this policy is to ratify that "community colleges are the engines for workforce development in this country" by "examining ways to enhance the community colleges' growing role in workforce development" by reexamining federal policies that "inadvertently discourage community college activity in workforce development" (D'Amico 2002).

For-profit organizations. Unlike community colleges, proprietary schools tend to be more flexible and have a greater tendency to use open-entry exit programs. They also tend to have shorter, more intensive courses that were commonly perceived to be more appropriate for WIA participants. Proprietary schools often tracked performance for accreditation or for their own internal records. As a result, proprietary schools generally do not have as many concerns with reporting data or outcomes. One-stop staff generally had the sense that proprietary schools provided active counseling and were more experienced and equipped to manage progress and reporting requirements (D'Amico et al. 2002).

However, not all proprietary schools feel at ease with the transition to WIA. Some proprietary schools that have depended largely on JTPA customers have not been able to transition to the unpredictable flows of customers that came with the new ITA system. Some have begun to market themselves to other non-WIA customers, while others have closed down. These types of proprietary schools, like the CBOs that depended heavily on JTPA customers, are not likely to continue successfully as providers under the ITA system (D'Amico 2002). Additionally, providers that do not offer placement services, or have not been successful in placing customers into employment, are also likely to be at risk during subsequent eligibility (Macro, Almandsmith, and Hague 2003).

Nonprofit organizations. Under JTPA, many CBOs held group contracts for classroom training. CBOs are usually established in the localities and specialized with serving specific populations, especially harder-to-serve populations. The use of open competition and vouchers instead of group contracts could affect their participation in the WIA system. For example, CBOs in Boston expected to lose about one-third of their enrollees during the transition to WIA, based on their experiences with vouchers under a previous pilot program (Buck 2002). Other localities also believed that CBOs would participate less under WIA due to the focus on vouchers instead of contracts (D'Amico 2002).

Unlike contracted group training where CBOs could be guaranteed a certain number of enrollees based on their contractual agreement with localities, the use of ITAs could no longer provide such a guarantee. CBOs have observed fluctuations in registered students but have little experience with planning or responding to unpredictable flows. As a result, many small nonprofits with modest budgets can be vulnerable to financial risk when they experience erratic customer flow, which may lead them to discontinue WIA participation (D'Amico et. al. 2002; Macro, Almandsmith, and Hague 2003). On the other hand, some CBOs have tried to improve their competitive positions within the WIA training environment by changing the format of their programs into shorter, more intense programs that are similar to the programs of proprietary schools (D'Amico et al. 2001).

CBOs also have other alternatives if they continue to experience difficulty connecting with the ITA system, such as by offering their services elsewhere, e.g., the welfare system (Buck 2002). CBOs generally have a history with other federal programs that support training for special populations of customers who are harder to serve, such as TANF recipients. Because welfare programs have a larger funding stream than WIA in many localities, and because CBOs are specialized in serving specific populations, CBOs may be able to turn to the TANF system as a source of training customers.

Brokering and Consulting Services

Local boards, one-stop operators, and service providers constantly make operational decisions to improve their management and delivery of services in the workforce development system. Assistance with these types of decisions are offered by brokering and consulting organizations that specialize in working with stakeholders to help them achieve their goals. The Council for Adult and Experiential Learning (CAEL) and the Structured Employment Economic Development Corporation (Seedco) are examples of nonprofit organizations that provide assistance on topics such as capacity building, strategic planning, and program and financial management. CAEL, for example, provides technical assistance with seeking funding and developing partnerships with business, government, labor and higher education (CAEL 2003).[31] Seedco, which is discussed further in the next section, provides technical assistance to small organizations and also helps foster partnerships among stakeholders. Macro, Almandsmith, and Hague (2003) reported that a number of the local boards in the intermediary study contracted with for-profit firms most often for consulting services such as information systems development, research, monitoring services, and marketing and public relations. These intermediaries can play an important role in improving the quality of services and management in the one-stop system.

UTILIZATION OF ECONOMIES OF SCALE

This section describes the benefits from economies of scale that can assist organizations maintain their competitiveness in the workforce investment system. We then identify four organizations, Goodwill Industries, Affiliated Computer Services, Employment Services, and Seedco, that actively participate in the system.

Larger organizations, regardless of whether they are nonprofits, for-profits, or public organizations, have the ability to consolidate functions and offer to their local offices or affiliates important services that may not be readily available to smaller organizations. These advantages include important access to capital as well as expertise on program and financial management (Winston et al. 2002). National headquarters can devote full-time staff to focus on specific subject areas, such as grantwriting or legislation, and provide technical assistance on program and financial management to the local offices. Local offices can also receive access to listservs, newsletters, policy updates, and conferences (Macro, Almandsmith, and Hague 2003). Additionally, centralized purchasing of supplies and other items, particularly software and hardware for management information systems, can contribute to cost-efficiency.

Financial stability and access to capital can affect an organization's participation with WIA programs. When an organization has a diverse set of funding sources, they are less likely to be affected by changes in WIA funding. For example, Goodwill received $80–$90 million in ETA Welfare-to-Work grants and has found that the Welfare-to-Work program is easier to participate in than WIA itself (Crosby 2002). Organizations that are not reliant on WIA can more easily decide to opt in or out of the system. On the other hand, organizations who do not have access to other funding sources can be more vulnerable to WIA changes. Preliminary observations showed that CBOs and for-profit training providers alike were susceptible to folding if they were heavily dependent on JTPA funding but could no longer obtain guarantees of funding from ITAs (D'Amico and Salzman forthcoming; Macro, Almandsmith, and Hague 2003). Also, poor financial management and lack of access to a sufficient line of credit to operate under a cost-reimbursement contract were often issues that resulted in turnover for one-stop operators (Macro, Almandsmith, and Hague 2003). Although smaller organizations may be more susceptible to these problems, Seedco President William Grinker suggests that developing networks of small organizations can help them achieve similar benefits of the larger organizations (Grinker 1999).

Goodwill Industries International, Inc. Goodwill Industries is one of the largest nonprofit providers of workforce development services in the United States, with a mission to serve primarily disadvantaged workers. In 2002, 179 local affiliates served over 500,000 workers, providing services in more than 94 percent of the counties in the country. Goodwill has grown rapidly during a period of shrinking JTPA programs. Local affiliates of Goodwill workforce services are autonomous 501(3c) organizations that operate under local-national agreements. Local affiliates benefit from the Goodwill name and logo, the exclusive use of the local area to operate its retail stores, and a range of services provided by the national office.

In 2000, Goodwill's revenues of $1.85 billion included $364 million in workforce development revenues, as grants from government agencies. Goodwill operated 55 temporary services agencies and was the one-stop operator in 19 localities (Goodwill Industries International 2001). More than 60 affiliates provide services to more than 125 one-stop centers. Goodwill provides a range of employment and training services to customers, including placement services, welfare-to-work services, case management, and job readiness (Crosby 2002).

The largest customer for Goodwill's workforce development services is TANF, followed by Vocational Rehabilitation and WIA. The revenue from retail stores provides a majority of the funding (about 80 percent) to deliver employment and training services to customers. WIA funds are a small proportion of Goodwill's public funding sources and are used to supplement revenues generated from the Goodwill stores that are used to subsidize their workforce development activities. WIA is important to Goodwill because Goodwill staff is better linked to customers when they work on-site or closely with the one-stop centers to deliver services (Crosby 2002).

Local affiliates receive a wide array of services from the national headquarters that help them with bidding for services and improving operations. The national headquarters provides grant writing assistance to local affiliates by making available a certified federal grants administrator and full-time grant writers, sponsoring workshops on grant writing, providing a collection of successful proposals, and offering online tools. The national headquarters or field staff, who may contract with consultants, provide technical assistance on an on-going basis, which can be particularly helpful if new affiliates struggle with service delivery. The benefits of economies of scale are apparent when the national headquarters researches and brokers purchasing deals for items used nationwide, such as computer hardware and software. Goodwill also develops its own software and plans to create a standardized client tracking system with financial data to provide the national headquarters and affiliates with real time data on customers (Crosby 2002).

Affiliated Computer Services (ACS). Formerly Lockheed Martin IMS, ACS is one of the leading for-profit organizations that provide workforce development services. ACS is an information technology and business process outsourcing Fortune 1000 company that acquired the Lockheed-Martin IMS unit in June 2001. Lockheed Martin IMS was the workforce development services portion of Lockheed Martin that specialized in welfare and workforce services, child support enforcement, child care management, and electronic toll collection. The unit has about 4,100 employees located in 275 locations, and is now called the "Workforce and Community Solutions" unit of ACS, with headquarters based in Austin, Texas.[32] In 2003, ACS provided services to about 50 local boards and served as the one-stop operator of 103 one-stop centers. In Texas and Florida, ACS was the one-stop operator and organization responsible for core and intensive services, while in California ACS provided services for local areas but did not serve as the one-stop operator (Zeitler 2003).

The ACS headquarters provides assistance to the local office staff in various ways. These include using "train the trainer" sessions and employing subject matter experts to oversee quality and project status. Grant writing is centralized at the ACS headquarters, which relieves local offices from having to devote much of their resources performing the task. Proprietary software and a client tracking system have been developed and are available for local offices, but are not required if the local board prefers to use a different system. Hiring is generally conducted at the local office, but headquarters can provide assistance to the local levels if necessary. Despite the recent acquisition to ACS, the same processes and much of the same staff, in place when the organization was under Lockheed Martin, remain the same under ACS (Zeitler 2003).

ACS has financial and staff resources to provide many of the services that a national nonprofit organization provides, such as technical assistance and consolidated functions in a national headquarters. Unlike Goodwill, which has local affiliates that are autonomous and responsible for their own financial and accounting mechanisms in place, ACS retains overall responsibility for local offices. Since ACS provides numerous services outside of its workforce development unit, it can likely withstand fluctuations, including decreases, in WIA funds because of other funding opportunities. ACS receives funds for workforce development services primarily through WIA, but has seen a decrease in WIA funding over the past few years. TANF is the next largest source of funding for these services. ACS is involved primarily with direct service delivery and limits its involvement to providing management and consulting services to local boards. Few for-profit firms in the ETA intermediary study provide youth services, but ACS plans to expand in this area (Zeitler 2003).[33]

In 2000, Lockheed Martin IMS had $580 million in revenue, and ACS estimated that it would increase to $700 million in 2001 (Wakeman and Welsh 2001). The President and CEO of ACS stated, "Our objective is to be premier provider of diversified business process outsourcing services, delivering a full range of services to multiple vertical markets." According to an ACS press release, the company expected a greater percentage of government expenditures to be outsourced due to a "rise in fiscal pressures, changing regulations, and increased accountability . . . to streamline program operations" (Intelligent Transportation System Access 2001).

The Employment Service (ES). The ES is a governmental agency with over 60 years of experience providing labor exchange and other services in locations nationwide. Each local ES office is part of a larger state workforce security agency that operates under a national legislative mandate and has experienced a relatively fixed though stagnant funding level. The national office provides information and guidance about new rules and procedures. Automated labor market information and labor exchange programs provide a national system of labor exchange and labor market information.[34] In addition to the national system, each state ES agency also maintains an automated state labor market information system and has an established network of employers across the state that local offices can access. State ES agencies are able to put in place exclusive hiring agreements with private employers and provide training and capacity building for local offices, with services standardized across localities. Staffing and financial functions are also standardized, and local offices benefit from central purchasing. Another important feature is the state ES agencies' authority to open new local offices in areas that are determined to be in need of ES services.[35] Additionally, WIA regulations mandating ES as a required partner in the one-stop center can provide ES with a physical advantage of co-location within the centers. ES has a long-standing history of providing labor exchange services, and most localities from studies on early WIA experiences selected ES as a primary provider of core services (D'Amico 2001; Macro, Almandsmith, and Hague 2003).

Structured Employment Economic Development Corporation (Seedco). Seedco is a national nonprofit intermediary that assists organizations improve in areas such as workforce operations, capacity-building, and performance and financial management. It assists small organizations consolidate functions, such as accounting and reporting, to improve their performance so that organizations can focus on direct service provision. The purpose is to allow small intermediaries to better compete with larger intermediaries through sharing of resources. Seedco also helps nonprofits establish a diverse set of funding sources to become economically sustainable. To further assist with financial independence and stability, Seedco brokers funds for community groups with cash flow needs. Seedco also develops tools, such as the Performance Measurement and Management (PM&M) system, to assist nonprofits measure and manage performance (Seedco 2002).

Seedco has provided technical assistance to numerous organizations, and grants from foundations and the government have helped support these efforts. For example, a USDOL grant was awarded to Seedco to provide assistance to CBOs to increase their participation in the workforce investment system.[36] Seedco has customers located in twenty states, and Washington, DC (Seedco 2002).

SUMMARY AND CONCLUSIONS

Intermediaries have greater participation in the system under WIA as a result of new one-stop centers that were created nationwide and local boards being prohibited from delivering direct services. Based on early accounts of WIA implementation, the following summarizes what has been observed of intermediary characteristics and service provision.

Intermediary Provision of Services

- **Nonprofit organizations and consortiums are generally selected to serve as one-stop operators**. Few local boards decide to deliver one-stop operator services themselves, choosing instead to use a variety of other providers.

- **ES plays a large role in providing core services, especially as a primary provider of the services.** When ES is not the primary provider of core services, this responsibility is usually assigned to the one-stop operators, which tend to be nonprofits.

- **Nonprofit organizations are major providers of intensive and youth services.** Intensive services are often the responsibility of the organization selected as the one-stop operator. CBOs with established histories are generally used to deliver services for specific populations, such as youth, dislocated workers, low-wage workers, and ex-offenders.

- **Certain types of training providers, especially community colleges and smaller CBOs, are reluctant to participate in an ITA/ETPL system, but for different reasons**. Many community colleges are not willing to provide customer data because of the resources needed to collect and maintain information for initial and subsequent eligibility, especially when the WIA customer is a small fraction of the colleges' student population. Community colleges would prefer to submit data that they have already collected, or data that is easier to collect than the current ETPL requirements. Smaller CBOs, on the other hand, tend to rely more on WIA customers and funding. Because of this, they are more vulnerable to the uncertainties of a voucher system that replaces group-contracted training. These CBOs may find it financially beneficial to diversify and provide training elsewhere, outside of the WIA system.

Intermediary Advantages in the One-Stop Environment

- **Larger organizations, regardless of whether they are for-profits or nonprofits, can have an advantage over smaller organizations when competing for WIA services.** Larger organizations have resources to support full-time staff to specialize in services where smaller organizations may find it difficult to do so, e.g., establish networks with federal government and other stakeholders, provide technical assistance and training, and assist with the bidding process. Larger providers may also better withstand the implementation of a voucher system that utilizes open competition, and are less reliant on WIA funding because they can seek other sources of funding.

- **Small community-based organizations dominate youth services.** More competition (and more choice for local boards) appears to exist among intermediaries for youth services. For-profits are generally not involved in youth services; there may be too much competition from other organizations, or not enough profit.

Notes

The content of this chapter reflects the opinions of the authors and does not represent the policy or positions of the U.S. Department of Labor. We thank John Colborn and Norton Grubb for helpful comments.

1. The term *intermediaries* has been recently defined and applied in the workforce investment system in different ways. In this chapter, we apply a broad definition used by Macro, Almandsmith, and Hague (2003) in an ETA study that referred intermediaries to public and private organizations who receive funding from local

boards to serve WIA customers or perform WIA-related functions. A separate U.S. Department of Health and Human Services study conducted by Pavetti et al. (2000) defined intermediaries as organizations that hold formal relationships with the welfare office (or other administrative entity) responsible for moving welfare recipients into the labor market, including training providers that provide place-ment services. In Workforce Intermediaries for the Twenty-First Century, Leete et al. (2004) broadly define *labor market intermediaries* as organizations that work at various levels of the labor market (such as job placement, training, and support services) to help link individuals to jobs. These would include temporary place-ment agencies and head hunters, unions, CBOs, nonprofits, governmental organi-zations, community and technical colleges, vocational schools, and associations. In the same book, Osterman (2004) also considers labor market intermediaries to include Internet job-matching agencies (such as www.monster.com and www.guru.com).

However, Giloth (2004) distinguishes another set of intermediaries, which he labels as *workforce intermediaries*, as a much narrower subset of organizations under labor market intermediaries. According to Giloth, workforce intermediar-ies, among other objectives, specifically serve both employers and low-income/less-skilled individuals, create and manage different funding streams, and provide job placement with other services. However, it is the broader definition, and not this narrow one, that we and (other sources) are more likely to associate with the term intermediaries.

2. The Employment Service (ES) is also referred to as Job Service in some states. The responsibilities of ES have evolved over the years as a result of changing leg-islation and priorities. See National Commission for Employment Policy (1991).

3. See Wandner and Javar (2001) for further discussion of privatization efforts under UI and ES. See Balducchi and Pasternak (2000) for a discussion of the issue of privatization of ES.

4. Employers, state apprenticeship agencies, trade associations, unions, and non-profit community agencies provided most of the on-the-job training (Levitan and Mangum 1969). In an MDTA longitudinal evaluation sample of 10 metropolitan areas, of the 54 training facilities that held contracts funded by the federal govern-ment (with some facilities receiving more than one contract), approximately two-thirds were public intermediaries and one-third were private intermediaries. Of the public intermediaries, most were either skill centers or community colleges.

5. Three large CBOs in particular, the National Urban League, Opportunities Indus-trialization Centers, and SER, significantly increased their work (Snedeker and Snedeker 1978).

6. In FY 1975, 700 ES positions were cut as a result of decreased contracts (Snede-ker and Snedeker 1978).

7. This figure does not include Public Service Employment funding.

8. ES also defined cost categories differently than JTPA programs and did not have a 15 percent limit on administrative costs, which may be another factor for why ES was selected.

9. Welfare-to-Work grants were awarded to local governments, local boards, and other entities (such as community development corporations and CBOs, community action agencies, and other private organizations) that applied with a local board or local government.

10. Six states (Florida, Texas, Kentucky, Pennsylvania, Utah, and Vermont) became early implementers of WIA. D'Amico et al. (2001) visited these states and localities as part of their study on early WIA implementation experiences.

11. In developing ETA's Five-Year Strategic Plan for pilots, demonstrations, research, and evaluation for July 2000–June 2005, an Expert Panel meeting was convened to discuss high priority research topics for ETA to focus on in the next five years. The Expert Panel agreed that intermediaries play a large role in the workforce development system, but that little information was known about these entities, and to what extent they were working with local boards in serving the locality's customers.

12. According to figures on January 27, 2003, there were 1,933 comprehensive one-stop centers nationwide, 1,604 affiliate centers, and 591 local workforce investment areas (www.servicelocator.org).

13. Results are based on data collected from the Workforce System Information and Evaluation (WSIE) survey (D'Amico et al. 2001).

14. Minimizing staff training and transitional costs, or desiring continuity of staff, are some reasons why former staff may be rehired by the new operator, e.g., the Lower Rio Grande local board (Texas) switched from a for-profit to a nonprofit to serve as the one-stop operator. The for-profit and nonprofit proposals were rated as a statistical tie, but the for-profit had an $800,000 cost difference for an 8 month period. Interestingly, the nonprofit that hoped to receive the new contract was previously the administrative arm of a private industry council, but had been a separate organization for five years (Lower Rio Grande Workforce Development Board 2002).

15. Nearly half (48 percent) of the comprehensive one-stop centers were operated by nonprofits (Macro, Almandsmith, and Hague 2003).

16. Although collaboratives and consortiums both are associations that band more than one organization together, Macro et al. (2003) distinguishes "collaboratives" from "consortiums" because collaboratives do not consist of at least three required WIA partners.

17. Milwaukee grandfathered the TANF service providers as one-stop operators. The decision to transform existing employment and training service locations into new one-stop centers, and select existing organizations as the one-stop operators or lead operators, has been evident in other localities as well. Consortiums in localities that transformed their existing ES buildings into new one-stop centers often had ES staff act as the lead in the consortium (D'Amico et al. 2001).

18. In this case, Lockheed Martin IMS was the former one-stop operator that decided not to re-compete for the contract (Jacobson 2002).

19. In 7 of the 9 localities, ES was the primary provider of core services (D'Amico et al. 2001).

20. Gulf Coast (Texas) was the only locality that used a for-profit organization (which was also the one-stop operator) to deliver core services (Macro, Almandsmith, and Hague 2003).

21. Only about one-sixth of the local boards nationwide received a waiver to provide core and intensive services, as of October 2000 (D'Amico et al. 2001). In the intermediary study, none of the local boards delivered intensive services (Macro, Almandsmith, and Hague 2003).

22. Intensive services have also been delivered out of affiliate centers, in addition to the comprehensive one-stops. Table 5.1 underestimates the total number of intensive service providers that are used in the one-stop system because it represents those used only in comprehensive one-stops.

23. The two national for-profit companies included Sylvan Learning Centers and ACS (Macro, Almandsmith, and Hague 2003).

24. Boston went from 24 to 34 providers, primarily with the entry of new proprietary schools, but almost one-third of the providers that held contracts under JTPA did not apply. In Charlotte, the number of providers remained the same at 16, but the mix of providers was not the same. Houston experienced a decrease from 120 to 95 providers, and officials believed that this was a result of a voluntary loss of CBO participation due to required performance benchmarks. Philadelphia increased from 56 to 64 providers, with nearly half of all providers being new to the workforce development system (Buck 2002).

25. Seventeen of the twenty-seven states requested to extend the initial period of provider eligibility to June 30, 2004. In fact, several states had submitted second requests to extend their previously approved dates of initial eligibility to a new end date of June 30, 2004.

26. In the ITA/ETP Demonstration report, California, Connecticut, Georgia, Maryland, Nebraska, Oregon, and Pennsylvania instituted these types of state certification or licensing from the state higher education commission, or equivalent (D'Amico et al. 2002).

27. Other providers were the TANF programs ($70 million), Welfare-to-Work grants ($25 million), secondary vocational education ($9.5 million), and a Community Services Grant ($3.6 million) (Buck 2002).

28. As of October 2002, the Southwest Connecticut local board changed the benchmark payment structure to 50 percent payment when the customer attends the first class, instead of 50 percent payment after the customer attends half of the training program.

29. Other states with an extensive system of technical colleges include Georgia, North Carolina, Texas, and Indiana (D'Amico et al. 2002).

30. Numbers based on April 2002 meeting on WIA reauthorization held in Los Angeles.

31. CAEL also works with localities to improve program services, such as working with Chicago to serve as the Training Assessment and Review Agency in the local ITA system.

32. The ACS company has about 30,000 employees (Zeitler 2003).

33. Although ACS has had youth service contracts since 1996, the effort in expanding these services is fairly new.
34. America's Job Bank and America's Career Kit are part of ES services for nationwide networks. State ES also maintain electronic labor exchange services for the state.
35. The ES office must be affiliated with the one-stop system, serving as either a satellite center, specialty center, or within a comprehensive one-stop center.
36. For more information on this and other grants awarded to Seedco, see "Fieldnotes," available at www.seedco.org/about/field/index.html.

References

Alssid, Julian L., David Gruber, Davis Jenkins, Christopher Mazzeo, Brandon Roberts, and Regina Sanback-Stroud. 2002. *Building a Career Pathways System: Promising Practicies in Community College-Centered Workforce Development*. Brooklyn, NY: Workforce Strategy Center.

American Association of Community Colleges (AACC). 2002. "Workforce Accountability Measures Proposed." http://www.aacc.nche.edu/Content/ContentGroups/Headline_News/May_2002/Wrkfrcaccb.pdf.

Baj, John, C. Trott, and David Stevens. 1991. *A Feasibility Study of the Use of Unemployment Insurance Wage-Record Data as an Evaluation Tool for JTPA*. Research Report 90-02. Washington, DC: National Commission for Employment Policy.

Balducchi, David E., and Alison J. Pasternak. 2000. "One-Stop Statecraft: Restructuring Workforce Development Programs in the United States." *Labour Market Policies and the Public Employment Service*. Prague Conference, July 2000. Paris: Organisation for Economic Co-operation and Development.

Buck, Maria L. 2002. *Charting New Territory: Early Implementation of the Workforce Investment Act*. New York, NY: Public/Private Ventures. http://www.ppv.org/pdffiles/charting.pdf.

Carnevale, Anthony, and Donna M. Desrochers. 1997. "The Role of Community Colleges in the New Economy." *Community College Journal* 66(5): 27–33.

Council for Adult and Experiential Learning (CAEL). 2003 Web site. www.cael.org. Accessed September 20, 2003.

Crosby, Kathy. 2002. Director of Workforce Development. Goodwill Industries, Inc. Personal communication with one author, August 2.

D'Amico, Carole. 2002. "Q & A with Carole D'Amico." *Community College Journal* 72(6): 22–23.

D'Amico, Ronald, and Jeffrey Salzman. Forthcoming. *An Evaluation of the Individual Training Account/Eligible Training Provider Demonstration: Draft Final Report.* Washington, DC: U.S. Department of Labor, Employment and Training Administration.

D'Amico, Ronald, Deborah Koga, Suzanne Kreutzer, Andrew Wiegand, and Alberta Baker. 2001. *A Report on Early State and Local Progress Towards WIA Implementation: Final Interim Report.* Washington, DC: U.S. Department of Labor, Employment and Training Administration.

D'Amico, Ronald, Alexandria Martinez, Jeffrey Salzman, and Robin Wagner. 2002. *An Evaluation of the Individual Training Account/Eligible Training Provider Demonstration: Interim Report.* Washington, DC: U.S. Department of Labor, Employment and Training Administration.

Eberts, Randall W. 2002. *Design, Implementation, and Evaluation of the Work First Profiling Pilot Project.* Washington, DC: U.S. Department of Labor.

Forde, Margaret L. 2002. "Community Colleges—The Center of the Workforce Development Universe." *Community College Journal* 72(6): 32–35.

Franklin, Grace A., and Randall B. Ripley. 1984. *CETA: Politics and Policy 1973-1982.* Knoxville, TN: University of Tennessee Press.

Giloth, Robert P. 2004. "Introduction: A Case for Workforce Intermediaries." In *Workforce Intermediaries for the Twenty-First Century*, Robert Giloth, ed. Philadelphia: Temple University Press.

Goodwill Industries International. 2001. "Statement of Corporate Capabilities." August 15. Bethesda, MD.

Grinker, William. 1999. Keynote speech at the conference, "Beyond JTPA and Welfare-to-Work: Building a Workforce Development Infrastructure." Held in Tarrytown, NY, November 11.

Grubb, W. Norton. 1996. *Working in the Middle: Strengthening Education and Training for the Mid-Skilled Labor Force.* San Francisco, CA: Jossey-Bass Publishers.

Intelligent Transportation System Access. 2001. "ACS Acquires Lockheed Martin IMS." http://www.itsa.org/itsnews.nsf.

Jacobson, Louis. 2002. Member, Montgomery County Workforce Investment Board. Personal communication with one author, March 29.

Leete, Laura, Chris Benner, Manuel Pastor Jr., and Sarah Zimmerman. 2004. "Labor Market Intermediaries in the Old and New Economies: A Survey of Worker Experiences in Milwaukee and Silicon Valley." In *Workforce Intermediaries for the Twenty-First Century*, Robert Giloth, ed. Philadelphia: Temple University Press.

Leonard, Paul. 1999. *Welfare to Work Block Grants: Are They Working?* Discussion paper prepared for The Brookings Institution, Center on Urban and

Metropolitan Policy. Washington, DC: The Brookings Institution. http://www.brook.edu/dybdocroot/es/urban/leonard.pdf.

Levitan, Sar A., and Garth L. Mangum. 1969. *Federal Training and Work Programs in the Sixties.* Ann Arbor, MI: Institute of Labor and Industrial Relations, University of Michigan, Wayne State University.

Lower Rio Grande Workforce Development Board. Minutes from meeting, October 25. http://www.wfsolutions.com/boardmeeting_112900_2.html. (Accessed on April 25, 2002.)

Macro, Bronwen, Sherry Almandsmith, and Megan Hague. 2003. *Creating Partnerships for Workforce Investment: How Services Are Provided under WIA.* Oakland, CA: Berkeley Policy Associates.

National Commission for Employment Policy. 1991. *Improving the Effectiveness of the Employment Service: Defining the Issues.* Washington, DC: National Commission for Employment Policy.

———. 1994. *A Guide to Major Federal Job Training Programs.* Washington, DC: National Commission for Employment Policy.

Operations Research, Inc. 1972. *Longitudinal Evaluation Study of Four Manpower Training Programs: Cost and Enrollee Data. Appendix A: MDTA Cost and Enrollee Data.* Washington, DC: Office of Economic Opportunity, Division of Evaluation.

O'Shea, Daniel, and Christopher T. King. 2001. *The Workforce Investment Act of 1998: Restructuring Workforce Development Initiatives in States and Localities.* Albany, NY: Nelson A. Rockefeller Institute of Government.

Osterman, Paul. 2004. "Labor Market Intermediaries in the Modern Labor Market." In *Workforce Intermediaries for the Twenty-First Century*, Robert Giloth, ed. Philadelphia: Temple University Press.

Pavetti, Donna, Michelle Derr, Jacquelyn Anderson, Carole Trippe, and Sidnee Paschal. 2000. *The Role of Intermediaries in Linking TANF Recipients with Jobs.* Washington, DC: Mathematica Policy Research.

Reville, Robert T., and Jacob Alex Kerman. 1996. "Job Training: Impact on California of Further Consolidation and Devolution." In *The New Fiscal Federalism and the Social Safety Net: A View from California*, James Hosek and Robert Levine, eds. Santa Monica, CA: RAND. http://www.rand.org/publications/CF/CF123/reville.

Seedco. 2002. *New Patterns, New Strategies: Corporate Report January 2001–December 2002.* New York, NY: Seedco. http://www.seedco.org/about/whatsnew/annrept1/index.html.

Snedeker, Bonnie B., and David W. Snedeker. 1978. *CETA: Decentralization on Trial.* Salt Lake City, UT: Olympus Publishing Company.

U.S. Department of Labor. 2000. Annual Report. *U.S. Employment Service Program Report Data: Program Year 1998*. Washington, DC: United States Department of Labor.

Wakeman, Nick, and William Welsh. 2001. "ACS to Buy Lockheed Martin IMS in $825 Million Deal." *Washington Technology*, July 19, 2001.

Wandner, Stephen A. 1997. "Early Reemployment of Dislocated Workers in the United States." *International Social Security Review* 50(4): 95–112.

Wandner, Stephen A., and Janet O. Javar. 2001. "Trends in Private Sector Involvement in the Delivery of Workforce Development Services in the United States." In S*ocial Security at the Dawn of the 21ˢᵗ Century*. Donate Dobernack, Dalmer D. Hoskins, and Christiane Kuptsch, eds. New York: Transaction Publishers.

Westat, Inc. 1985. *Implementation of the Job Training Partnership Act: Final Report*. Rockville, MD: U.S. Department of Labor.

Winston, Pamela, Andrew Burwick, Sheena McConnell, and Richard Roper. 2002. *Privatization of Welfare Services: A Review of the Literature*. Washington, DC: Department of Health and Human Services.

Zeitler, Amy. 2003. Director of Business Developments. ACS State and Local Solutions. Personal communication with one author, July 17.

6
Individual Training Accounts, Eligible Training Provider Lists, and Consumer Report Systems

Paul Decker
Irma Perez-Johnson

A crucial change brought about by the Workforce Investment Act (WIA) of 1998 has been the requirement that local workforce agencies use training vouchers, known as Individual Training Accounts (ITAs), to provide training to their customers. Training vouchers are intended to maximize customer choice in training decisions. Theoretically, if individuals use vouchers to choose the training occupations and providers they value the most, the use of training vouchers should also generally maximize social welfare. However, the success of training vouchers in maximizing social welfare depends on individuals making sensible choices based on reliable information. In an actual training market, it may be difficult for individuals to collect reliable information about occupational opportunities and training providers or to use this information effectively in making sensible training choices. Hence, the use of a pure, unrestricted training voucher with no further government role is probably unrealistic. Instead, the government training agency needs to 1) ensure that information about occupations and providers is available and accessible to customers, and 2) help customers in evaluating the information appropriately.

Under WIA, ITAs are intended to empower adult and dislocated worker customers to choose the training services they need and to raise the accountability of states, local areas, and service providers for meeting these needs. Rather than have counselors in local workforce agencies decide who receives what kind of training from which providers, under WIA, customers use their ITAs to make their own training choices. The thinking behind this legislative shift was consistent with the general argument for vouchers described above—that customers would improve the quality of training choices by selecting the programs and providers that were most appropriate for them. The use of training vouchers was also anticipated to increase competition among training providers, thereby increasing their responsiveness to customers' needs and the overall quality of their offerings.

The ITA system established under WIA also recognizes the need to maintain an important and appropriate role for local training agencies in the administration of ITAs. WIA gives states and local areas a great deal of flexibility in both setting the value and other parameters of ITAs to maximize customer access to training and deciding how much guidance and direction counselors provide to customers as they formulate their training decisions. This flexibility allows state and local officials to specify and administer their ITAs in a way that is best suited for their local customers.

Although customers who are determined eligible for training and are awarded an ITA can use their ITAs to purchase training, their selection of a provider is constrained to approved training programs—those included on the state's Eligible Training Provider (ETP) list. To be included on the list, programs must be certified by the state and local workforce areas as meeting acceptable levels of performance. States also provide customers with data on provider performance through the Consumer Report System (CRS), which is intended to help customers make effective training decisions.

This chapter describes the shift to the use of ITAs under the new law and some of the issues that local workforce agencies have faced in designing and implementing ITA programs. Our objectives are to evaluate the degree to which local areas have been able to implement the ITA system envisioned in WIA and, based on this evaluation, discuss issues that may need to be addressed in WIA reauthorization. In the first section, we describe the experience of local workforce agencies with training vouchers prior to WIA. In the following section, we describe key provisions of WIA relating to the administration of ITAs and the selection of training providers. Then we describe the ITA Experiment, which is being sponsored by the U.S. Department of Labor (USDOL) to investigate the implications of different designs for specifying and administering ITAs. In the fourth section, we summarize the experiences of the six local areas participating in the experiment in implementing ITAs, both in the early days of WIA prior to the experiment and under the ITA Experiment. Finally, we discuss the overall feasibility of ITAs as an ongoing approach to providing training and several challenges that may be addressed in WIA reauthorization.

EXPERIENCE WITH TRAINING VOUCHERS PRIOR TO WIA

To some extent, the establishment of ITAs under WIA is a reflection of a trend that had already been ongoing for years at the local level. For example, D'Amico et al. (2001) found that in 13 sites in which they studied early WIA implementation, almost all had already moved away from exclusive use of contracted training and toward individual referral methods during the Job Training Partnership Act (JTPA) era. Furthermore, half of the sites had previous experiences with using vouchers for training, either as a grantee under the Career Management Account demonstration (Public Policy Associates 1999) or as part of some other pilot program.

Moreover, a few local training agencies experimented with training vouchers many years prior to WIA. For example, the Atlanta Regional Commission first used vouchers in 1991 as a means to provide training services to about 13,000 dislocated Eastern Airlines workers when the company went bankrupt. Given the existing training infrastructure and the size of the dislocation, the commission could not handle the number of prospective trainees using the contracted class-size training approach that predominated under JTPA. The commission therefore established a voucher system and let dislocated workers choose whatever training they wanted. It found that many of the dislocated workers who were issued a voucher made poor training choices, selecting training for occupations that paid low wages, or had limited opportunities for career development. In response to this experience, the commission began to build its vendor list and monitor vendor performance, long before these responsibilities were officially established under WIA (D'Amico and Salzman forthcoming).

Local agencies that experimented with voucher programs under JTPA specifically designed programs that allowed for customer choice but still required counseling and constrained choices so as to ensure customers made informed, appropriate choices. A Trutko and Barnow (1999) study of nine areas using voucher programs under JTPA found that eight of the nine areas used a "constrained choice" voucher model, in which the local training agency played a substantial role in approving individual training choices.[1] Under this model, the local agency screened approved vendors, limited occupational choices, provided assessment and counseling on appropriate training choices, and retained the agency's authority to reject a participant's training choice. Local administrators interviewed as part of the Trutko and Barnow study felt that a "pure" voucher model, without assessment or restrictions on training choices, would result in some participants making poor training choices and wasting resources. Many of the elements of this "constrained choice" voucher model are common under the emerging local ITA models, as we will describe later in this chapter. Local administrators in the sites studied by Trutko and Barnow felt that the use of vouchers in their sites had little effect on customer outcomes or costs, but that it improved the level of customer satisfaction (Trutko and Barnow 1999, pp. 35–37).

In the mid 1990s, in anticipation of the possible enactment of training vouchers as part of new workforce development legislation, USDOL sponsored the Career Management Account (CMA) Demonstration to test the feasibility of providing training for dislocated workers through vouchers. The CMA Demonstration was conducted from 1995 to 1997 in 13 sites (Public Policy Associates 1999). Sites continued to operate their nonvoucher programs, but they designed and operated voucher programs to be used for a subsample of their dislocated workers. The targeting of dislocated workers to receive vouchers varied widely and included, in various states, those determined most in need, profiled unemployment insurance claimants, nominations by one-stop staff, and those interested enough to apply for services. Customers were free to choose their training programs, but the local agencies required customers to participate in assessment and counseling to support their decisions. Local agencies felt that if customers had the choice of using these services or not, they would not invest adequate resources in planning their training strategy. Overall, the models developed by local agencies resembled the "constrained choice" models identified in the Trutko and Barnow (1999) research on voucher programs under JTPA. The research on the CMA Demonstration concludes that voucher systems in general are likely to work just as well as a contracted-training system, and lead to somewhat more satisfied customers and staff.

THE ESTABLISHMENT OF ITAs UNDER WIA

Under the tiered service structure established by WIA, adults and dislocated workers can receive training support from local workforce areas only after they have completed minimum core and intensive service requirements established by the local one-stop center.[2] Core services include basic services to assist individuals in obtaining and retaining employment. Intensive services generally include counseling, assessment, and short-term pre-vocational services.

Once individuals complete their core and intensive service requirements, they may be determined eligible for and in need of training. WIA regulations require that local workforce areas use ITAs to provide training to adults and dislocated workers, except in some limited circumstances, to ensure that these individuals can choose their training providers. Exceptions to the use of ITAs can include funding of on-the-job training or customized training provided by an employer or training provided by an organization designed to assist special populations facing multiple employment barriers.

ITAs enable individuals to purchase training from any eligible provider, subject to the limitations established by the states and local areas. The WIA regulations allow states and local workforce areas to restrict the type or duration of training they will fund. For example, training can only be funded for positions that relate to job opportunities in the local area or to a broader geographic area if the customer is willing to relocate. Similarly, states and local areas can impose limits on the duration or costs of training. These limits can be either based on individual circumstances or established across the board. For example, the amount of an ITA may be set for an individual based on that individual's training needs. Alternatively, the state or local area may establish a range of amounts or a maximum amount that is applicable to all ITAs.

States and local areas, through their one-stop centers, are also responsible for ensuring that the training choices made by customers are supported by high-quality information and guidance. A critical component in this effort is the ETP list, which specifies training programs approved for WIA-sponsored training. The WIA legislation specifies two objectives of the ETP list. First, the list defines the training programs that may be considered by adults and dislocated workers who are undertaking training funded by WIA. At the same time, it also serves as a resource for any individual who is interested in conducting research on training providers in the state. As pointed out by D'Amico and Salzman (forthcoming), there is some tension between these two objectives, because the first objective requires that the list exclude some providers while the other objective requires that the list include enough providers to be a useful resource.

To be included on the ETP list, providers must establish their eligibility to receive ITA funds. ITAs can be used to pay only for training provided by vendors whose programs have been certified by the states and local areas as meeting acceptable performance levels on a variety of outcomes measures, including

1) the percentage of all participants who completed training,

2) the percentage of all participants who obtained unsubsidized employment,

3) the average wages at placement of all participants,

4) the percentage of WIA-funded participants who completed training and obtained unsubsidized employment,

5) the percentage of WIA-funded completers who were employed six months after the start of employment,

6) the average wages received by WIA-funded completers, measured six months after the first day of employment, and

7) if applicable, the percentage of WIA-funded completers who obtained a license or certificate, an academic degree or equivalent, or other measures of skills.

States are responsible for establishing acceptable performance levels on these measures and administering the eligibility determination process. Performance levels for each program are to be adjusted to account for the characteristics of the local economy and the clients served.

Information on provider performance and other provider character-istics, including costs, are provided to customers through each state's CRS. The CRS is built on the ETP list and contains information pro-vided by the training providers during the eligibility determination pro-cess. According to WIA regulations, the system "must contain the information necessary for an adult or dislocated worker to fully under-stand the options available to him or her in choosing a program of training services." Although the CRS is built on the ETP list, some states have chosen to make the CRS as comprehensive as possible by also including non-ITA eligible providers (D'Amico and Salzman forthcoming).

The WIA regulations left considerable flexibility for local agencies to develop their own unique programs within the broad structure described above. Given this flexibility, together with the limited expe-rience with vouchers prior to WIA, several questions remained to be answered at the state and local levels as WIA implementation began, such as:

- What is the appropriate balance between customer choice and counselor guidance?

- How should scarce training dollars be allocated among customers through ITA awards?

- Are ITAs appropriate for adult customers as well as dislocated workers?

In the following section we describe the ongoing ITA Experiment, which is designed to specifically address some of these important ques-tions related to the design and administration of ITAs.

THE ITA EXPERIMENT

The ITA specifications set out in WIA, as summarized above, allow states and local areas great flexibility in deciding how they will administer their ITAs. The ongoing ITA Experiment (Perez-Johnson et al. 2000) is providing a test of different approaches to managing customer choice in the administration of ITAs.[3] The experiment is testing three alternative ITA approaches. These approaches differ with respect to both the resources made available to customers to help them access training and the involvement of local counselors in guiding customer choice.

The ITA approaches are being tested side-by-side in six local areas using an experimental design. That is, new customers determined to be eligible for training are randomly assigned to one of the three ITA approaches and are directed to participate in the activities of the ITA approach to which they have been assigned. All eligible customers receive some type of ITA offer—there is no control group of customers who are denied ITAs. The experiment also works with the existing ETP list and CRS in each of the six sites. Intake in the study sites began between December 2001 and August 2002 and continued for approximately 18 months. By the end of intake, in February 2004, 8,331 local training customers had been enrolled in the ITA Experiment and randomly assigned to one of its three ITA approaches.

The findings from the ITA Experiment will reveal how different approaches generate different training choices, employment and earnings outcomes, returns on training investments, and customer satisfaction. Importantly, this study will not assess the merits of a voucher-based approach relative to other approaches (for example, prenegotiated contracts) to helping individuals access training. Rather, the ITA Experiment departs from the premise that vouchers are the required approach and asks the questions: "What is the best way to operate voucher-based training programs?" and "When or for whom might approaches offering more or less customer choice be most appropriate?" Hence, the objective of the ITA Experiment is to provide state and local administrators with the information they need to determine which ITA approach, or combination of approaches, is most appropriate for their customers.

Selection of the ITA Approaches Being Tested

The selection of approaches to be tested in the ITA experiment was based largely on research on voucher models that existed prior to WIA or that were emerging in the early days of WIA.[4] The information gathered through this research was used to identify ITA approaches that were consistent with WIA, had the potential for generating different training choices and outcomes, and seemed both feasible and likely to be of interest to sites implementing WIA.

In making the final selection of the three approaches being tested in the ITA experiment, we had two broad objectives in mind. First, we wanted the approaches to generally represent the spectrum of voucher models that were emerging prior to WIA and in the early days of WIA. Based on our examination of these emerging models, we developed a spectrum of ITA approaches that represent different balances between customer choice and counselor guidance in the formulation of training decisions. In the middle of the spectrum, we specified the model that sites were most likely to adopt in the absence of the experiment. Then, at one end of the spectrum, we specified an ITA approach that placed greater emphasis on customer choice and less emphasis on counselor guidance. At the other end of the spectrum, we specified an approach that reversed this emphasis to depend more on counselor guidance and somewhat less on customer choice. The limit on the amount of the voucher varied along this spectrum as well, so that the resources available to a customer were more limited in the approaches that entailed greater customer choice of training options.

The second objective in selecting the three approaches to test was to promote innovation in the use of vouchers. In the early days of WIA, most local agencies designed ITA models that looked similar to the "constrained choice" model identified by Trutko and Barnow, and there was little deviation from this model. That is, because of the limited evidence on the effects of alternative approaches and their own limited experience with vouchers, states and local areas appeared reluctant to develop voucher models that provided substantial customer choice or, alternatively, restricted customer choice in notable ways. Hence, to make the experiment as informative as possible, we selected approaches that, while feasible, pushed sites a bit beyond their comfort zone in the spectrum described above. Thus, we selected models that offered either greater customer choice or more intensive counseling than local workforce agencies were inclined to provide on their own.

Description of the Approaches Being Tested

The approaches being tested in the ITA Experiment vary along three dimensions related to the management of customer choice: 1) the method used to control each customer's ITA spending, 2) the type of counseling provided and whether it is mandatory or voluntary, and 3) the ability of local counselors to restrict the choices of customers. We use these dimensions of variation as the basis for the three ITA approaches, whose basic features are summarized in Table 6.1.

The approaches range from a highly structured approach, which we call Approach 1 or structured customer choice, to a true voucher approach, which we call Approach 3, or maximum customer choice. In the middle of the spectrum, Approach 2, or guided customer choice, is intended to broadly represent what most sites are doing on their own under WIA. In contrast, Approaches 1 and 3 are designed to be more or less structured than what most sites are doing on their own.

- **Approach 1** is the most directive of the three approaches. Customers assigned to Approach 1 participate in a series of mandatory assessment and counseling sessions designed to identify promising training opportunities. During these sessions, customers are guided by their counselor through the estimation of the benefits and costs of alternative training options and directed toward options expected to yield a high return—that is, programs that will generate earnings on a new job that are high relative to the resources invested in training. Counselors can reject training selections that are not consistent with this approach. Once appropriate training has been chosen, customers receive an ITA to fully cover the costs of training. Therefore, the amount of the ITA is considered to be customized to the individual based on the training program approved by the counselor.

- **Approach 2** broadly represents the approach that most local areas have adopted in the transition to WIA. In comparison with Approach 1, Approach 2 reduces the service requirements and allows greater customer choice, but at the same time it offers a limited, fixed ITA amount to all customers. As in Approach 1, Approach 2 customers are required to participate in structured counseling activities, but the activities are less intensive and are

Table 6.1 Summary of the Approaches Being Tested in the ITA Experiment

	Approach 1: Structured customer choice	Approach 2: Guided customer choice	Approach 3: Maximum customer choice
Award amount	Customized	Fixed	Fixed
Counseling	Mandatory, most intensive	Mandatory, moderate intensity	Voluntary
Can counselors reject choices?	Yes	No	No

not specifically focused on the return to the training investment. Once Approach 2 customers have completed their required counseling, they are free to choose any training program from the state ETP list—counselors cannot reject choice. Although Approach 2 customers can choose any training program, they receive a fixed ITA award, which limits the resources they can spend on training.

- **Approach 3** is the least structured of the approaches. It is intended to represent a true voucher program, where customers are free to spend a fixed amount of resources on any training program they choose. As in Approach 2, all Approach 3 customers receive the same fixed ITA amount and have final authority to choose their training providers from the ETP list. Unlike in Approach 2, however, Approach 3 customers are not required to participate in any counseling activities (although they may participate if they wish) prior to pursuing the training of their choice.

LOCAL EXPERIENCES IMPLEMENTING ITAs AND ETP LISTS

The six local areas participating in the ITA Experiment are located in or near Phoenix, Arizona; Chicago, Illinois; Atlanta, Georgia; Jacksonville, Florida; Bridgeport, Connecticut; and Charlotte, North Carolina, and include recognized leaders in the workforce development field. For instance, Phoenix and Atlanta participated in the CMA Demonstration. Most of the local areas also operated individual purchase or voucher-based models for training services for five or more years prior to implementation of the ITA Experiment. Jacksonville, for example, implemented a program of "scholarship accounts" for its training customers in 1995. As we described earlier, Atlanta used vouchers in 1991 to provide training assistance to workers displaced by the bankruptcy of Eastern Airlines. Chicago had abandoned the traditional JTPA approach of contracted training 10 years ahead of the passage of WIA, relying instead on voucher-based training purchases for all of its customers since 1988. In the next section, we describe the experiences of these innovative localities implementing ITAs and related WIA training provisions.

Local ITA Models Prior to Implementation of the Experiment

In the design phase of the ITA Experiment, we visited each of the six local areas to develop an understanding of their procedures under WIA.[5] Table 6.2 summarizes the components of their training programs in the early days of WIA. Overall, we found that these local areas had, by late 2001, made substantial progress implementing WIA's training provisions.

- **Local areas included in the experiment had well-established policies on the amount and duration of their ITAs prior to the experiment.** For instance, all sites placed caps on ITA awards, ranging from $3,000 to $8,900, and awards were valid for one or two years. Customers were not generally aware of the cap unless they requested training that cost more than the cap. Some local areas had tiered caps, offering additional support to customers choosing longer programs.

- **Local areas had Internet-based ETP lists available or under development.** Five of the six areas in the experiment had electronic databases that were accessible via the Internet, while the sixth area had a system under construction. The systems varied in the extent to which they could be sorted or searched. Hard-copy versions of the ETP lists were also available.

- **All local areas had voucher procedures in place.** Most local areas retained their pre-WIA provider payment systems. All but one local area used paper vouchers to demonstrate their "promise to pay" the training provider to serve an approved customer. None of the local areas used "smart cards" or other high-tech strategies to handle ITA administration.

Despite their extensive experience operating voucher-based training programs prior to WIA, the local areas participating in the experiment still faced several important challenges associated with building a system to administer ITAs.

- **Getting programs onto ETP lists.** Local training providers that were active under JTPA programs did not automatically qualify to serve WIA customers. All local areas indicated that they lost training offerings in the transition to WIA because some providers chose not to apply for WIA certification. Public education institutions, such as community colleges, objected to the performance-reporting requirements, as well as the requirement that they submit an application for each program at each location (as opposed to one application for a given program at all locations or even one application for the entire institution). In many cases, these institutions did not apply for WIA certification, since WIA customers represented a small proportion of their clientele. In contrast, proprietary providers more actively sought certification because WIA customers tended to represent a far larger share of their students.

- **Revising counseling.** Some local areas needed to revise their counseling activities. To implement WIA's tiered structure of services, local areas needed to boost the ability of their staff to assess customers and to provide more intensive career counseling. Local areas also needed to focus training-related counseling on options included in the ETP list (subject to local constraints as well).

- **Building the CRS.** Development of the CRS proved to be an ongoing effort. In each local area that we visited, the CRS can be accessed via the Internet, usually through the ETP list. The CRS typically contains information on program costs, duration, and so on. However, these systems still contain little information on program performance.

- **Making ETP lists and the CRS user-friendly.** Both information systems are continuously being refined to improve user sorting,

Table 6.2 Key Characteristics of Preexperiment Training Programs in the ITA Experiment Study Sites

	Phoenix and Maricopa County, AZ	Bridgeport, CT	Jacksonville, FL	Atlanta and Northeast GA	Northern Cook County, IL	Charlotte, NC
Maximum value and duration of ITA awards	**Phoenix:** $3,000 for programs less than 6 mo. in duration; $4,000 for longer programs; no maximum duration of award **Maricopa County:** $3,500 regardless of program duration; no maximum duration of award	$3,000 regardless of program duration; staff encouraged short-term training options	Tiered caps according to entry-level wages for occupation: • $4,600 if less than $8.78 per hour • $5,800 if $8.79 to $14.44 per hour • $8,900 if more than $14.44 per hour • Training support for up to 2 years	**Atlanta:** Tiered approach with $5,000 for first year and $3,000 for second year **Northeast GA:** Tiered approach with $3,000 for first year and $2,000 for second year	$3,000 per year, for up to 2 years	$4,000 in total support, usable over up to 2 years
Counseling services typically delivered prior to determination of training eligibility	• Resume workshop • Workshop on job readiness and transferable skills • Interests/aptitudes testing • Supervised job search or job club	• Assessments of basic skills and interests/aptitudes *if requested by customer or deemed necessary by counselor* • Individual counseling • Review of recent job search activities	• Assessments of basic skills and interests/aptitudes • Review of recent job search activities and/or supervised job search for 2 to 4 weeks	• Assessments of basic skills and interests/aptitudes • Career counseling • Review of recent job search activities	• Testing for reading/math skills (unless postsecondary degree) • Interests/aptitudes assessment • Occupational counseling • Review of recent job search activities	• Testing for reading and math skills (unless postsecondary degree) • Interests/aptitudes assessment • Individual counseling • Review of recent job search activities

Criteria used to determine eligibility for and need of training services[a]	• Unable to find employment offering self-sufficiency wages or 89% replacement of pre-dislocation wages • No basic skills deficiencies • No severe barriers to participation in training	• Counselor completes "Most In Need Assessment" based on customer's educational level and occupational skills • No severe barriers to participation in training	• Conducted "valid" job search for "suitable" employment of self-sufficiency wages or 80% replacement of pre-dislocation wages • No basic skills deficiencies • No severe barriers to participation in training	• Unable to find employment offering self-sufficiency wages or reasonable wage-replacement rate • No basic skills deficiencies • No severe barriers to participation in training	• Unable to find employment offering self-sufficiency wages or 89% replacement of pre-dislocation wages • No basic skills deficiencies • No severe barriers to participation in training	• Part of mass layoff; dislocated and long-term unemployed; or unable to find employment offering self-sufficiency wages • No basic skills deficiencies • No severe barriers to participation in training
Counseling services typically provided in support of decisions about training	• Occupational counseling • Labor market research • Research and comparison of training programs • Evaluation of training budget and overall feasibility	• Occupational counseling • Research and comparison of training programs	• Occupational counseling • Labor market research • Research and comparison of training programs • Evaluation of training budget and overall feasibility	• Occupational counseling • Labor market research • Research and comparison of training programs	• Research and comparison of training programs • Evaluation of training budget and overall feasibility	• Occupational counseling • Exploratory interviews with potential employers • Research and comparison of training programs
Criteria for approval of training selections	Directed/guided choice: • Completed counseling requirements • Demand occupation • Feasible selection	Guided/free choice: • Completed counseling requirements	Directed/guided choice: • Completed counseling requirements • Demand occupation • Feasible selection	Directed/guided choice: • Completed counseling requirements • Demand occupation • Feasible selection	Guided/free choice: • Completed counseling requirements	Directed/guided choice: • Completed counseling requirements • Demand occupation • Feasible selection

(continued)

Table 6.2 (continued)

	Phoenix and Maricopa County, AZ	Bridgeport, CT	Jacksonville, FL	Atlanta and Northeast GA	Northern Cook County, IL	Charlotte, NC
Implementation status and key characteristics of ETP list	• Fully developed, operational • Available to staff and customers online (www. ade.az.gov/ arizonaheat) • Links to CRS	• Fully developed, operational • Available to staff and customers online (www. ctdol.state.ct.us / cgi-bin/ wiapub.pl)	• Web-based system under construction; accessible online; links to CRS (www.ften. labormarketinfo.com) • Hardcopy lists of approved vendors for region, linked to Regional List of Targeted Occupations	• Fully developed, implemented • Available to customers online (www.gcic.ed/ gawia) • Links to CRS	• Fully developed, operational • Available to customers online (www.ilworkforce .org/slep.htm) • Links to CRS	• Fully developed, operational • Available to customers online (www.ncstars.org) • Links to CRS

Implementation status and key characteristics of CRS	• Operational • Available to staff and customers online (www.arizonaheat.com) • Includes information on certification date, entry requirements, program length and costs, Pell grant eligibility, location, accessibility by public transit, child care availability • Placeholders for performance info. (number enrolled, completion/placement rates, average hourly wages at placement); information not yet available for many programs	• Under construction • Not available to customers	• Operational, integrated with ETP system, but still being fine-tuned • Available to staff and customers online • Includes program description plus information on program location, duration, costs, and credentials attained • Placeholders for performance information (placement rate, training-related placement rate, number completing, annual earnings at placement); information not yet available for many programs	• Operational • Available to customers online • Placeholders for performance information (students obtaining employment, average weekly earnings after employment); information not yet available for many programs	• Operational, but still being fine-tuned • Can be accessed online by staff or customers • Placeholders for type of training, program cost, length, location, rates of completion and employment, average quarterly earnings 6 mos. after graduating; information not yet available for most programs	• Operational, integrated with ETP system • Available online • Includes program description plus location, application date, duration, costs, credentials attained, Pell eligibility, how long organization has been in business, and business accreditation • Complete information not available for all providers • Does not include performance information

(continued)

Table 6.2 (continued)

	Phoenix and Maricopa County, AZ	Bridgeport, CT	Jacksonville, FL	Atlanta and Northeast GA	Northern Cook County, IL	Charlotte, NC
ITA payment systems	• Customers receive paper voucher to provider/vendor when enrolling • Vendors invoice grantee directly for training costs; No funds released directly to customers	• Counselors submit paper voucher to provider/vendor • Vendors invoice grantee directly for training costs; no funds released directly to customers	• Grantees issue a list of approved trainees for individual vendors • Vendors invoice grantee directly for training costs; no funds released directly to customers	• Counselors submit paper voucher to provider/vendor • Vendors invoice grantee directly for training costs; no funds released directly to customers	• Customers receive paper voucher to take to provider/vendor when enrolling in classes • Vendors invoice grantee directly for training costs; no funds released directly to customers • Use *American Fundware* to track obligations and payments	• Counselors submit paper voucher to provider/vendor or customer receives paper voucher to take to vendor when enrolling • Vendors invoice grantee directly for training costs; no funds released directly to customers
Allowable uses of ITA funds	• Tuition and fees • Books and other required supplies	• Tuition and fees • Books and other required supplies	• Tuition and fees • Books and other required supplies uniforms • Certifications	• Tuition and fees • Books and other vendor-required supplies	• Tuition and fees • Books and other required supplies	• Tuition and fees • Books and other required supplies
WIA-funded assistance with support service needs while in training	Available on need basis: • Child care • Transportation • Support payments	Limited resources available on a need basis: • Child care • Transportation	Available on a need basis; means-tested support levels: • Child care • Transportation	Available on a need basis: • Child care • Transportation	None offered	Limited resources available on a need basis for transportation • Customers referred to local agency for assistance with child care

195

| Monitoring / follow-up requirements while in training | • Counselors follow up with customers about every two weeks once they begin training • Vendors submit periodic attendance/grade reports to the grantee | • Customers asked to meet periodically with assigned counselors • Vendors required to submit periodic attendance/grade reports to grantee to receive benchmark payments | • Customers were required to submit *monthly* attendance sheets, in person, to their counselors and to submit grade reports | **Atlanta:** Customers are required to maintain *monthly* contact with counselor (or *bimonthly* if receiving supportive services) and submit attendance/grade reports (signed by instructor) **Northeast GA:** Vendors required to submit periodic attendance/grade reports to grantee | Customers are required to maintain *monthly* contact with counselor and to submit attendance/grade reports to counselor Counselors follow up with customers periodically to discuss their progress in training |

(continued)

Table 6.2 (continued)

	Phoenix and Maricopa County, AZ	Bridgeport, CT	Jacksonville, FL	Atlanta and Northeast GA	Northern Cook County, IL	Charlotte, NC
Non-ITA training options for WIA customers	• Adult basic education and GED instruction offered as intensive services • On-the-job training placements used on need basis only • Customized training; employers cover 50 percent of training costs	• Adult basic education and GED instruction offered as intensive services • On-the-job training placements used rarely (on need basis only)	• Adult basic education and GED instruction offered as intensive services • Customized training ("Skills upgrade" program); employers to cover at least 50 percent of training costs • Other special grants ("Operation Paycheck")	**Atlanta:** • Adult basic education and GED instruction offered as intensive services • On-the-job training placements on need basis only • Customized training • Other special grants **Northeast GA:** • Adult basic education and GED instruction offered as intensive services • No other forms of non-ITA training	• Adult basic education and GED instruction offered as intensive services • No on-the-job training placements or customized training • Other special grants (National Emergency grant, Information Technology grant)	• Adult basic education and GED instruction offered as intensive services • On-the-job training placements used rarely (on need basis only) • No other forms of non-ITA training

[a] All grantees followed WIA requirements for sequential eligibility for core, intensive, and training services. Hence, in addition to the criteria listed in this table, customers must have been determined eligible for WIA services and received at least one staff-assisted core service and one intensive service.

searching, and comparison capabilities. Substantial progress has been made over time. For example, the Georgia systems can be used to search training programs and providers and generate comparisons more effectively now than a year ago.

Implementation of the ITA Experiment

Based on the findings from our exploratory visits to participating local areas, we selected a site to pilot-test the experiment's proposed operational procedures. Chicago was selected to serve as the pilot site and began operations in December 2001. The ITA Experiment operated as a pilot at this site for about six months, and we used the site's experiences to refine the experiment's procedures before starting operations in the five remaining local areas.[6] The other localities began operating the experiment in stages, from May through August 2002.

Commonalities across local ITA programs

The experiment's ITA approaches are operated fundamentally in the same way across the participating local areas. That is, each local area is testing all three approaches side by side and counselors work with customers assigned to all three approaches. ITA operations are also the same in other important ways.

- **Counseling services made available.** The same types of training-related counseling services are made available to *all* ITA customers, regardless of the approach to which they are assigned. What varies across the approaches is whether participating in particular services is mandatory or not. Moreover, the experiment's counseling services represent the minimal set made available to customers. Local areas can offer, though not require, additional counseling.

- **Allowable uses of ITA funds.** Study participants have access to ITA funds to cover the same types of training-related expenses. The ITAs of customers assigned to all three approaches include funds to cover only their direct training costs—that is, tuition, fees, and other expenses directly related to the program chosen (for example, books and supplies). Customers can still access support for other training-related needs not covered by their ITAs (for example, child care or transportation). If offered with WIA funds, such assistance must be provided through methods other than the ITA (supportive payments, for example).

- **Use of other sources of support for training.** Consistent with WIA regulations, when approving release of ITA funds, local staff always take into consideration other sources of support available to the customer (for example, state scholarships or Pell grants). As part of the experiment's counseling activities, local staff help their assigned ITA customers identify and apply to all relevant sources of training support before tapping WIA funds. There are no restrictions on customers' use of training funds from sources other than WIA.

- **Case manager approval of ITA expenditures.** Study participants do not have direct control of the funds in their ITA accounts. After a training program and vendor have been approved, disbursement of ITA funds still requires authorization by local staff. Thus, customers cannot receive approval for a program and then decide unilaterally to apply the approved ITA funds to a different selection.

Differences across local ITA programs

Implementation of the ITA Experiment did not completely homogenize WIA training operations across the participating local areas. Differences in their ITA programs reflect practices left unchanged by the experiment, local circumstances, or both:

- **Services delivered prior to random assignment.** For the most part, implementation of the ITA Experiment left unchanged the core and intensive services that local areas delivered prior to determining a customer's eligibility for WIA-funded training. Prior to the experiment, the local areas varied in how they formulated sequential eligibility procedures under WIA and their minimal service requirements prior to approving a customer for training. For instance, to ensure that a "valid" job search has been conducted, Jacksonville requires customers to document fully recent work search efforts, participate in supervised job search activities, or both. In contrast, in Chicago, counselors may approve WIA training services based solely on semistructured discussions with the customer. These philosophical differences persist under the ITA Experiment.

- **ITA values.** Across all local areas, the cap on Approach 2 and Approach 3 fixed ITA awards is more modest than the maximum potential value of Approach 1 customized awards. However, the actual caps for fixed and customized ITAs vary across the local areas, reflecting differences in their WIA training budgets, expected client flow, and the prices of local training options.

- **ETP lists and CRS.** The experiment relies on the ETP lists and CRSs available at each of the participating local areas. As required by WIA regulations, all study participants are instructed to make their selection from their states' ETP lists. Similarly, customers are encouraged to use the CRS when researching their training options. These systems vary nevertheless in the range of available training options, the costs and durations of these options, and the information that is available to customers to support their decisions about training.

Preliminary Implementation Findings from the ITA Experiment

Once the local areas began operations, we held regularly scheduled telephone conferences with key staff to discuss issues related to implementation of the ITA Experiment. These conversations served as an opportunity to answer staff questions, clarify procedures, and provide technical assistance when it was needed. About 1½–2 months after the start of operations, we also conducted intensive in-person monitoring and technical assistance visits. In preparation for these visits, we reviewed selected case files of participants assigned to each of the experiment's approaches.[7] In addition, evaluation staff have been periodically reviewing data entered into the experiment's Study Tracking System, which collects information on ITA counseling activities completed by participants, ITA award amounts, training selections (including program costs and other training resources tapped prior to ITA funds), and payments made out of the customers' accounts.[8]

Implementation of the experiment in six local areas has demonstrated that each of the ITA approaches is broadly feasible, in the sense that local staff report no major difficulties in the administration or operation of any approach. The key distinctions among the three approaches are clear to staff, and customers are generally reported to be completing their ITA requirements with few questions or objections. Local staff confirm that Approach 2 is similar to the local programs that were in place prior to the experiment, except that the forms and worksheets used in the experiment provide a bit more structure and consistency in the counseling process. In contrast, Approaches 1 and 3 clearly differ from the preexperiment ITA programs—Approach 1 in requiring more intensive counseling and in attempting to match individual customers to the training choice expected to generate high earnings relative to resources invested (high return), and Approach 3 in having no counseling requirements and allowing customers full control over their training decisions. Staff have generally expressed satisfaction with the forms and worksheets used under Approach 1, although some counselors feel that Approach 1 is too intensive to be applied to all customers seeking an ITA, particularly those that have already developed their own training plans.

Our observations of the early operations of the ITA Experiment suggest additional tentative conclusions, which we will eventually test more rigorously in our data analysis.

- **Counseling can influence customer choice.** Local staff report that the structured mandatory counseling for Approaches 1 and 2 has helped some customers explore their training options more broadly and more carefully. Staff cite cases in which customers who come into a one-stop center with a specific training plan have reconsidered their initial plans and have instead selected alternative training plans that promise higher earnings, better opportunities for advancement, or greater compatibility with their personal circumstances. For example, counselors in Florida report that they have persuaded some Approach 1 customers that were originally focused on information technology (IT) training to instead pursue careers in a medical field that would better match their skills and offer better local employment prospects.

- **Some staff struggle with being directive under Approach 1.** Although many counselors appear to be influencing customer training decisions in Approach 1, some counselors struggle with being as directive with these customers as is required under the

approach. These counselors are reluctant to disapprove customers' training choices, even when those choices are expected to
generate relatively low returns. They tend to weigh heavily non-
cost factors—such as a school's proximity to the customer's
home, the program's start date and duration, or the vendor's reputation—when evaluating training alternatives. One challenge is
that many counselors are relatively young and inexperienced,
which makes it hard for them to confidently guide their customers, especially when they are highly experienced workers. The
Chicago site responded to this challenge by having a senior staff
member sit in on Approach 1 counseling sessions to provide rein-
forcement in guiding customer choices.

- **ITA caps may constrain customer choice.** Local staff assert that
customers prefer shorter, intensive programs (typically offered by
proprietary schools), since these programs help customers return
to work sooner. However, these programs tend to be expensive—
often costing more than the Approach 2 and 3 fixed ITA
awards—and few customers qualify for alternative sources of
support for training. Hence, many Approach 2 and 3 customers
are not able to access these programs, while these selections are
often approved and fully covered for Approach 1 customers.
Examples of this difference in training access were observed in
Chicago, where one customer who was laid off from an IT
employer and assigned to Approach 1 used his customized ITA to
fully pay for a proprietary school IT certification course costing
$8,000. In contrast, a customer who was laid off from the same
employer and assigned to Approach 2 received a fixed ITA of
$3,000, which did not fully cover the costs of the same IT certifi-
cation program. Since this customer could not afford to pay the
remaining training costs, he decided not to enter that program.

- **Customers seldom use voluntary services.** Although counseling
services are offered on a voluntary basis to customers assigned to
Approach 3, most of these customers are not taking advantage of
the services. Among customers enrolled in the ITA Experiment
for one month or longer as of late January 2003, only 5 percent of
Approach 3 customers participated in any ITA counseling beyond
their mandatory orientation, compared with 56 percent of

Approach 2 customers and 60 percent of Approach 1 customers.[9] Local staff report that many Approach 3 customers submit their program selections immediately after orientation, based on information they have gathered on their own prior to orientation.

- **Training rates may vary by approach.** While data on actual enrollment in training and program completion are still scarce, rates of program approval already appear to vary across the three ITA approaches. Tracking system data show that 65 percent of Approach 3 customers secured ITA program approval, compared to 58 percent of Approach 2 customers and 59 percent of Approach 1 customers.[10] The higher program approval rate for Approach 3 customers is not surprising given the approach's "pure voucher" design. However, the lower approval rates for Approaches 1 and 2 could also reflect delays as these customers complete their counseling requirements. We are confident that the differences in training rates by approach are not due to differences in the timing of customers' program approval. Tracking system data show that, at the time of our data extract, study participants had been enrolled in the ITA Experiment for an average of 14 months. Tracking system data also show that study participants secured program approval, on average between six and eight weeks after random assignment, depending on their approach assignment. This suggests that tracking system data are likely to capture entry into training for the vast majority of ITA customers who reached this milestone.

ISSUES IN DESIGNING AND ADMINISTERING ITA PROGRAMS

In this chapter, we have sought to answer important questions related to the implementation of ITAs and other training-related provisions of the WIA. The information presented herein represents some of the most current evidence available to evaluate the program changes introduced by WIA and to help manage programs sponsored by the legislation. In this section, we attempt to shed light on important policy questions likely to be debated in preparation for WIA reauthorization, in particular:

- Should prominent WIA innovations—ITAs, ETP lists, and CRSs—be preserved as part of reauthorization?
- What legislative or regulatory modifications might help ease some of the challenges that states and localities have encountered implementing key WIA provisions?

Overall Soundness of the ITA Approach

Our observations suggest that local areas are able to implement ITA programs that are consistent with the objectives of WIA in the following sense:

- **Local areas are able to use ITAs as their principal method of paying for training.** The local areas participating in the ITA experiment have moved decisively away from prenegotiated contracts for training. At the same time, they continue to make some use of alternative training arrangements, such as on-the-job training or customized training. These alternatives extend customer choice beyond ITAs and help workforce agencies respond to special customer and employer needs (for example, when a customer needs to upgrade skills while working or when an employer has difficulties finding applicants for desirable job openings).
- **Local areas can specify ITAs so as to achieve different balances between customer choice and counselor guidance.** Local areas are apprehensive about the effect of customer choice on local WIA performance. Thus, in the absence of the ITA experiment, local areas have tended to develop similar programs that constrain the training choices and resources available to any customer. Yet, the ITA Experiment demonstrates that local areas can operate alternative programs that either minimize the constraints on customer choice (as under Approach 3) or maximize the role of counselors in directing customers to promising opportunities and matching the training resources to those opportunities (as under Approach 1).

- **The ETP lists provide sufficient training options to support the ITA approach.** Despite widespread and ongoing concerns about provider participation in the ITA system, the ETP lists in the local areas participating in the ITA Experiment have provided most urban customers with a real choice of providers. Hence, the current system seems to provide a foundation from which to build and enhance customer choice.

Importantly, the kind of institutional change envisioned by WIA may take longer to occur in other local areas. As we noted, the local areas participating in the ITA Experiment are recognized leaders for innovation and relatively experienced in the operation of voucher-based training programs. Hence, their experiences implementing ITAs, ETP lists, and CRSs likely represent a better-than-typical or best-case scenario. At the same time, they demonstrate the overall feasibility and soundness of the ITA approach.

Further Consideration Needed: ETP Lists and the CRS

As WIA reauthorization proceeds, there are several issues related to the ETP lists and the CRS that may require further attention and revision.

- **States could play a larger role in building the training provider network.** Future legislation and regulations could specify, or at least highlight the potential for, a larger role for states in promoting the ITA system. Local staff tend to recruit local providers and support them in the certification process. However, they lack sufficient leverage with larger providers to gain their support for and participation in the system. States could do more, such as requiring public educational institutions to comply with WIA requirements. For example, prior to WIA, Florida had already mandated that all state-funded postsecondary educational institutions (including community colleges) provide data on various performance measures. Once WIA was passed, these same data provision requirements were simply carried over to the WIA provider approval process.

- **The certification and performance reporting requirements should be reexamined.** To become an eligible provider of training services and maintain such eligibility, WIA requires educational institutions to submit information on program costs and (at least annually) verifiable, program-specific information on a variety of "all student" and "WIA student" performance measures. Providers that serve relatively few WIA customers find these performance-reporting requirements burdensome and, therefore, a disincentive to participation in the ITA system. As evidenced by the limited availability of performance information in CRSs, they have also proven challenging to meet for those providers that have elected to participate in the ITA system. Some states have attempted to make participation in the ITA system less burdensome for providers by working out data-sharing agreements to enable workforce agency staff to evaluate provider performance using UI wage records. For example, Georgia worked out agreements with the governing agencies of the two postsecondary systems by which the workforce agency would match and compile data on customers from the UI wage records and provide those data to the postsecondary agencies.

- **Building user-friendly systems will take time.** Local areas have made important progress in developing and implementing their ETP lists and CRSs. Progress has been slow, since the technical development of the systems and the assembly of program information has required substantial time, effort, and resources. Nearly every state now has a Web-accessible ETP list and CRS containing descriptive information on approved programs. However, many states still need to fill gaps in the program information provided on the CRS—especially on provider performance. Improvements to user sorting, searching, and comparison capabilities also continue to be made. Refinements to both systems are likely to continue for some time.

CONCLUSION

Empowering customers and increasing accountability are key goals of the workforce investment system established under WIA. The use of ITAs and the creation of ETP lists and CRSs are important elements in the overall strategy for achieving these goals. By enabling customers to choose training from among a menu of eligible providers, ITAs are intended to empower customers to obtain the training services that best fit their needs. Training providers, in turn, have to demonstrate successful performance to remain eligible to receive funds under WIA. The CRS makes available key information on the performance of training providers, empowering customers—with their ITAs and the guidance and support of one-stop staff—to make well-informed training decisions.

Looking ahead to WIA reauthorization, the emerging ITA systems appear to provide the customer choice and empowerment intended by the legislation. If adjustments are needed, they are less in the overall approach and more in the infrastructure that is used to control and monitor access to training providers. Securing broad participation of training providers in the ITA system and getting reliable performance data on the providers remain a challenge. The incentives for provider participation and the burden of performance reporting requirements could be better balanced.

The ITA Experiment will eventually provide information on how three distinct ITA approaches affect the training decisions and outcomes of training customers. We will use these data to evaluate the relative cost-effectiveness of the approaches. Intake into the experiment continued for a total of 18 months, with an additional 6 months for the pilot site. Over that period, we have conducted additional visits to each site to observe intake and operations, and continue to gather feedback on the experiment from customers, training providers, counselors, and other local staff. A 15-month follow-up survey of the customers in the experiment is already under way. This survey collects information on customer satisfaction, service and training use, employment and earnings, and a variety of other outcomes. Along with the 15-month follow-up survey, UI wage records will be the primary source of employment and earnings data for the evaluation. Employment and earnings will be measured for the full sample in the four calendar quarters after random assignment; additional quarters may be available for early enrollees. An interim report on the preliminary findings from the experiment will be produced in the summer of 2004, and a final report will be produced in 2005.[11]

As evidenced by President Bush's proposal of a new program of Personal Reemployment Accounts (PRAs), the appeal of "pure vouchers" continues to be strong. Embodied in H.R. 444, the Back to Work Incentive Act, which was introduced in Congress on January 29, 2003, the goal of PRAs is to provide unemployed workers who are likely to exhaust their unemployment insurance benefits with additional assistance and incentives to help them get back to work sooner. The proposed PRAs would have two components—a reemployment bonus and a broad service voucher component. Under the service voucher component, PRA recipients could use their accounts, containing up to $3,000 each, to pay for intensive services, training, supportive services, and even assistance to purchase or lease an automobile the worker needs to accept a promising job offer. Moreover, as in Approach 3 of the ITA Experiment, PRAs would have no counseling requirements. Recipients would be able to choose the combination of services that best meet their needs and use their PRAs to pay for those services. Thus, PRAs would extend the application of vouchers to the full range of assistance offered by one-stop centers, not just training, and give individuals even greater flexibility and control over the use of these resources. This suggests that the findings from the ITA Experiment should be of interest not only to local areas charged with implementing ITA programs, but to the wider workforce development community and potentially to proponents and critics of vouchers alike.

Notes

We thank Ralph Smith for helpful comments.

1. The one exception was the Thumb Area Employment and Training Consortium located in eastern Michigan. The program in this area was closer to a pure training voucher model. Customers in this site were eligible to open a Tool Chest, which was essentially a checking account against which customers could spend down resources to purchase education, training, and a wide range of support services. Customers could spend these resources at virtually any public or private school in the local area, as well as at a range of retail stores (for example, for work clothes). The size of the account was set for customers based on their eligibility for various programs run by the consortium.

2. Some local workforce agencies originally interpreted the tiered service structure specified in WIA as requiring that local agencies use a work-first approach in serving customers. That is, agencies felt they were to focus most of their effort

and resources on getting customers into jobs and provide training only as a last resort for customers who failed to find a job. However, USDOL subsequently clarified that WIA did not require a work-first philosophy and emphasized the importance that should be placed on customers' needs.

3. The ITA Experiment is being conducted by Mathematica Policy Research, Inc., and its subcontractor, Social Policy Research. A related project, the Individual Training Account/Eligible Training Provider (ITA/ETP) Demonstration, was conducted primarily by Social Policy Research under the same contract. The ITA/ ETP Demonstration examined a set of pilot sites that have designed and implemented their own models for providing ITAs to one-stop customers who seek training. D'Amico and Salzman (forthcoming) describe the ITA/ETP Demonstration in detail.

4. During the design phase of the experiment, MPR staff visited one-stop centers in Phoenix, Arizona; Baltimore, Maryland; Lowell, Massachusetts; Marlette, Michigan; and Killeen, Texas. These localities were selected principally because of their experience with training vouchers. All except Michigan had participated in the CMA Demonstration. Michigan had been operating a voucher program for all of its JTPA customers since 1996. The information from these visits was supplemented with information from 1) a review of findings from the evaluation of the CMA demonstration (Policy Research Associates 1999) and 2) site visits to two WIA early implementation states (Pennsylvania and Texas) conducted by staff from Social Policy Research.

5. These visits were conducted between July and December 2001.

6. No major changes to the experiment's operational procedures were implemented as a result of pilot operations. The only adjustments needed were providing additional guidance on Approach 1 implementation and developing some tools in Excel form to facilitate counselor use.

7. MPR staff selected these cases from lists of all individuals enrolled to date in the study. Generally, we selected two to three cases for each of the staff delivering ITA services to study participants. To allow sufficient time for participants to have received at least some ITA counseling services, we only selected cases that had been assigned to one of the experiment's approaches at least three weeks earlier.

8. Data from this system showed that, by the end of intake, a total of 8,331 customers had been enrolled in the ITA Experiment across our six study sites. As of mid-May 2004, 99 percent of these customers had been enrolled in the study for one month or longer; 92 percent had been enrolled for six months or longer.

9. The differences in participation rates for Approaches 1 and 2 relative to Approach 3 are statistically significant from zero at the 0.01 confidence level, two-tailed test.

10. The differences in program approval rates for Approaches 1 and 2 relative to Approach 3 are also statistically significant from zero at the 0.01 confidence level, two-tailed test.

11. An important limitation of the evaluation is its relatively short follow-up period (12 months for wage records and about 15 months for the survey). Because many

people in the sample will be in training for most of the follow-up period, they are likely to work less or possibly not at all in the short term. Some sample members may still be in training one year after random assignment. Thus, it may not be possible to assess posttraining impacts on employment and earnings. We will assess these impacts within the context of the proportion of the sample still in training.

References

D'Amico, Ronald, Deborah Kogan, Suzanne Kreutzer, Andrew Wiegand, Alberta Baker, Gardner Carrick, and Carole McCarthy. 2001. *Interim Report: A Report on Early State and Local Progress Towards WIA Implementation.* Washington, DC: U.S. Department of Labor, Employment and Training Administration, February.

D'Amico, Ronald, and Jeffrey Salzman. Forthcoming. *An Evaluation of the Individual Training Account/Eligible Training Provider Demonstration: Final Report.* Oakland, CA: Social Policy Research Associates.

Perez-Johnson, Irma L., Paul T. Decker, Sheena McConnell, Robert B. Olsen, Jacquelyn P. Anderson, Ronald D'Amico, and Jeffrey Salzman. 2000. *The Evaluation of the Individual Training Account Experiment: Design Report.* Washington, DC: Mathematica Policy Research, Inc., September 2000.

Public Policy Associates. 1999. *Dislocated Worker Program Report: Findings from the Career Management Account Demonstration.* Washington, DC: U.S. Department of Labor, Employment and Training Administration.

Trutko, John W., and Burt S. Barnow. 1999. *Experiences with Training Vouchers under the Job Training Partnership Act and Implications for Individual Training Accounts under the Workforce Investment Act.* Direct report to the U.S. Department of Labor. Washington, DC: U.S. Department of Labor, Employment and Training Administration.

7

The Scope of Employer-Provided Training in the United States

Who, What, Where, and How Much?

Robert I. Lerman
Signe-Mary McKernan
Stephanie Riegg

Only 12 years ago, former Secretary of Labor Ray Marshall and Marc Tucker (1992) suggested that frontline workers in the United States were the least skilled among all industrial nations. Sparked by this concern that U.S. workers lacked the skills to compete in an increasingly technological global economy, policymakers in the early 1990s called for increased investments in human capital. And although the rapid U.S. productivity growth of the late 1990s demonstrated that U.S. workers were, in fact, able to keep pace with their foreign competitors, improving education and training is still a key ingredient in achieving long-term economic growth (Hanushek 2002; Griliches 1997). Not only is a well-trained workforce better able to implement new technology (Bartel and Lichtenberg 1987), but the returns to education and training are high for workers themselves (Mincer 1994).

Encouraging or even requiring employers to sponsor more worker training is among the many proposals for dealing with skill shortfalls. Certainly, some firms are active trainers, but are they the exception or the rule? A *Wall Street Journal* article (Wessell 2001) featured the apparent exceptionally generous training subsidies provided by United Technologies Corporation. This large manufacturer not only covers the cost of college tuition and fees for any credit course its employees want to take, but it also offers up to three hours off each week—with pay—to study. The article suggested that United Technologies is the exception. But, are other firms so far behind? Are employers increasing the amount of training they sponsor in response to their rising demand for skilled workers? Despite high returns and the rising demand for skill, employer investment in training may be falling short of the socially optimal level. Some firms (especially small ones) and workers face capital constraints that limit their ability to invest in training. Workers face the risk that the training will be poorly tailored to their careers and do little to raise their wages. For firms, a key problem is that spending to train workers might yield little reward if the trained workers are bid away by other employers or if their wages are bid up to reflect their added productivity. Still, firms like United Technologies offer employees substantial amounts of training and even sponsor education in fields not related to the worker's current or next job.

Theory offers clues about why firms may or may not sponsor training, and we briefly review the relevant hypotheses. Our focus, however, is empirical; we describe the actual amounts of employer-provided training using data from four different surveys. Guiding the analysis are the following questions:

- *How much*: What is the incidence and intensity of employer-provided training overall and by size of employer? Have employers increased the amount of training they sponsor over the last two decades?
- *Who*: Which workers receive employer-provided training?
- *Where*: Which employers provide the most training?
- *What*: What types of training do employers provide?

EXPECTATIONS OF EMPLOYER-PROVIDED TRAINING

Becker's (1964) classical view of human capital emphasizes the distinction between training for general and specific skills. General skills increase a worker's productivity at any firm, while specific skills raise the worker's productivity only for his or her current employer. Once workers receive general training, they become more valuable to all employers and can consequently demand a higher wage or opt to take their skills elsewhere. Because workers, not employers, will reap the full benefits from general training, Becker suggests that employers have no incentive to pay for general training. In contrast, employers may well sponsor training in specific skills since they can reap at least some of the benefits of the training-induced productivity gains. Because the skills are specific to the individual firm, trained workers are no more valuable to outside firms than they would have been without the training.

Given the differences in returns to general and specific training, we would expect to see employers providing specific training, but not general training. If so, United Technologies is an obvious exception, since it pays for workers to get general training—they can take credit courses in any subject. But maybe United Technologies is not such an exception. Barron, Berger, and Black (1999) find that when firms were asked about the composition of the training they provide, nearly 70 percent claimed that most or almost all of the skills learned by new employees were general training. Veum (1999) also cites evidence that employers are paying for general training. Still, as Barron, Berger, and Black (1997) point out in an earlier study, firms may overstate the amount of training they provide, and some training that they claim is general may very well be specific.

If employers do provide general training, do their workers tend to leave the firm in search of higher wages, as Becker's theory suggests? When United Technology's go-back-to-college program began, managers were concerned that employees would be "educated on our nickel and then take off and go work for someone else" (Wessel 2001, p. 1). However, most workers who participated in the program stayed. In fact, attrition was much lower among those who received company-financed degrees—just 4 percent, compared to 9 percent among those who did not participate in the go-back-to college program (Wessell 2001).

So what is the role of general training? Might general training promote worker loyalty, as it seems to do in the case of United Technologies? Do workers regard access to general training a worthwhile fringe benefit? Or are there alternative explanations for the apparent employer funding of general training?

Acemoglu and Pischke (1999) challenge the applicability of Becker's theory to many employers and provide theoretical and empirical findings showing why employers often have incentives to offer general training. They argue that the presence of transaction costs in the labor market, including matching and search costs, makes it difficult for workers to quit their jobs and costly for firms to replace their employees. By avoiding turnover, employers and workers reduce these transaction costs, allowing both to benefit when the training-induced addition to productivity exceeds the increase in the worker's wage.

Asymmetric information is another reason why general training may raise productivity faster than wages and thereby create a gain for employers. Firms providing the training may know more about the content and value of training than outside firms. As a result, outside firms will not be willing to compensate the newly trained workers by an amount equal to their increased productivity (Chiang and Chiang 1990; Katz and Ziderman 1990). A second form of asymmetry arises when high-ability workers benefit more from training than other workers (Acemoglu and Pischke 1999). As Barron, Berger, and Black (1999) argue, since firms are most likely to lay off the low-ability workers who receive occupational training, outside firms will assume that the trained workers available in the market are the least capable of those trained. High-ability workers will not be able to quit and demonstrate their high ability to outside firms. Thus, the firm providing the training can keep the highly productive worker without paying the full value of the enhanced productivity.

The complementarity between specific and general skills is another reason firms may sponsor training. The ability to benefit from general training (for example, knowing how to use a specific piece of software) may increase when the worker knows the strategy of the company (specific training). Thus, the higher the worker's general skills, the more valuable the employer-provided specific training is to the company.

The theory also sheds light on which workers we expect to receive the most training. Because specific and general skills are often complementary, employers are more likely to invest in those who already have a high level of general skills. Several studies have corroborated the latter point, finding that those with higher education levels receive more training (Lillard and Tan 1986; Brown 1990; Lynch 1992; Barnow, Giannarelli, and Long 1996; Barron, Berger, and Black 1997; Lynch and Black 1998; Holzer and Reaser 1999). In addition, these studies often have found differences by race and gender, with white males typically receiving more training than other groups.

Which firms do we expect to provide the most training? According to Becker's theory, training levels should be sensitive to the turnover in the organization because the higher the turnover, the greater the chance that workers will leave before the firm can reap the benefits of the training—especially when it comes to general training. In addition, past studies typically find that large firms offer more training (Barron, Berger, and Black 1997; Lynch and Black 1998; Holzer and Reaser 1999), but there is no dominant theory as to why this is the case. Because larger firms pay higher wages, they typically have lower turnover and a more qualified workforce (Holzer and Reaser 1999; Leuven and Oosterbeek 1999). They may also face fewer capital constraints and can gain from economies of scale in the operation of formal training programs.

Other expectations relate to the connection between technical change and training. Firms trying to achieve high levels of technical change are most likely to invest in training. Indeed, Bartel and Sicherman (1998) find that rapid technical change causes companies to invest more in production workers, thereby narrowing the training gap between the more- and less-educated workers. As more companies pursued strategies to increase their rates of technical change, especially in the early to mid 1990s, we should observe an increase in the level of training and a narrowing of the training gaps between types of workers.

Expanding the amount of employer-provided training may or may not affect wage levels and wage differentials. If the benefits from training accrue largely to firms making the investments rather than the employees, differences in the receipt of training by groups of workers may not influence wage differentials.

This chapter adds to the empirical literature by compiling and analyzing estimates of the overall extent and composition of employer-sponsored training in the United States. Keeping in mind theoretical considerations, we describe the patterns and trends in employer-provided training, the distribution of training by type of worker, and differences in the types of employer-provided training across workers and firms.

RECENT SURVEYS WITH DATA ON
EMPLOYER-PROVIDED TRAINING

The four recent surveys that yield empirical evidence on the total amount of employer-provided training in the United States are the 1997 National Employer Survey (NES), the 1995 Survey of Employer-Provided Training (SEPT), the 1995 Adult Education Component of the National Household Education Survey (NHES), and the 1996 Survey of Income and Program Participation (SIPP) topical modules. Before presenting results, we describe the four surveys and their training questions.

1997 National Employer Survey

The 1997 NES, administered by the U.S. Bureau of the Census, is a telephone survey of over 3,000 establishments. These establishments represent more than 5,400 private U.S. establishments with 20 or more employees (Shapiro and Goertz 1998). The survey provides information on the incidence and intensity of formal employer-provided training by worker occupation. It also provides detailed information on establishment characteristics. The 1997 NES asks each employer if they pay for or provide any formal training either on-the-job or at a school or technical institute. It defines formal training as any type of training activity with a pre-defined objective that may occur during or outside working hours.

1995 Survey of Employer-Provided Training

The 1995 SEPT is a personal interview survey of approximately 1,000 establishments and approximately 1,000 employees at those establishments. It provides information on both formal and informal training from private establishments with 50 or more employees.

The Establishment Survey portion of 1995 SEPT collected information on formal training using two survey instruments—an employer questionnaire and an employer training log. Like the 1997 NES, the 1995 SEPT Employer Survey defines formal training as training that is planned in advance and has a structured format and defined curriculum. Employer-provided training is formal training provided or financed by the establishment. With its emphasis on financing, this measure should include tuition reimbursement programs and other training that takes place off-site and outside working hours.

The Employee Survey portion of the 1995 SEPT collects information from up to two employees from each establishment using survey instruments similar to those in the Employer Survey, but the training questions in the Employee Survey are quite different. The Employee Survey focuses on training that the employees received from the employer and does not mention training that the employer paid for. Also, the Employee Survey log provides information on hours of training that took place from May to October 1995, a time when many educational institutions are closed, rather than a full year period. For these reasons, the Employee Survey may not capture training that was paid for by the employer, but provided off-site and outside working hours. The SEPT Employee Survey also includes a broad measure of informal training. Informal training in the SEPT includes any unstructured and unplanned activities that taught a skill or provided information to help workers do their jobs better. Both informal and formal training activities need only have lasted five minutes to be recorded in employee logs.

1995 National Household Education Survey

The Adult Education component of the 1995 NHES is a cross-sectional telephone survey of approximately 20,000 adults age 16 and older who were not enrolled in elementary or secondary school. The survey emphasizes formal courses and programs since it first asks its respondents to focus on education and training programs, courses, workshops, and seminars that they took during the past 12 months. The survey then asks about English as a second language, basic skills and GED preparation, credential classes, apprenticeships, and career or job-related courses. For non-self-employed workers, the survey also asks whether the employer provided instruction for these courses and whether the employer supported the courses in various ways. We define employer-provided training to include all apprenticeships, and any type of training for which an employer provided instruction, gave time off from work with or without pay, provided classroom space, or paid all or part of the cost.

1996 Survey of Income and Program Participation Topical Modules

The 1996 SIPP is a national survey of approximately 36,000 households (including roughly 90,000 individuals) conducted by the U.S. Census Bureau. In addition to its core survey data, the SIPP includes a number of topical modules that ask about specific subjects of interest. The Education and Training History topical module administered in Wave 2 (August to November 1996) provides information on work-related training apart from high school or college, specifically training that 1) helps persons search for or be trained for a new job, and 2) training that helps improve skills in a person's current job. Both training types are included in our formal training definition. Next, the survey asks how many training activities of each type, lasting one hour or more, were received by the worker in the past 12 months. Only then is the respondent asked who sponsored or paid for their *most recent* training. If the current or previous employer sponsored or paid for this training, we include it in our measure of employer-provided training.

The 1996 SIPP School Enrollment and Financing topical module administered in Wave 5 (August through November of 1997), provides information specifically on employer-financed educational assistance. It asked persons enrolled in school in the past year if they received financial assistance from their employers. It also asked if students could take classes during work hours and if the student is paid for time spent in class. We use these questions to assess the level of and reasons for employer-financed educational assistance.

Differences in the samples and training questions in the four surveys are likely to affect estimates of employer-provided training. Survey results from the 1997 NES and the 1995 SEPT exclude training in establishments with fewer than 20 employees (NES) and fewer than 50 employees (SEPT). Moreover, definitions of employer-provided training vary and play a crucial role in estimates of the scope of employer-provided training. The 1995 NHES focuses more on courses, the 1995 SEPT captures more informal and very quick training activities, and the 1996 SIPP emphasizes only the most recent training activities lasting over an hour. But considered together, the 1997 NES, the 1995 SEPT, the 1995 NHES, and the 1996 SIPP offer a comprehensive picture of the status of employer-provided training in the United States.

HOW MUCH: THE INCIDENCE AND INTENSITY OF EMPLOYER-PROVIDED TRAINING

Incidence

Most establishments offer some type of formal training. The 1997 NES and the 1995 SEPT employer surveys find that 78 percent (NES) to 93 percent (SEPT) of establishments with 50 or more employees provided formal training over the past year. Considered with the additional NES finding that 72 percent of establishments with 20 or more employees provided formal training, the results suggest that approximately 85 percent of establishments with 50 or more employees provided formal training and approximately 70 percent of all establishments provided formal training.[1]

Turning to the incidence of employer-provided training among workers, rather than establishments, we find clear results for informal training but mixed results for formal training. Informal training is ubiquitous. The 1995 SEPT (the only one of our four focal surveys with this information) finds that over 95 percent of workers in establishments with 50 or more employees receive employer-provided informal training. Though this number sounds quite high, it makes sense when we consider the broad definition that the SEPT uses—a definition that includes training activities lasting just five minutes. Nonetheless, other studies have found similar incidences of informal training. Using the 1994 NES, Lynch and Black (1998) find that 97 percent of establishments with 20 or more employees provide informal training. Evidently, the networks of informal training are reaching most employees.

The incidence of formal training is less clear, with findings from the surveys varying substantially. The 1995 SEPT finds that 70 percent of workers in establishments with 50 or more employees receive formal employer-provided training, while the 1995 NHES finds that just 37 percent of all workers receive formal employer-provided training. But lower still is the 1996 SIPP. Though this survey asked respondents only if their most recent training was employer-provided (only 24 percent of workers received), adding in employer-provided educational assistance (another 2 percent) and the probabilistic incidence of employer-provided training for those whose most recent training was not employer-provided over the past year would still only raise this figure to just over 26 percent.

Part of the difference between these results can be accounted for by samples—the SEPT includes only workers at larger firms, while the NHES and SIPP include all workers age 16 and over. And, as mentioned above, the NHES's focus on classes may result in a narrower measure of training than that used in the SEPT. Moreover, the SEPT's requirement that training activities last just five minutes, rather than the 1 hour required by the SIPP and the "programs, courses, workshops, and seminars" emphasized in the NHES, may account for the large difference in magnitude between these figures. The SIPP figure provides a lower bound (26 percent of workers reporting most recent training paid for by their employer), and the SEPT yields an upper bound (up to 70 percent of workers in large establishments received at least some short formal training).

Intensity

How many hours of training do workers receive? Averaged over all workers, whether they received training or not, the hours per worker of employer-sponsored training vary widely by survey. As with incidence, the amount of training is highest for informal training. The SEPT Employee Survey reports an average 31 hours of informal training per worker over six months. But average amounts of formal training are much less. The 1995 SEPT Employer and Employee Surveys yield estimates of 11–13 hours of training per worker over the six-month period from May to October 1995. The SIPP, which measures only the most recent training activity, yields an average of 14 hours per worker. The proximity of these figures is no surprise. Both the SEPT and the SIPP typically omit coursework from the employer-provided training definition and the SEPT's six-month focus is likely to capture a measure of intensity similar to that of the most recent training in the SIPP, since the most recent training likely occurred in the past six months. The slightly higher SIPP number makes sense because the SIPP survey takes place a year after the SEPT and we expect that training is growing over time. The 1995 NHES finds a much higher number—an average of 33 hours per worker per six-month period. This is likely due to its emphasis on coursework, activities that tend to have much higher intensity.

These modest levels of mean intensity across all workers do not reflect the extent of training among workers actually trained.[2] On average, trained workers engaged in 15–19 hours of training in the 1995 SEPT over a six-month period, 60 hours in the SIPP during the most recent training, and 89 hours of training in the 1995 NHES over a six-month period.

The effectiveness of training would be questionable if almost all workers received very few hours of training. But, as shown in Figure 7.1, about 21 percent of all workers (57 percent of trained workers) participated in more than one full week of training over the past year.[3] A small percentage, about 10 percent of workers, report more than one month of training. These are likely to be workers enrolled in courses and degree programs. The Figure 7.1 results come from NHES data, but we find a very similar distribution using the SIPP data. Holzer and Reaser (1999) also find that a small but significant percentage of firms (about 5 percent) report providing more than one month of training to their most recent hire.

Training over Time

How has the incidence of employer-provided training changed over time? Have employers responded to the increased importance of skill by sponsoring more training? Figure 7.2 presents the incidence of employer-provided training over time by data source. The evidence within surveys shows large increases in employer-provided training in the past two decades.

According to the NHES, the percentage of workers receiving training appears to have doubled, from 19 percent in 1990 to 37 percent in 1994. However, the gains may be overstated because of differences in the training questions in the two years. The 1991 initial training question asked: "Not counting full-time school or courses taken toward a degree . . . have you been involved in . . . educational or training activities given by an employer or labor organization . . . in the past 12 months?" (Barnow, Giannarelli, and Long 1996). On the other hand, the 1995 questions, as discussed above, enable us to measure any type of training (including English as a second language, basic skills and

Figure 7.1 Distribution of Training by Hours of Training Received in One Year (1995 NHES)

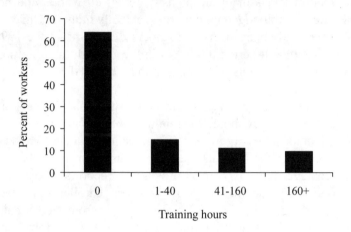

Figure 7.2 Percentage of Workers Receiving Training across Surveys and over Time

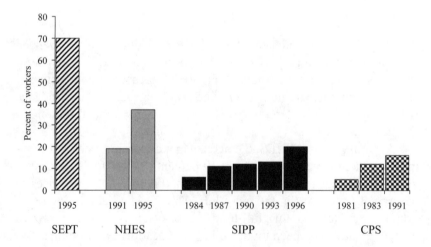

GED preparation, credential courses, career or job-related activities, and apprenticeships) provided or *supported* by the employer. But if we focus only on employer-provided or -supported career or job-related courses in the 1995 NHES, we find that the percentage of workers receiving training in 1995 falls from 37 percent to 27 percent. The additional questions in the 1995 NHES instrument that enable us to include employer support may account for a few more percentage points, further lowering the comparable 1995 NHES estimate to 25 percent of workers. This would leave a lower, though still respectable, six-percentage-point change between 1991 and 1995.

The SIPP provides more accurate data over time by using the same universe and questions in each survey. It shows the percentage of all persons age 18–64 that receive training rising from 6 percent in the 1984 SIPP, to 20 percent in the 1996 SIPP—with the largest jump between 1993 and 1996.[4] The CPS also shows increases in employer-provided training over time, from 5 percent in the 1981 CPS to 16 percent in the 1991 CPS.[5] These steady increases add up to a 14 percentage point increase over a 12-year period in the SIPP and a comparable 11-point increase over a 10-year period in the CPS.

Previous research also has found evidence that training increased over this period. Lynch and Black (1998) find that 57 percent of firms reported that they increased the amount of training they offered between 1991 and 1994, and only 2 percent of firms reported decreases over that period (all others presumably experienced no changes in the amount of training offered). Rapid technological change is responsible, as Bartel and Sicherman (1998) find. This is especially plausible given the boom in personal computing and Internet technology in the early 1990s. Or, perhaps the increase is due to higher corporate profits with a good economy, or simply a shift in corporate culture that now emphasizes lifelong learning.

WHO: THE WORKERS RECEIVING EMPLOYER-PROVIDED TRAINING

Who is receiving employer-provided training? Table 7.1 presents tabulations on the incidence and intensity of employer-provided training by various worker characteristics for each of the three surveys. Despite absolute differences in the numbers due to survey design and universe, as discussed in previous sections, we find patterns of training common to all three surveys, together with some important exceptions. Although the data show that employer-provided training does not reach all types of workers equally, many disadvantaged groups are apparently receiving higher amounts of training than previously thought.

In all surveys, the incidence of employer-provided training increases with education—a finding consistent with other empirical studies (Lillard and Tan 1986; Lynch 1992; Brown 1990; Barnow, Giannarelli, and Long 1996; Barron, Berger, and Black 1997; Holzer and Reaser 1999). Figure 7.3a confirms this common view that training levels rise with formal education. In all three employee surveys, workers with a high school diploma or less are the least likely to receive training of any educational group while those with a bachelor's degree or higher are the most likely to receive training. This tendency suggests the worker's existing stock of training may raise the benefits to employers of additional training.

More surprising are the data on the intensity of training in Figure 7.3b. The NHES, which captures substantially more educational activities than the other surveys, shows that the "some college" group has by far the highest intensity of training, suggesting that employers are helping these workers go back to school.

To further investigate this hypothesis, we examine data from the SIPP School Enrollment and Financing topical module, data not included in our SIPP measures of employer-provided training. These data provide further evidence that more-educated workers do not necessarily receive more employer-provided training, when the training comes in the form of educational assistance. In the SIPP, workers with some college experience almost exactly the same incidence of employer-provided educational assistance as workers with at least a bachelor's degree.

Similar variations by data set arise with regard to training by earnings level, age, and job characteristics. Both the SEPT and the SIPP report that workers with the lowest earnings receive the least amount of employer-provided training—both in incidence and intensity. This finding again supports the findings of past research. All three surveys reveal that the incidence of employer-provided training is positively

Figure 7.3a Incidence of Employer-Provided Training, by Education

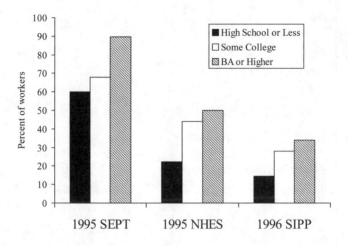

Figure 7.3b Intensity of Employer-Provided Training, by Education

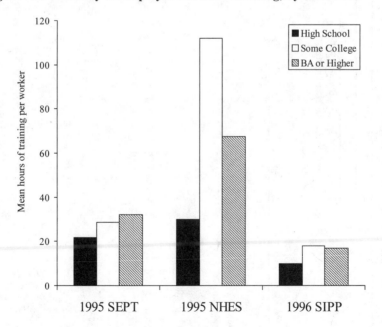

Table 7.1 Incidence and Intensity of Employer-Provided Formal Training, by Worker Characteristics

	Survey					
	1995 SEPT		1995 NHES		1996 SIPP	
Worker characteristics	% workers in estabs. w/50+ employees (past year)	Mean hours per worker in estabs. w/50+ employees (6 months)	% workers in all estabs. (past year)	Mean hours per worker in all estabs. (6 months)	% workers in all estabs. (most recent)	Mean hours per worker in all estabs. (most recent)
Total (formal training)	69.8	13.4	36.7	32.7	23.6	14.2
Educational attainment						
High school graduate or less	60.1	10.9	22.2	15.0	14.5	9.9
Some college	67.8	14.3	44.1	55.6	28.1	18.0
Bachelor's degree or higher	89.7	16.1	50.0	33.8	33.9	16.9
Earnings quartile						
First	61.8	4.1	27.1	41.6	10.9	6.2
Second	74.5	11.6	31.3	25.9	17.8	12.9
Third	62.0	15.9	42.1	27.6	29.6	18.3
Fourth	84.0	22.8	49.3	27.7	35.4	18.6
Age						
25 and younger	63.4	2.7	43.1	83.9	16.4	12.6
25–34	78.5	14.0	37.3	32.5	26.5	17.0
35–44	74.7	15.4	39.5	23.8	27.3	15.7
45–54	64.7	17.2	36.9	17.7	26.2	14.4
55+	50.7	5.7	20.3	7.9	14.3	6.5

Usual hours worked per week					
Under 35	56.1	4.8	34.8	52.7	14.7	7.5
35 or more	71.6	14.6	38.6	25.4	28.6	17.5
Tenure with current employer					
Up to 2 years	67.5	8.9	32.8	35.1	—	—
More than 2 years and up to 5 years	56.8	4.5	36.5	36.7	—	—
More than 5 years and up to 10 years	79.7	19.5	36.7	32.3	—	—
More than 10 years	75.3	21.1	39.4	20.9	—	—
Gender					
Men	66.5	12.2	36.0	34.1	22.1	14.3
Women	73.1	14.6	37.5	31.2	25.3	14.0
Race and origin					
White	70.4	13.6	37.8	31.7	24.2	14.1
Black	70.6	13.8	32.5	35.3	20.9	16.2
American Indian/Alaskan Native	—	—	36.5	29.9	22.3	13.3
Asian/Pacific Islander	—	—	36.3	44.9	17.2	10.0
Hispanic	73.7	11.0	24.6	52.5	14.5	9.2

NOTE: — = data unavailable.
SOURCE: 1995 Survey of Employer-Provided Training (SEPT) figures are from Frazis et al. (1998). 1995 National Household Education Survey (NHES) figures are from authors' weighted tabulations of the 1995 NHES public-use data. 1996 Survey of Income and Program Participation (SIPP) figures are from authors' weighted tabulation of the 1996 SIPP public-use data.

related to earnings, but the results on intensity differ for the NHES. The SEPT and SIPP both show a lower training intensity among workers in the lowest earnings quartiles while the NHES shows a higher training intensity—the lowest earnings quartile report obtaining far more training than higher earning workers in the NHES. Workers earning below $15,000 per year were receiving 42 hours of training on average over six months, well above the 28 hours of training reported by workers earning over $39,000. This reversal of expected patterns is apparently explained by the NHES's emphasis on credit courses. Workers taking advantage of employer-sponsored tuition often have lower than average earnings, are younger and less-experienced, and spend less time at work.

The estimates by age follow similar patterns. In the SEPT and SIPP data sets, workers 25 years old and younger are less likely to participate in employer-provided training than all other age groups except the 55 and older group. The youngest cohort also engages in far fewer hours of training than most older cohorts in these two surveys. The NHES, on the other hand, shows that workers age 25 and younger are experiencing a higher incidence and intensity of training than any other age group. The survey reports that 43 percent of workers age 25 and younger receive employer-sponsored training compared to 37 percent of workers age 25–34. Moreover, according to the NHES, this youngest cohort is averaging 84 hours of training per six months, compared to 33 hours for workers age 25–34.

The pattern is even the same by job characteristics. Full-time workers and workers with longer tenure have a higher incidence of training in all surveys, but the NHES reports that part-time workers and those with less tenure have a much higher intensity of training. According to the NHES, workers who put in less than 35 hours per week receive more than double the number of hours of training than their full-time counterparts—53 hours per week compared to 25.

All of these results for education level, earnings, age, and job characteristics are likely attributable to the NHES's measure of training. As the survey includes for-credit vocational and college programs in its definition of training, it includes workers who are receiving employer support to attend school full or part time. These students are likely to be 25 years old or younger and recent high school graduates with "some college." The hours of training they receive are likely to be much higher than those of other workers as they are enrolled in formal college or vocational classes, often for several weeks at a time.

Unlike past research, we find no significant differences in the receipt of training by sex or race and ethnicity in any of the surveys.

In general, we find a more mixed picture of differences in training by worker characteristics than reported in most other studies. On one hand, we find evidence for the commonly cited result that employer-provided training is disproportionately reaching more-educated workers and higher-income workers. Data from SEPT and NHES confirm this pattern with regard to the incidence of training. However, in an important departure from other studies, we find average hours of training per worker are generally higher (rather than lower) for young, part-time, and less-experienced workers in the NHES—presumably because these characteristics are common to workers enrolled in credit courses. Still, overall, less advantaged workers average fewer hours of training across all workers than more advantaged workers because their higher NHES intensity figures do not fully compensate for their lower incidence of training.

WHERE: THE EMPLOYERS OFFERING THE MOST TRAINING

The 1997 NES and both the 1995 SEPT Employer and Employee Surveys provide information on which employers offer the most training. As shown in Table 7.2, the estimates for all three of these surveys indicate that the amount of training steadily increases with establishment size and number of workplace benefits. According to the 1997 NES, 69 percent of small establishments (20–50 employees) provided formal training, while 93 percent of large establishments (1,000 or more employees) provided formal training. And though the magnitudes of the SEPT surveys are different, the pattern is the same as in the NES—larger establishments provide more training. Measures of the intensity of training indicate the same result—workers in large establishments receive considerably more hours of training than workers in small establishments. These findings are consistent with the literature

Table 7.2 Incidence and Intensity of Employer-Provided Formal Training, by Establishment Characteristics

| | Survey | | | | | |
| | 1997 NES | | 1995 SEPT employer | | 1995 SEPT employee | |
Establishment characteristics	% estabs. w/20+ employees (past year)	% estabs. w/50+ employees (past year)	% estabs. w/50+ employees (past year)	Mean hours per worker in estabs. w/50+ employees (6 months)	% workers in estabs. w/50+ employees (past year)	Mean hours per worker in estabs. w/50+ employees (6 months)
Total (formal training)	72.4	77.6	92.5	10.7	69.8	13.4
Number of employees						
20–50	69.2	—	—	—	—	—
50–99	72.4	—	90.8	5.7	61.6	8.2
100–249	82.3	—	—	—	—	—
250–999	86.5	—	—	—	—	—
100–499	—	—	94.4	12.1	73.0	13.5
500 or more	—	—	98.1	12.0	71.0	16.6
1,000 or more	93.0	—	—	—	—	—
Turnover						
Low	71.5	73.4	92.7	10.8	78.3	27.3
Medium	73.0	81.9	96.0	12.5	74.7	15.6
High	72.6	72.9	88.6	7.2	60.7	7.6
Union presence						
No employees represented	72.3	78.3	92.9	11.0	71.6	14.0

Some employees represented	74.2	73.7	90.6	9.7	65.7	12.1
Number of selected benefits						
Six or fewer	63.6	63.6	89.5	7.1	62.9	10.2
Seven or more	84.3	87.0	99.6	14.8	76.9	16.7

NOTE: — = data unavailable.
SOURCE: 1997 National Employer Survey (NES) figures are from authors' weighted tabulations of the 1997 NES public-use data. 1995 Survey of Employer Provided Training (SEPT) figures are from Frazis et al. (1998).

(Lynch and Black 1998; Barron, Berger, and Black 1997; Holzer and Reaser 1999) and with expectations from theory.

Employer-provided training rises with the number of benefits a firm offers. Benefits may include perks such as paid vacation, paid sick leave, health insurance, pension plans, family leave, and child care. Establishments that provide more of these types of benefits also provide more formal training, both in incidence and intensity. According to the SEPT, the percentage of establishments providing training and the percentage of workers receiving training is at least 10 percentage points higher in establishments that provide seven or more selected benefits, than in establishments that provide six or fewer of these benefits.

A powerful expectation is that employers provide less training in establishments with high turnover, because of the greater chance that workers will leave before the firm can recoup their investment in training. But surprisingly, the evidence on training by turnover is mixed. The 1995 SEPT incidence and intensity measures presented in Table 7.2 generally support the expected negative relationship between turnover and training. Fewer high-turnover establishments report providing formal training and fewer workers in high-turnover establishments receive formal training than workers in low-turnover establishments. On the other hand, the 1997 NES reports that the percentage of establishments providing training does not vary significantly with turnover.[6]

Previous studies find mixed results on differences in training by union presence. Using the 1992 Small Business Administration–funded survey, Barron, Berger, and Black (1997) find that newly hired workers receive more training if they belong to a union. But the authors find no significant difference for firms with and without unions when using the 1982 Employment Opportunity Pilot Project survey. We also find that employer-provided training varies little by union status in both the 1997 NES and the 1995 SEPT. There is a small difference of two percentage points by union status in both the NES and the SEPT Employer Survey, but this difference is not statistically significant. The same is true of intensity measures.

WHAT: THE TYPES OF TRAINING
EMPLOYERS PROVIDE

So far, the surveys suggest the importance of looking not only at employer-provided general versus specific training, but at a particular form of general training—employer-sponsored educational assistance. Is this form of general training widespread? When fully accounting for educational assistance, is the mix of training still in accord with Becker's theory and with the common view that that lower-earning, younger, and less-educated workers have limited access to employer-sponsored training?

In Table 7.3, where we report the scale of various types of employer-provided training, there is evidence for Becker's theory that firms choose to provide more specific than general training. The 1997 NES, 1995 SEPT, and the 1995 NHES all find that employers emphasize occupational safety training (66 percent, 72 percent, and 43 percent, respectively), which is generally firm-specific, and provide little basic or remedial skill training (17 percent, 9 percent, and 2 percent, respectively), which is general. Lynch and Black (1998) find similar results in the 1994 NES. They find that roughly three-fourths of employers provide specific training, but only one-quarter of establishments provide remedial skills.

In our focal surveys, the high percentage of establishments offering computer training might be an exception to this pattern and to Becker's theory, but some computer training could involve a combination of specific and general training. In any event, note that the NES finds that 73 percent of firms with more than 50 employees offered computer skills training in the past year—the highest incidence of any type of training. Similarly, training intensity measures are highest for computer skills in both the SEPT Employer and Employee Surveys. More information on the specific versus general content of computer training would be necessary before judging whether the high levels of this form of training constitute employer-provided general training. Nonetheless, these findings on computer training suggest that rapid technological growth may have played a large role in encouraging increased employer investments in training over the 1990s.

Table 7.3 Incidence and Intensity of Formal Employer-Provided Training, by Type of Training

	Survey							
	1997 NES		1995 SEPT Employer		1995 SEPT employee		1995 NHES	
Type of training	% estabs. w/20+ employees (past year)	% estabs. w/50+ employees (past year)	% estabs. w/50+ employees (past year)	Mean hours for workers in estabs. w/50+ employees (6 months)	% worker in estabs. w/50+ employees (past year)	Mean hours for workers in estabs. w/50+ employees (6 months)	% of all workers (past year)	Mean hours for all workers (6 months)
Total (formal training)	72.4	77.6	92.5	10.7	69.8	13.4	36.7	32.7
Type of training								
Management	—	—	66.8	0.8	16.3	0.6	—	—
Professional and technical skills	—	—	49.4	1.3	21.4	1.9	—	—
Computer skills	63.5	72.8	65.5	2.1	23.5	5.1	—	—
Clerical and administrative support	—	—	38.1	0.5	8.4	0.6	—	—
Sales and customer relations	58.9	58.5	50.5	0.8	15.1	0.6	—	—
Service-related	—	—	27.0	0.6	5.9	0.3	—	—
Production and construction-related	—	—	29.6	1.1	11.3	2.0	—	—
Basic or remedial skills	16.4	17.3	9.4	0.1	2.3	0.0	—	—

Occupational safety	58.5	65.8	71.7	1.2	42.8	0.6	—	—
Communication, employee	—	—	45.7	1.4	22.8	1.5	—	—
Development and quality								
Employee wellness	—	—	37.3	0.1	—	—	—	—
Orientation	—	—	72.5	0.2	—	—	—	—
Awareness	—	—	51.7	0.6	—	—	—	—
Other	—	—	0.3	0.1	1.4	0.2	—	—
Teamwork and problem solving	62.8	69.4	—	—	—	—	—	—
English as a second language	—	—	—	—	—	—	0.2	0.1
Basic skills or GED prep	—	—	—	—	—	—	0.4	0.3
Credit courses/ programs	—	—	—	—	—	—	10.3	20.7
Apprenticeship	9.1	9.9	24.4	—	—	—	1.6	1.9
Career or job-related courses	—	—	—	—	—	—	27.1	9.7
Mentoring programs	9.5	10.1	44.1	—	—	—	—	—

NOTE: — = data unavailable.

SOURCE: 1997 National Employer Survey (NES) figures are from authors' weighted tabulations of the 1997 NES public-use data. 1995 Survey of Employer Provided Training (SEPT) figures are from Frazis et al. (1998) and (1997). 1995 National Household Education Survey (NHES) figures are from authors' weighted tabulations of the 1995 NHES public-use data.

The NHES provides a different breakdown of training—one that helps explain the wide variation in incidence and intensity figures between the SEPT and the NHES and gives us an insight into the incidence and intensity of employer-supported education. The NHES's nearly exclusive focus on courses and the SEPT's lack of focus on courses mean that the NHES misses many of the higher incidence, but lower intensity types of training captured in the SEPT (e.g., occupational safety), and the SEPT misses many of the lower incidence, but higher intensity types of training captured in the NHES. For example, the NHES reports that 10 percent of workers were enrolled in employer-supported credit courses or programs in the last year. Though the incidence of this type of training is low, the intensity is high. Workers engaging in this employer-sponsored training attend an average of 21 hours of class time in six months. Adding this type of training to the equation nearly triples the number of hours of training for all workers in the NHES figures.

Taking workers receiving employer-supported credit courses out of the NHES calculations would lower the number of hours of training for all workers to 12 hours—almost equal to the SEPT figure of 13 hours, which is based on a sample of only large firms. We are not advocating omitting employer-supported credit courses from the definition of employer-provided training, but think it worthwhile to distinguish employer-supported education from other forms of employer-provided training.

As suggested above, keeping employer-supported credit courses in the calculations appears to modify the conventional conclusions about training patterns that appear in the literature and are present in the SEPT data. Because many of the workers who take advantage of credit courses are likely more traditional college students or only slightly older, they tend to be younger, less-educated, in a lower earnings quartile. They also may work fewer hours per week, as they are likely to be spending more time in the classroom. As discussed above, the NHES reports both higher levels of employer-sponsored education and much higher amounts of training for younger, less educated, and low earning workers than does the SEPT.

The 1996 SIPP offers additional insights about the levels and reasons for employer-financed educational assistance in its School Enrollment and Financing topical module. First, the topical module shows employer-provided educational assistance as affecting only 2 percent of workers, far less than the 10 percent found in the NHES. Part of the reason is that the NHES uses a broader definition, one that includes any type of employer support (such as time off to go to school), while the SIPP includes only those whose employer actually paid directly for some part of the education.

The low share of workers reporting employer-provided educational assistance in the SIPP does not mean that employers are not offering tuition support. In a separate question in the NES (not included in our prior tabulations of employer-provided training), firms were asked if they reimburse the cost of tuition for an approved course. Surprisingly, more than 82 percent of firms reported offering this type of tuition reimbursement to managers, supervisors, and administrators and 69 percent offered the same support to frontline workers. Data from other employer surveys reported by Cappelli (2002) confirm the high shares of employers offering tuition subsidies.

Although only a minority of workers use the tuition and paid leave subsidies in a given year, the impact on adult education is substantial. Of all adults enrolled in postsecondary degree–granting programs, 24 percent received an employer-provided tuition subsidy and 53 percent obtained employer support either from tuition or paid leave.[7]

The SIPP School Enrollment and Financing topical module yields information on why employers might sponsor educational assistance. Of workers taking courses with employer support, almost 50 percent are required to enroll in courses to maintain skills (25 percent), retrain (3 percent), or receive a promotion or salary increase (21 percent). And only 27 percent of those employees are paid for their time spent in class. According to Cappelli (2002), a major reason employers offer the apparently general training is the reduction in turnover and the ability to attract above average workers. Employers believe workers stay longer with the firm because of the chance to use the educational subsidies.

The picture based on the observed types of training is only partly consistent with Becker's theory. Employers are indeed providing a significant amount of specific training, such as orientation and occupational safety, but the widely prevalent computer skills training is likely to have a significant general component. Finally, a large percentage of establishments offer employer-provided educational assistance and a small but significant proportion of workers use this support for courses related to jobs or careers.

SUMMARY AND IMPLICATIONS OF EMPLOYER-PROVIDED TRAINING PATTERNS

What generalizations can be made about recent patterns and trends in employer-provided training? First, employer-provided training increased substantially over the 1980s and early 1990s. The percentage of workers receiving training grew about one percent per year with even more rapid growth in the mid 1990s. The question remains, however, as to what drove this increase. Rapid technological growth, a booming economy, or a shift in corporate culture that now emphasizes lifelong learning, may all be possible explanations. Whether we can sustain this growth in employer-provided training through an economic downturn remains to be seen.

Second, alternative data sets yield similar estimates concerning the large percentages of establishments (about 85 percent of establishments with 50 or more employees and 70 percent of all establishments) providing formal training. But, the data sets differ on the share of workers participating in employer-sponsored formal training; the range runs from 26 to 65 percent of workers.

Third, the surveys providing measures of intensity of training report widely different amounts. Among workers participating in employer-sponsored training, the average number of hours in training over a six-month period ranged from 15–19 hours in the 1995 SEPT to 89 hours in the 1995 NHES. The primary reason for these disparate estimates is apparently the inclusion of employer-supported formal schooling in the NHES, but not in the SEPT.

Fourth, the distribution of hours of formal training in the NHES and SIPP suggests that some workers are receiving intensive employer-provided training. Fifteen percent of all workers in the NHES received more than two full weeks of employer-provided formal training in 1994. Although 15 percent may sound like a low share obtaining training of at least moderate intensity, over a three- to four-year period, the share of the workforce participating in some intensive training could reach 40–60 percent, depending on whether workers intensively trained in one year do so in the adjacent years.

Fifth, unlike formal training, informal training is ubiquitous. The 1995 SEPT finds that nearly all workers—over 95 percent—at establishments with 50 or more employees receive informal training. This finding is not surprising, given the SEPT's broad definition of informal training. The SEPT also finds that workers receive an average of 31 hours of employer-provided informal training per worker for the six-month period from May through October, 1995.

Sixth, how employer training varies by worker characteristics is sensitive to the inclusion of employer-sponsored educational assistance. Ignoring such educational assistance, the data support the commonly cited result that employer-provided training is disproportionately reaching more advantaged (e.g., well-educated, higher earnings) workers. However, the NHES survey, which best captures data on employer assistance in education, finds surprising evidence that the intensity of training is generally higher for young, part-time, and less-experienced workers.

Seventh, the amount of training received varies by employer characteristics. The 1997 NES, 1995 SEPT, and the 1995 NHES estimates indicate that the amount of training provided rises substantially with establishment size and number of work place benefits, but is only modestly affected by turnover and barely affected at all by union status.

Finally, the data support Becker's theory that employers emphasize specific training, but we also find evidence of a considerable amount of employer-supported general training, both in the form of computer training and employer-provided educational assistance.

What are the implications of these findings for policy? Certainly, employers are already receptive to training and, on average, are spending more on training than the one percent of payroll requirement proposed as a mandate by the Commission on the Skills of the American Workforce (Marshall and Tucker 1992). The spending covers a broad spectrum of workers, though it is least concentrated on the less-educated workers but more concentrated on workers in the middle than at the top. Not surprisingly, much employer-supported training is for tasks specific to the employer. However, almost all employers offer tuition subsidies or paid leave to workers taking an approved course in a postsecondary degree–granting institution—although only a minority of workers take up these offers. The widespread availability of employer-subsidized tuition suggests that substantial increases in employer-sponsored training could take place if more workers chose to take advantage of existing offers.

With evidence pointing to substantial growth in employer-sponsored training and to widespread offers of employer-subsidized tuition, the case for a government training mandate receded somewhat in the 1990s. Although progress has been made, it is far from clear that employer-provided training on its own can achieve and sustain a socially optimal level of training or that current training practices are effective.

As the United States continues its transition from an industrial economy to an information economy, academic and technical literacy will become increasingly important for workers and for continued U.S. productivity growth. This growing need for training may well outpace increases in training opportunities provided by employers, especially in a recession, making the gap between the need and level of training ever wider. Rather than simply requiring firms to spend a percentage of their payroll on employee training, government policies should instead focus their efforts on increasing access to training for underrepresented groups, encouraging take-up of existing opportunities, and ensuring that training is of high quality to help U.S. workers keep their competitive edge. At the same time, the government should recognize that many if not most companies are, like United Technologies, willing to play an active role in raising the skills of American workers.

Notes

The authors would like to thank Kevin Hollenbeck, Harry Holzer, and other participants at the Conference on Job Training and Labor Exchange in the United States for their comments and suggestions. The authors are grateful to the U.S. Department of Labor for research support.

1. The 1993 SEPT also found that approximately 70 percent of all establishments provided formal training (Frazis, Herz, and Horrigan 1995).
2. To compare our results from the 1995 NHES with Frazis et al.'s (1998) results from the 1995 SEPT, we report results for all workers not just workers trained (i.e., we average in the zeros for workers who did not receive training). Results for

workers trained can be derived by dividing the average hours of training for all workers by the incidence rate.

3. These figures indicate higher hours of training than found by Holzer and Reaser (1999) for training provided to newly hired workers in Atlanta, Boston, Detroit, and Los Angeles.

4. The 20 percent incidence among all persons reported here for the 1996 SIPP differs from the 24–26 percent incidence among all workers because of the difference universes (all persons age 18–62 versus all workers age 16+) used in the calculations.

5. Note that the training questions in the CPS are much narrower than those in the other surveys and hence result in much lower and (not very comparable) figures of employer-provided training. The CPS includes only training to improve skills taken in a formal company training program. Moreover, the CPS asks about training with the current employer not training over the past year (NHES and SEPT) or the most recent training (SIPP).

6. Turnover in the 1995 SEPT is measured as the ratio of hires and separations to employment during a 3-month period. The low-, medium-, and high-turnover categories contain 7, 49, and 44 percent of establishments, respectively (Frazis et al. 1998). We measure turnover in the 1997 NES as the ratio of separations to employment during a one-year period. The low-, medium-, and high-turnover categories contain 19, 49, and 33 percent of the weighted establishments, respectively.

7. These data come from Hudson's report on the Adult Education Survey, as cited in Cappelli (2002).

References

Acemoglu, Daron, and Jorn-Steffen Pischke. 1999. "Beyond Becker: Training in Imperfect Labor Markets." *Economic Journal Features* 109: F112–142.

Barnow, Burt, Linda Giannarelli, and Sharon Long. 1996. "Training Provided by Private Sector Employers." Washington, DC: The Urban Institute.

Barron, John M., Mark C. Berger, and Dan A. Black. 1997. *On-the-Job Training.* Kalamazoo, MI: W.E. Upjohn Institute for Employment Research.

———. 1999. "Replacing General with Specific Training: Why Restricting Alternatives Makes Sense." *Research in Labor Economics* 18: 281–302.

Bartel, Ann P., and Frank R. Lichtenberg. 1987. "The Comparative Advantage of Educated Workers in Implementing New Technology: Some Empirical Evidence." *Review of Economics and Statistics* 69(1): 1–11.

Bartel, Ann P., and Nachum Sicherman. 1998. "Technological Change and the Skill Acquisition of Young Workers." *Journal of Labor Economics* 16(4): 718–755.

Becker, Gary. 1964. *Human Capital.* Chicago: University of Chicago Press.

Brown, Charles. 1990. "Empirical Evidence on Private Training." *Research in Labor Economics* 2: 97–113.

Cappelli, Peter. 2002. "Why Do Employers Pay for College?" NBER working paper no. 9225. Cambridge, MA: National Bureau of Economic Research.

Chiang, Shin-Hwan, and Shih-Chen Chiang. 1990. "General Human Capital as a Shared Investment under Asymmetric Information." *Canadian Journal of Economics* 23(1): 175–188.

Frazis, Harley J., Diane E. Herz, and Michael W. Horrigan. 1995. "Employer-Provided Training: Results from a New Survey." *Monthly Labor Review* (May): 3–17.

Frazis, Harley, Maury Gittleman, Michael Horrigan, and Mary Joyce. 1997. "Formal and Informal Training: Evidence from a Matched Employee-Employer Survey." *Advances in the Study of Entrepreneurship, Innovation, and Economic Growth* (9): 47–82.

———. 1998. "Results from the 1995 Survey of Employer-Provided Training." *Monthly Labor Review* (June): 3–13.

Griliches, Zvi. 1997. "Education, Human Capital, and Growth: A Personal Perspective." *Journal of Labor Economics* 15(1, Part 2): 330–344.

Hanushek, Eric A. 2002. "The Long Run Importance of School Quality." NBER working paper no. W9071. Cambridge, MA: National Bureau of Economic Research.

Holzer, Harry, and Jess Reaser. 1999. "Firm-Level Training for Newly Hired Workers: Its Determinants and Effects." *Research in Labor Economics* (18): 377–402.

Katz, E., and A. Ziderman. 1990. "Investment in General Training: The Role of Information and Labor Mobility." *Economic Journal* 100(December): 1149–1158.

Leuven, Edwin, and Hessel Oosterbeek. 1999. "The Demand and Supply of Work-Related Training." *Research in Labor Economics* (18): 303–330.

Lillard, Lee A., and Hong W. Tan. 1986. *Private Sector Training: Who Gets It and What Are Its Effects?* Report prepared for the U.S. Department of Labor. Santa Monica, CA: The Rand Corporation.

Lynch, Lisa. 1992. "Private Sector Training and the Earnings of Young Workers." *American Economic Review* 28(1): 299–312.

Lynch, Lisa M., and Sandra E. Black. 1998. "Beyond the Incidence of Training." *Industrial and Labor Relations Review* 52(1): 64–81.

Marshall, Ray, and Marc Tucker. 1992. *Thinking for a Living: Education and the Wealth of Nations*. New York: Basic Books.

Mincer, Jacob. 1994. "Investment in U.S. Education and Training." Working paper no. W4844. Cambridge, MA: National Bureau of Economic Research.

Shapiro, Daniel, and Margaret E. Goertz. 1998. "Connecting Work and School: Findings from the 1997 National Employers Survey." Unpublished manuscript, University of Pennsylvania, Philadelphia, PA.

Veum, Jonathan R. 1999. "Training, Wages, and the Human Capital Model." *Southern Economic Journal* 65(3): 526–538.

Wessel, David. 2001. "Loyalty Comes by Degrees." *The Wall Street Journal*, May 17.

8

International Experience with Job Training

Lessons for the United States

Lori G. Kletzer
William L. Koch

During the last three decades, concern about the skills of the U.S. workforce has emerged as a persistent public policy issue. In the late 1970s and early 1980s, sluggish U.S. labor productivity growth generated alarm over a perceived gap between the skills of U.S. workers and workers in other industrialized countries. In the 1990s, concerns arose about Americans being left behind as substantial changes in the labor market reduced the real earnings and labor force participation of less-skilled workers. The current focus on skills and their importance in the working lives of Americans is not new, rather a renewal. Federal training policy has its roots in New Deal public works programs. Today's programs are the descendants of programs initiated during the Johnson Administration's War on Poverty.

Several factors can be tied to the renewed public interest in skill development. Globalization, technological change, and the reorganization of work have combined to produce dramatic changes in the demand for workers' skill. Into the late 1970s, workers without any college experience could anticipate a (manufacturing) job at good pay with attainable skill requirements. Most necessary skills could be acquired on the job. Today, "good" jobs increasingly require a strong base of analytical, quantitative and verbal skills.[1] In the United States, these skills are produced, for the most part, by the educational system, followed in sequence by private employers. For most Americans, training occurs within firms as part of the normal course of business. Publicly provided job training is different; these programs (and other active

245

labor market policies) offer a second chance to many workers. In nearly all countries, these programs have a stated goal of integrating the unemployed and economically disadvantaged into the workforce.

In this chapter, we review recent evidence on training programs for a small group of mostly industrialized countries, and try to distill some lessons for the United States in its employment and training policy. We concentrate primarily on publicly funded programs targeted at unemployed and economically disadvantaged workers. Where appropriate, we make note of a country's overall training environment. We are not the first authors seeking an international perspective on employment and training policy. Interested readers are directed to two highly useful and readable earlier papers, Haveman and Saks (1985) and Casey and Bruche (1985).

Training is just one tool in the kit of active labor market policies (ALMP). Active labor market policies are geared toward enhancing the employment and long-run earnings prospects of unemployed workers and those with low skill levels and/or little work experience. These measures include public employment services and administration (job placement, information, counseling, job matching, referrals, administrating unemployment benefits); training for adults (vocational and remedial training for the unemployed and training for labor market reasons for the employed); youth programs (training and employment for unemployed youth and apprenticeship training for school leavers); programs for the disabled; and subsidized employment for the unemployed and other groups, excluding the disabled and youth (hiring subsidies, assistance in self-employment, direct job creation). Active labor market policies are grounded in a widely shared value that people need opportunities to work and advance themselves.[2]

For the most part, we will not discuss passive labor market policies, such as unemployment compensation and subsidies for health insurance.[3] These policies are part of the social safety net, and are geared toward reducing economic hardship resulting from joblessness.

We acknowledge at the outset that private training expenditures vastly exceed spending by governments. As we show in Table 8.1, the United States spent 0.04 percent of GDP on public training in 2000. Public spending is estimated at just under 10 percent of total training expenditures (see Chapter 1). Even in Sweden, where spending on

Table 8.1 Public Expenditure on Labor Market Policies as a Percentage of GDP for 2000

	Total labor market policy expenditures (active + passive)	Passive measures	Active measures	Active measures categories[a]				
				Public employment services and admin.	Labor market training	Youth measures	Subsidized employment	Measures for the disabled
Canada	1.49	0.98	0.50	0.40	0.34	0.06	0.16	0.06
Germany	3.13	1.89	1.23	0.19	0.28	0.07	0.25	0.22
Hungary	0.87	0.48	0.39	0.28	0.18	—	0.56	—
Japan	0.82	0.54	0.28	0.39	0.11	—	0.46	0.04
Korea	0.55	0.09	0.46	0.09	0.20	0.02	0.67	0.02
Sweden	2.72	1.34	1.38	0.19	0.22	0.01	0.20	0.38
United Kingdom	0.94	0.58	0.37	0.35	0.14	0.41	0.03	0.05
United States	0.38	0.23	0.15	0.27	0.27	0.20	0.07	0.20
Cross-country average[b]	1.36	0.77	0.60	0.24	0.23	0.07	0.28	0.19

NOTE: — = data unavailable.
[a] Categories for each country may not sum to 1 due to rounding error.
[b] Unweighted average.
SOURCE: OECD (2000, Table H).

active labor market policy is much higher, public expenditures on training in 2000 amounted to 0.31 percent of GDP.

The countries in our sample are Canada, Germany, Hungary, Japan, Korea, Sweden, United Kingdom, and the United States. All are members of the Organisation for Economic Co-operation and Development (OECD), with Hungary joining the organization in 1995 and Korea joining in 1996. We chose these countries as examples of different approaches to labor market policy in general and training in particular. Most clearly for the advanced industrialized countries, we were looking for countries with potential to yield useful lessons for the United States. Hungary was added as an interesting case of labor market policy in a transition economy, and Korea as an example of a rapidly developing economy.

The chapter is organized as follows. First, we examine recent patterns of public spending on labor market programs in general and job training specifically. Then we review recent cross-country trends in access to training, both in the private and public sectors. The third section briefly discusses what is known about training programs and the evaluation literature that provides these findings. The fourth section is devoted to country profiles, followed by profiles of displaced worker programs. In the final section, we offer concluding remarks, including lessons for the United States.

PUBLIC SPENDING ON LABOR MARKET POLICIES

As background to our discussion of spending, Table 8.2 presents standardized national unemployment rates and measures of the incidence of long-term unemployment. Unemployment rates generally fell over the late 1990s, with the exception of Japan. Unemployment fell dramatically in Canada, Hungary, and Sweden, and it reached a contemporary historic low in the United States. Long-term unemployment is a serious concern in Germany and Hungary and is a much greater problem now in Sweden than it was in the late 1980s. Long-term unemployment remains a problem in the United Kingdom, although it has diminished somewhat from the late 1980s. Canada has more long-

Table 8.2 Unemployment Rates and Incidence of Long-Term Unemployment, by Country

| Country | Standardized unemployment rate as a percentage of total labor force | | | | Long-term unemployment as a percentage of total unemployment | | | | | |
| | | | | | 6 months and over | | | 12 months and over | | |
	1985–88	1998	1999	2000	1998	1999	2000	1998	1999	2000
Canada	9.1	8.3	7.6	6.8	24.1	21.4	19.5	13.7	11.6	11.2
Germany	6.5	9.3	8.6	8.1	69.6	67.2	67.6	52.6	51.7	51.5
Hungary	—	8.0	7.1	6.5	71.0	70.4	69.7	49.8	49.5	48.9
Japan	2.7	4.1	4.7	4.7	39.3	44.5	46.9	20.9	22.4	25.5
Korea	—	—	—	4.3	14.7	18.6	14.3	1.6	3.8	2.3
Sweden	2.3	8.3	7.2	5.9	49.2	45.2	41.5	33.5	30.1	26.4
United Kingdom	10.2	6.3	6.1	5.5	47.3	45.4	43.2	32.7	29.6	28.0
United States	6.4	4.5	4.2	4.0	14.1	12.3	11.4	8.0	6.8	6.0

NOTE: — = data unavailable.
SOURCE: OECD Employment Outlook (2001, Tables A and G).

term unemployment than the United States, and both countries have seen little change since the late 1980s.

The OECD has been collecting comparable data on public spending on labor market measures since 1985. As reported in Martin and Grubb (2001), the typical OECD country spent just over two percent of GDP on active and passive labor market measures in 2000. Spending by the countries in our sample for the year 2000 is reported in Table 8.1. Our sample contains both some of the highest spending countries (Sweden and Germany), as well as the lowest spending countries (the United States). The (unweighted) average for these countries is 1.36 percent of GDP. Passive spending accounts for around one-half to two-thirds of total spending on labor market policy. Korea is an exception, where passive policies account for just 16 percent of total spending. For the most part, spending on passive programs in 2000 was a lesser share of GDP than it was for 1985–1988 (see Table 8.3). Germany, Japan, and Sweden are exceptions, where passive spending was higher in the late 1990s than in the mid-to-late 1980s. Since both passive and active spending are positively correlated with the unemployment rate, and passive more so than active, higher unemployment in these countries may explain the increase in spending (see Martin and Grubb 2001).

The relative importance accorded to active labor market policy varies considerably across the countries in our study. The average for the sample in 2000 was 0.6 percent of GDP on active measures, compared to an average of 0.8 percent of GDP for OECD countries. It is the variation in spending in our sample of countries that is remarkable. Sweden devotes the greatest share of GDP to these measures, but its spending as a share of GDP has fallen. Spending was almost two percent of GDP over the late 1980s, and as recently as 1997, it was 2.03 percent of GDP (see Table 8.3). But spending dropped to 1.38 percent of GDP in 2000. Germany is the only other country in our sample with significant resources devoted to ALMP, just over 1 percent of GDP in 2000. Other countries in the sample spend far less; the United States is the lowest, at 0.15 percent of GDP in 2000, down from a 1985–1988 average of 0.26 percent of GDP. Despite widespread recognition that governments should shift the balance of spending toward active labor market policies, the active share of spending has increased in a few countries (Canada, the United Kingdom, the United States, Japan), but

Table 8.3 Labor Market Expenditures as a Percentage of GDP, by Active and Passive Categories

	Active measures					Passive measures				
	1985–88 Average	1997	1998	1999	2000	1985–88 average	1997	1998	1999	2000
Canada[a,b]	0.58	0.56	0.47	0.46	0.50	1.74	1.29	1.16	1.01	0.98
Germany	0.95	1.23	1.26	1.30	1.23	1.36	2.52	2.28	2.12	1.89
Hungary	—	0.44	0.39	0.40	0.39	—	0.63	0.62	0.56	0.48
Japan[a,c]	0.19	0.34	0.33	0.25	0.28	0.40	0.40	0.41	0.50	0.54
Korea	—	0.09	0.46	0.69	0.46	—	0.02	0.01	0.19	0.09
Sweden	1.96	2.03	1.96	1.82	1.38	0.80	2.10	1.93	1.68	1.34
United Kingdom[a,d]	0.80	—	0.39	0.34	0.37	1.89	—	0.80	0.64	0.58
United States[e]	0.26	0.17	0.17	0.17	0.15	0.51	0.26	0.25	0.25	0.23

NOTE: — = data unavailable.

[a] Fiscal years starting April 1.

[b] Data are from 1995–96 to 1996–99.

[c] Data are from 1996–97 to 1999–2000. Japanese LMP data have been revised.

[d] Excluding Northern Ireland.

[e] Fiscal years starting on October 1.

SOURCE: OECD (2001) and Leigh (1995, Table 2.1).

fallen in others (Germany, Sweden). As noted, the share of ALMP in total labor market policy spending varies across the business cycle, with some similarities across countries. In general, the active share falls as unemployment rises.[4]

Turning to the separate active measures, training and retraining programs are the traditional core of government labor market policy, perhaps most strongly so in Western Europe. Training accounts for the largest share of total public spending on active measures for the OECD as a whole. In 2000 on average, OECD countries devoted 23 percent of total active spending to training programs, and that fraction has remained fairly constant since 1985 (see Martin and Grubb 2001, Figure 2). Our sample of countries acts somewhat similarly, spending on average 21 percent of total active spending on training, but the average masks a wide variation. Canada spends 34 percent of their total active expenditures on training, with Germany at 28 percent, the United States at 26 percent, and Sweden at 22 percent, while Hungary and Korea spend just under 20 percent and the United Kingdom 13 percent. Qualitatively, Sweden and Germany have stable, nationwide employment and training programs (as does Japan, in a fundamentally different way). The Public Employment Service (PES) is the largest share of total active spending for a number of countries in our sample (Canada, Japan, United Kingdom). For most countries, the PES serves two central functions: 1) as a clearinghouse between potential employers and workers (as the central labor exchange), and 2) as the interface for sources of assistance for the unemployed (payment of unemployment benefits, providing job search assistance).

CROSS-COUNTRY TRENDS IN PRIVATE AND PUBLIC TRAINING ACCESS

The International Adult Literacy Survey (IALS) is our primary source of information on private and public training access and participation.[5] There are some clear patterns in the data (see Table 8.4). In the overall population, about one-third to one-half of adults ages 25–64 were engaged in some form of education or training outside of formal schooling. Employed adults were considerably more likely to receive

Table 8.4 Cross-Country Comparisons for Adults Aged 25–64 of All Education and Training, by Labor Force Status, Gender, Age, and Educational Attainment (%)

		Labor force status			Gender		Age group			Educational attainment		
	All	Em-ployed	Unem-ployed	Inactive	Men	Women	25–34 years	35–44 years	45–64 years	Below upper secondary	Upper secondary	Tertiary
Canada	36.5	41.9	30.1	23.1	37.0	36.0	43.6	41.9	26.6	19.6	31.1	54.9
	(29.5)	(37.5)	(22.0)	(9.9)	(33.4)	(25.8)	(35.3)	(32.3)	(22.8)	(13.6)	(25.1)	(46.5)
Sweden[a]	54.3	60.2	46.0	28.9	52.6	56.0	55.7	61.1	49.2	36.4	55.7	68.0
United Kingdom	44.9	56.0	33.1	14.3	45.7	44.2	53.7	53.7	33.6	33.3	53.6	71.4
	(39.7)	(51.9)	(24.0)	(7.0)	(42.6)	(36.8)	(49.2)	(49.0)	(27.5)	(28.3)	(48.3)	(65.7)
United States	41.9	49.0	30.2[b]	17.1	41.8	42.1	45.7	45.9	37.1	13.3	32.6	62.4
	(37.8)	(45.6)	(28.5)	(10.1)	(39.0)	(36.7)	(41.8)	(41.9)	(32.8)	(10.5)	(28.9)	(57.2)

NOTE: Values in parentheses are for job-related training only.
[a] Job-related training data unavailable.
[b] Less than 30 cases in sample cell.
SOURCE: O'Connell (1999).

training than either the unemployed or the inactive (individuals out of the labor force). Separating job-related training from all education and training, we see that for the employed, most training is job-related.[6] In our sample of countries, women tend to receive roughly the same overall level of education and training as men, but somewhat less job-specific training. Younger workers were more likely to receive training than older workers.

Perhaps the most striking pattern in access to training is the direct relationship it has with the level of formal educational attainment. There are three main educational attainment categories used in the IALS: 1) below upper secondary, equivalent to less than a high school diploma; 2) upper secondary, equivalent to a high school diploma; and 3) tertiary, equivalent to a college or university degree. Across three of the four countries in Table 8.4, adults in the tertiary category were more than twice as likely to receive education and training than adults in the below upper secondary category.[7] The differences are particularly large for Canada and the United States, with the ratio of tertiary to below upper secondary in the range of 2.8–4.7. Even in Sweden, the ratio of tertiary to below upper secondary receiving training was close to 2 (1.87). Given these numbers, the overall message is clear: those who are employed, young, and with some college education are likely to receive some kind of training, whether job-related or not, in any given year. A virtuous cycle, with respect to the recent literature on labor market trends and skill-biased technological change, seems to exist for workers fitting this description. Skill upgrading is provided for the already skilled, and for the lesser-skilled, there is far less access to training. This pattern of providing services (skills) to those most likely to succeed is strikingly consistent across countries, despite their diverse labor market policies. It is not surprising, given the prevalence of employer-provided training. Employers can be expected to provide training to workers for whom it will yield the highest return.

When the focus is shifted to employed adults and their job-related training, similar patterns across groups are evident (see Table 8.5). Several observations stand out. Training participation in Hungary is quite limited, focused on the young, somewhat more on women, and in particular, on those with a university degree. Training participation in the United States is much broader, with about half of all employed adults involved in some kind of job-related training. The United States

Table 8.5 Cross-Country Differences in Various Training Indicators, Employees Aged 25–64 in the 1990s

Country[a]	Participation rate in career or job-related training	Volume of career or job-related training (avg. hours of training per employee)	Ratios of participation rates for women to men	Ratios of participation rates for workers aged 25–29 to 50–54	Ratios of participation rates for workers with a university degree to those not having finished upper secondary schooling
Canada	37.70	41.10	0.94	1.96	2.34
Germany	20.00	40.50	1.15	1.79	1.96
Hungary	4.20	13.50	1.15	3.67	12.05
Sweden[b]	55.50	11.60	1.09	0.93	1.58
United Kingdom	58.00	52.10	1.00	1.56	1.70
United States	48.80	46.60	1.00	0.97	4.09

[a] Hungary source: ELFS 1997, other countries IALS 1994–1995.
[b] Source for average hours of training: ELFS 1997.
SOURCE: OECD Employment Outlook (1999).

also displays a strong association between educational attainment and access to training. A college-educated worker is four times more likely than a high school dropout to receive training (in Hungary, the difference is 12:1). In Canada, Germany, Sweden, and the United Kingdom, the education bias in training access is considerably weaker, on the order of 2:1. It is clear from the evidence that an adult high school dropout begins his working career at a large disadvantage and that disadvantage is compounded by the lack of job-related training opportunities.

Sweden provides not only the highest level of training access, but is also the most egalitarian provider of training across groups differing in gender, age, and education. From Table 8.5 we see that Sweden also provides more training to unemployed workers than the other countries. However, even from its egalitarian perch, Sweden is a strong illustration of the literacy-training association.

Job-related training is just one type of human capital investment, and at the country level, enhancements to human capital are strongly positively related. Analyses reported in OECD (1999) reveal that participation rates in job-related training are positively correlated with school spending, educational attainment, spending on research and development, and the share of the labor force working as researchers (see OECD 1999, Table 3.10). We find it striking the degree to which literacy is a foundation for skill training. Literacy skills themselves are mostly acquired in school, but there is an interaction between literacy and the labor market. Improved literacy is associated with more employment opportunities (and less unemployment), and within the employed, training is more readily available to the more literate. Given the fact that basic literacy skills are developed in school, it is not surprising that cross-country differences in education are associated with literacy differences. But even within education categories, stronger literacy skills are associated with greater access to training.[8]

Information on the financing of training further highlights the pervasiveness of privately provided and sponsored training (see Table 8.6). Among workers with access to training, about one-third report employer financial support (slightly more for the employed), with workers and families contributing the next largest share (about one-fifth report self financing). Government financing plays a considerably

Table 8.6 Percent of the General and Employed Populations in Adult Education Who Receive Financial Support from Various Sources, 1994–1998

Country		General population		Employed population	
		Men	Women	Men	Women
Canada	Self or family	22.9	27.7	25.7	23.9
	Employers	26.0	19.8	31.9	24.2
	Government	9.8	13.9	8.2	10.3
	Other	5.9	5.2	5.9	5.3
Hungary	Self or family	19.2	23.0	16.3	22.1
	Employers	27.4	31.3	29.3	34.2
	Government	6.4[a]	8.8	7.0[a]	9.1
	Other	7.4[a]	7.9	6.4[a]	7.9
Sweden	Self or family	—[b]	—	—	—
	Employers	48.5	51.5	48.7	51.3
	Government	—	—	—	—
	Other	—	—	—	—
United Kingdom	Self or family	9.6	14.4	9.2	11.7
	Employers	37.7	29.2	42.3	32.9
	Government	9.6	10.6	7.8	8.2
	Other	5.2	3.7	5.1	3.2
United States	Self or family	16.1	21.1	17.1	17.8
	Employers	32.4	30.1	35.4	31.3
	Government	4.8	6.5	5.1	5.9
	Other	3.2	5.0	3.1	4.5

[a] Unreliable estimate.
[b] Data unavailable.
SOURCE: OECD (2000).

reduced role. Across countries, women report more government financing than men, even among the employed.

To summarize, most access to training is through employers, with more educated, full-time, large-firm workers more likely to receive training. Numerous studies have shown firm-based training to have a higher rate of return than other forms of postschooling training. We consider it most likely that in the United States, private sector training will continue to yield a (much) higher return than publicly financed job training, and that the vast majority of job training will continue to be provided by the private sector. Yet it is important to recognize that private sector training has a strong skill/literacy bias; the more literate and skilled, the greater the access to private training. The relative lack of private training access for less-skilled workers seems likely to further disadvantage them, creating a need for training funded by the public sector.

WHAT WE KNOW ABOUT PUBLICLY FUNDED TRAINING

Before turning to our country profiles of training programs, it is useful to discuss how we know what we know about program impacts. The central question any program evaluation has to answer is whether and to what degree the treatment had an impact on the treated. For the most part, it is generally accepted that the most reliable evidence on the efficacy of training programs is provided by formal statistical evaluation of program impacts, whether experimental or nonexperimental. Experimental evaluations, where the treatment and control groups are randomly assigned, are commonly seen to be the state of the art in statistical evaluations, due to relative ease of methodology and interpretation of results. Experimental approaches do have limitations, particularly in situations where programs are ongoing with potential substitutes. Random assignment evaluations also raise ethical questions, and have institutional limitations and potentially considerable implementation costs.[9] In nonexperimental evaluations, it is more difficult to answer the counterfactual question of what would have happened to the treatment group in the absence of the program. This is a considerable challenge, and there have been important recent methodological advances in nonexperimental evaluations that address this challenge. These advances are centered on improving data quality and designing matching techniques that yield more reliable comparison groups.[10]

With its legislative mandates requiring program evaluation, the United States has a more extensive statistical evaluation history than does Europe, although the evaluation "gap" is likely to narrow when recently established European multi-country evaluation efforts bear fruit.[11] The difference between the United States and Europe on this point is quite sharp. Europe has its well-funded, stable nationwide programs aimed at reducing unemployment, particularly long-term unemployment. In the United States, government funding for programs is at a low level and subject to instability, with uneven management, aimed at improving the earnings prospects of the disadvantaged. Although we can expect these differences to narrow in the near future, within the OECD, the understanding of what works and for whom is currently based heavily on evaluations of U.S. programs (see Martin and Grubb 2001).[12]

In their comprehensive review of active labor market policy evaluations, Heckman, LaLonde, and Smith (1999, p. 2053) conclude, "The evidence both from North American and European studies indicates that government employment and training programs have at best a modest positive impact on adult earnings." Most gains are in employment, not in wages.[13] Formal classroom training appears to help women, whether displaced workers, welfare recipients, or reentrants. Best results are seen when classroom training is strongly linked to employers. Displaced men and otherwise unemployed men with low levels of educational attainment gain little from classroom training. One exception for displaced men is rigorous technical training in community college settings that does produce gains (see Jacobson, LaLonde, and Sullivan 2001). On-the-job training similarly appears to help women, but not men, provided again that the training is closely linked with local employers.

The United States has very little funding for out-of-school youths, with the exception of Job Corps. Job Corps results are positive, with results likely associated with its considerable per-participant costs. Early studies indicated modest positive effects on employment and earnings, and a recent study found significant earnings gains (Burghardt

2001). Reduced participation in criminal activities is an additional important positive impact.

Due in part to a different political culture surrounding employment and training programs and the absence of legislative mandates on evaluation, European evaluations are later entries and less numerous in the literature. Heckman, LaLonde, and Smith (1999) discuss evaluations up to the early 1990s, and Kluve and Schmidt (2002) provide a review into the late 1990s.[14] Youth programs are a particular European focus, due to concerns about high youth unemployment. In general, studies of European youth programs find increased employment rates, and the increases can be substantial. Higher youth employment rates are thought to be due to improved transitions out of unemployment. There is much more limited evidence of program effects on European youth wages. For comparison purposes, it is important to note that European youth are generally less economically disadvantaged than targeted American youth.

Across the number of European studies reviewed by Heckman, LaLonde, and Smith (1999), a common finding is a significant impact of training on employment, but not on wages (where point estimates of a positive impact on wages are large, statistical significance is often lacking). The same is true for the somewhat smaller number of late 1990s studies reviewed by Kluve and Schmidt (2002). Kluve and Schmidt (p. 438) take a slightly nuanced view, concluding that training (and job search assistance), "are more likely than subsidy-type schemes to display a positive impact on programme participants." This conclusion rests more on the failure of job creation and subsidy schemes than on the success of training programs. Recent studies do find positive impacts of training on employment, although not for all groups in all countries.

While outside the direct focus of this chapter on job training, job search assistance (JSA) appears to help most unemployed workers, particularly displaced workers. Both European and U.S. evidence supports the provision of JSA. Its key advantage is its low-cost, but it also offers many unemployed workers what they most need, an upgrading of search skills. Access to JSA raises employment rates.

COUNTRY PROFILES OF PUBLICLY FUNDED JOB TRAINING PROGRAMS

This section offers a profile discussion of key features of publicly funded training programs for each country in our select sample. Our aim is to convey a sense of how each country approaches training, the target populations, and the basic institutional structure of service provision. With an eye to distilling lessons, our sample of countries concentrates on those with a history of active labor market programs, along with a few countries that have successfully adapted key elements of these systems. We start with Sweden, Germany, and the United Kingdom, recognizing the European history of (mostly) well-established ALMPs. Hungary is included as part of the region, and as an example of how programs can be adapted to transition economy needs. From Europe we turn to North America, to discuss Canada and the United States. We conclude with Japan and Korea.

Sweden

Haveman and Saks (1985) denote key characteristics of a Western European employment and training model. These characteristics describe well both Sweden and Germany and are 1) a single primary agency established by the national government but often independent, 2) an extensive network of local offices with outreach, 3) participation by employer groups and trade unions in policy formation and implementation, and 4) money is spent developing a professional staff. Sweden has a broad-based, large-scale training and retraining system that is grounded in its stable, comprehensive nationwide employment and training system.

Sweden's ALMP is best understood within the country's overall policy of wage solidarity, and with that, some uniqueness. If the wage policy establishes a floor on wages, workers with low productivity will find it difficult to obtain employment. This aspect increases the benefit of enhancing worker productivity through training. With wage equalization, ALMP is needed to facilitate worker mobility because the signaling aspects of wage movements are reduced. Firms are required to list vacancies with the Employment Service, and relocation expenses are funded by the government. These policies explicitly entail a work principle, with a focus on employment rather than income transfers.

Although more recently decentralized, up to the early 1990s, training was centralized through the National Employment Training Board (AMU). This entity sold training services to any customer willing to pay, although its primary customer was the National Labor Market Board (AMS) and its Employment Service offices. The national AMU board operates a system of 100 skill centers located across the country. We note that this training system is independent of the educational system. The training system offers about 450 general curricula, available in all 100 centers. Each of the 25 regions may develop additional curricula. Most training courses are vocationally oriented and aimed at the upper secondary level. There are also basic education courses. Courses may last up to one year. AMU training is widely used, by both the employed and the unemployed. Training of unemployed workers is by referral from the Employment Service and is free, with a stipend roughly equivalent to unemployment compensation. Using data for 1990, Forslund and Krueger (1994) estimate that 62 percent of Swedish unemployed participate in government training.[15]

The Swedish training system was decentralized more recently, moving away from standardized training in government training centers to firm-based training meeting the needs of employers with a more flexible curriculum.

Forslund and Krueger (1994) surveyed a small number of early studies, noting a percentage wage effect in the range of –0.2 to +0.4 (and four studies are between –0.05 and +0.05).[16] Three recent evaluations of Swedish training programs (reviewed in Kluve and Schmidt 2002, Table 2) show very modest (zero to some negative) impacts on employment and earnings for programs targeted at youth and adult unemployed. With these studies as the evidence, one is hard-pressed to conclude for Sweden that the payoff from training is more than modest.

Germany

Germany's "dual" apprenticeship system gets its name from the way vocational training and education are provided simultaneously by employers and the state. The state is responsible for the financing, curricula, and provision of general training along with the theoretical aspects of vocational education. Firms provide the setting for practical, "hands-on" aspects of vocational training. This setup strengthens the connection between education and employment and is seen as an effective method of maintaining both low youth unemployment and supplying an adequate number of skilled workers for the German economy.[17]

Educational tracking is an element of the German system. Secondary schools lead either to a university or to vocational education and training (VET). There are outlets, however, where students can go to university after completing VET (and the reverse). For VET student apprentices, the dual system consists of one or two days a week spent in the classroom at vocational schools. Other workdays are spent at the firm usually under the guidance of an older "meister" worker or in specialized training centers organized by the firm (Gill, Fluitman, and Dar 2000).

The government organizes all aspects of training regulations, laws, and curricula for a given industry, along with monitoring costs and effectiveness of training via periodic national surveys. Curricula are drawn up by groups consisting of employers' associations, unions, and government officials. The vocational schools themselves are run by state education ministries and financed by local governments that provide equipment and material, and state (länder) governments that provide personnel.

Employers are all part of 480 regional employer associations (chambers) that regulate vocational training via vocational training committees (VTCs). Employers pay vocational training costs including wages for the apprentice. Supervision of training is performed by VTCs. These committees also include union and vocational teacher representatives.

One strength of the dual system is the cooperative and stable relationship among parties and participants. Overall societal acceptance of the need for such a system is high, the division of responsibility between government and private firms is clear, and long-term financing, both through general government monies and firm contributions, is assured. Secure financial and political support insures that training is provided for both employed and unemployed workers throughout the business cycle.

The apprenticeship system is the most visible component in German labor market policy. The Federal Employment Service (FES) administers unemployment insurance, job matching, and training programs. One-stop job centers are the starting point for the unemployed and for employed workers looking to upgrade skills.[18] Unemployed workers in training programs are eligible for unemployment insurance.

Although the dual system is seen as a model for other countries to emulate—Korea in particular, for the purposes of this chapter—it does have some fundamental weaknesses and limitations. First, it is expensive. In 1990–1991 annual figures, total cost per student in U.S. dollars was $21,000, and since then costs have been rising faster than formal university expenses. Second, small firms take part in the system at a much lower rate than larger firms (between 35 percent and 60 percent for firms with 5–49 workers versus greater than 90 percent for firms with 100 or more workers). Smaller firms also have a lower retention rate of apprentices after completion of training as compared to larger firms (65 percent or less compared to over 80 percent for larger firms). Third, given its size, and the extent to which government, industry, and labor have a stake in the system, it suffers from institutional inertia. Any major changes in regulations concerning what is taught in vocational schools requires consensus among major societal groups. And even when consensus is reached and new curricula are drawn up, vocational schools are slow to respond. Curricular changes in certain subjects can take up to two decades. Firms are often accused of indifference where vocational education is concerned.[19] Thus, while government and firms acknowledge the other's legitimacy in the process, communication between the two is often lacking. These characteristics may not bode well for flexible skill-updating in a global economic environment characterized by rapid technological change.

The German government has been concerned with this problem since at least the mid 1990s. The concept of "modularisation/unitisation," a decentralization where training is offered in smaller, individually certified blocks within an occupation, has been discussed as a method of providing greater flexibility to both training providers and students (Reuling 2000). Smaller training units give firms greater flexibility to tailor courses to actual production requirements, and offer trainees greater opportunities to take targeted courses that address focused skill needs. Smaller, targeted classes could improve incentives for firms to provide training. Across the system, designing shorter, more targeted, and flexible training opportunities spells could allow market signals to play a greater role in determining training content and student enrollment.

One sticking point in the implementation of this more flexible plan is the need to accommodate certification with flexible focused training. Certification is an important and successful component of the German system. Certificated training enhances the transferability of skill and allows workers to be more mobile across firms. Yet, certification is built on a foundation of standardized and comprehensive training courses. It may be necessary to reform the certification process to bring in line the goals of flexible training with recognized credentials.[20]

United Kingdom

The United Kingdom's active labor market policy looked considerably different in 2000 than it did in the late 1980s. Overall spending fell, from 2.69 percent of GDP averaged over 1985–1988, to 0.94 percent of GDP in 2000. Spending on training, as a share of GDP, dropped by just more than half, although spending on active policies, as a share of total labor market policy spending, increased to 39 percent in 2000 from 29 percent in 1985–1988.

Following a set of 1988 reforms, a national network of Training and Enterprise Councils (TECs) was established as the central training institution. Following a common theme, these councils were intended to decentralize the provision of training services and increase the involvement of employers.[21] As part of a government reorganization in 2001, the Learning and Skills Council (LSC) superseded the TECs and became responsible for post–age 16 education and training (apart from the university sector). The LSC seems to reestablish the central authority of the government, with a national office in Coventry running a set of 47 local offices. This is in contrast to the TECs, which were structured as independent private sector enterprises, created when a group of local employers entered into a contract with the national Department of Education and Employment.[22] Moving back to a more unified approach, the LSC is charged with the planning and funding of work-based learning for young people; workforce development; adult and community learning; and information, advice, and guidance for adults. Local councils continue to include upper-level management from local private sector enterprises. The overall system remains decentralized in spirit, with considerable local authority over financing and curriculum.

Work-Based Learning for Adults (WBLA) (formerly Training for Work) is the main state-funded program for unemployed adults. Individuals aged 18–63 who have been unemployed six months or longer are eligible, with priority to those unemployed 12 months or longer. Access to services is facilitated for individuals needing basic skills training, those jobless from large-scale redundancies, and those returning to the labor force. The LSCs manage the program. State funding has been reduced over the recent past. The focus seems to be on placing workers with employers, and most training occurs on the job, in the context of ongoing production. Trainees continue to receive unemployment benefits. Employers are not obligated to hire the worker after the training period. Outcomes are not overly impressive, with about 46 percent of trainees who complete training finding jobs or entering self-employment, full-time education, or further training. It is not known whether this outcome would occur without any state intervention (Crowley-Bainton 1997).

Work-Based Training for Young People (WBTYP) (formerly Youth Training [YT]) is the main state-funded program for young people. YT was developed from the highly successful former Youth Training Scheme, and it offers a place for all young people ages 16–17 who are unable to find a job. Funding is administered by the LSC. About one-third of trainees are employed by an enterprise while in training. Nonemployed trainees receive a small training allowance. Trainees aim to achieve a National Vocational Qualification (NVQ) level 2 (craftsperson) qualification. According to Crowley-Bainton (1997), YT suffered from bad publicity regarding the quality of training provided by some schemes and the low attainments of some trainees.

A more traditional apprenticeship program, called Modern Apprenticeships, was started in 1994, and reformed in 2001–2002. There are two programs, both administered by the LSC. Foundation Modern Apprenticeship (formerly National Traineeship) is targeted at 16–17-year-olds, but also open to individuals over 18 if training can be completed before age 25. The goal is a NVQ level 2 qualification. Advanced Modern Apprenticeship is aimed at school and college leavers, and these work-based training options lead to at least a NVQ level 3. Starting with the 2001–2002 reforms, these apprenticeships are available in over 60 sectors, including some sectors without a tradition of apprenticeships, such as information technology and retail trade.[23]

It has been generally accepted within European countries that youth training should incorporate general transferable skills in addition to occupation-specific and industry-specific training. During the 1990s, concerns were voiced about a downgrading of the general and technical content of vocational training in YT, arising from the interests of local groups of firms (via the TECs) in reducing the general educational content of training curricula in favor of specific skills (see Oulton and Steedman 1994).

Hungary

Any assessment of Hungary's publicly funded training schemes requires a look at the macroeconomic context. With the disintegration of the Soviet bloc in 1990, Hungary experienced a dramatic decline in GDP and an increase in unemployment. The unemployment rate rose from a negligible level in 1990 to a peak of 13.4 percent in February 1993. Unemployment fell in the late 1990s, but a considerable part of the decline was due to a shrinkage in the labor force (due to early retirements and informal sector employment). Although there is considerable optimism about Hungary's prospects for completing the transition from a centrally planned economy to a market economy, the transition path for the Hungarian labor market has been bumpy, and difficulties remain. Long-term unemployment remains high (the highest for our set of countries). Industrial restructuring has resulted in a large number of unemployed workers needing retraining, along with training demands of students finishing formal education and desiring places in the training system (Gill, Fluitman, and Dar 2000). Large public sector budget deficits place a constraint on spending.

Despite these constraints, Hungary has an impressive array of active labor market policies. In 2000, spending on ALMP accounted for about 44 percent of total labor market policy expenditures, with training accounting for 18 percent of active program spending. Along with retraining, public service employment, a wage subsidy program, and self-employment assistance constitute the set of active labor market programs. O'Leary, Kolodziejczyk, and Lazar (1998) report that about one million people use Hungary's labor programs each year, with about 30 percent participating in an active program.

Hungary uses an extensive system of performance indicators to monitor the cost-effectiveness of active labor market programs. This system of indicators has been in place since 1994, and it tracks outcomes such as reemployment rates and costs. One issue, common across countries, that arises with performance indicators is "creaming." When program managers are encouraged to achieve a high reemployment rate as a measure of program success, they may react by selecting the most able individuals, those already equipped with the skills to find new jobs on their own. These individuals may be more skilled than the group of unemployed as a whole. If workers are positively selected into programs by management on the basis of ability, programs may produce high rates of reemployment (success), yet the impact of the program (the effect of the training) may well be lower. When the Hungarian performance indicator system was implemented, program managers were warned about creaming and were encouraged to target services to those most in need.[24]

O'Leary, Kolodziejczyk, and Lazar (1998) provide a comprehensive summary and assessment of ALMP in Hungary. Workers eligible for retraining include the unemployed, those expecting to lose their jobs, workers in public service employment, and recent school-leavers. Training programs are short-term, to provide workers for job vacancies. Participants receive a stipend worth 10 percent more than their unemployment compensation payment. Training costs are paid by the local labor office.

Hungary's retraining of the unemployed takes place within a backdrop of its vocational education and training system. There are two aspects: vocational schools that provide theory and general education, and firms and public and private institutes that provide practical training. Government financing relies on enterprise training levies. Regional Training Centers (RTCs), set up to augment other public and private training schools, are partially funded by the World Bank. Both public and private training schools bid for training contracts from the local labor offices to retrain the unemployed.

In a statistical analysis that controls for observed differences between unemployed workers participating in retraining and unemployed workers not participating, O'Leary, Kolodziejczyk, and Lazar

(1998) find that individual retraining produced an increase of 11 percentage points in the likelihood of finding unsubsidized work or self-employment, and an increase of 9 percentage points in those still in a job at their survey date. Similar to many other studies, these authors found no impact on average monthly earnings. Reemployment was higher for those bearing some of the direct costs of retraining. Group retraining produced similar, if a bit smaller, increases in reemployment and no effect on earnings.

At the beginning of the transition from a centrally planned to a market-based economy, enterprises provided the bulk of the training for workers. In the years since, enterprise training has collapsed as firms have gone bankrupt. RTCs and government-run vocational training institutes are attempting to pick up where enterprise training has fallen off. In addition, these government training institutes and RTCs are facing competition from an increasing number of private training institutes (UNEVCO 1998). Although this higher level of activity may eventually produce improved training opportunities, there is currently little if any official accreditation of these private institutes or certification of training results. This clouds the environment for assessing the impact of training.

For Hungary, ALMPs are likely to remain an imperative, given conditions of employment instability. Assessments yield mixed and modest results, outcomes that are well in line with the experience of other countries.

Canada

In Canada, the federal government is responsible for the state of the economy and the provincial governments have responsibility for education. Because training relates to both concerns, it falls under both federal and provincial responsibility. As in the United States, program initiatives undergo fairly frequent repackaging and reform (see Gunderson and Riddell 2001). A major reform was undertaken in 1996, when the federal government replaced Unemployment Insurance (UI) with Employment Insurance (EI), in the Employment Insurance Act. The revamped EI program reflects an emphasis on reemployment benefits and support measures targeted at unemployed workers available and able to work but unable to find a job. Also in 1996, the federal government began offering provinces and territories an opportunity to design and deliver EI-funded active employment measures.

Relative to other countries in our sample, passive labor market policies are used more extensively in Canada. Principally, this feature is due to Canada's comprehensive and generous EI (formerly UI) benefits. Within active measures, Canada has the highest ratio of spending for employment services of the countries in our sample (40 percent of active spending is on employment services). A number of support measures, including job search assistance, a labor exchange network, and an automated labor market information system, are provided by the National Employment Service. Spending on training is an even larger share of active measures, at 34 percent in 2000.

For the 30 years prior to the 1996 reforms, the Government of Canada ran a series of training programs to improve the reemployment prospects of adult workers. Classroom training from community colleges and other training institutions was available, and on-the-job training from private employers. Labor market assistance to various target groups was coordinated through the Canadian Jobs Strategy (CJS). These groups include the long-term unemployed (through a program called Job Development); reentry women (Job Entry); training in designated areas of current or anticipated occupational skill shortages (Skill Shortages); and UI claimants in training who remained eligible for UI without a search requirement paying the cost of training (Feepayer). CJS programs were available to employed workers as well as unemployed. Park, Power, Riddell, and Wong (1996) reported estimated impact on earnings for the Skill Shortages, Feepayer, and Job Entry programs that are large in size and highly statistically significant. The estimated impact of Job Development is insignificantly different from zero.

The revamping of the EI system set two explicit goals: getting people back to work, and producing savings to the EI account. To further these goals, there are four main areas of Active Employment Benefits: 1) targeted wage subsidies; 2) self-employment assistance; 3) job creation partnerships; and 4) skills development, which includes training. The Skills Development program provides financial assistance to help unemployed EI claimants (or recent EI exhaustees) pay for the costs of skills training and related expenses while they are enrolled in an approved training program. The level of financial support provided is based on need, and participants are normally required to pay a share of the cost. Skills Development participants currently on an EI claim may continue to receive their regular EI benefits until the end of the benefit period. The usual skills training duration is up to 52 weeks, with the potential for an extended period up to three years.

Although there is scant evaluation evidence regarding these recent reforms, we note that the direction of reform is consistent with earlier evaluation studies for Canada. As noted by Gunderson and Riddell (2001), there has been a reorientation away from basic and classroom training toward training in the private sector combined with work experience. Through the federal–provincial agreements that devolve responsibility to the provinces (Labour Market Development Agreements), there is more employer involvement in the delivery of training.

United States

Our discussion of U.S. federal job training programs will be brief here, as other chapters in this volume (see Chapters 1 and 3) offer more detailed perspectives. Our aim is to facilitate our own cross-country comparisons and to provide a background for the lessons we distill in the concluding section.

As summarized by Krueger and Rouse (2002), each decade since the 1960s has seen a major reform in federal job training programs. Unemployed and underemployed workers were the target of training initiatives introduced in the Manpower Development and Training Act (MDTA) in 1962, with particular focus on low-income and welfare recipients. The Comprehensive Employment and Training Act (CETA) was introduced by the Nixon Administration in 1973, and it continued to focus on unemployed and underemployed adult workers, with programs for disadvantaged youths. Decentralization, visible through a transfer of decision-making authority from the federal level to states and localities, emerged as a theme in CETA. State and local government gained responsibility for designing, implementing, and evaluating programs. CETA evaluations produced the first findings of no measurable program impacts for men and modest yet positive, significant impacts for women. The evaluations also found that on-the-job training was more effective than classroom training.

Program decentralization continued as a major theme in the 1983 replacement of CETA with the Job Training Partnership Act (JTPA). The steep recession of the early 1980s prompted the addition of displaced worker programs. The Private Industry Councils established under CETA were strengthened on the private employer side to limit training content to skills in demand by private employers. Public service employment, in place in MDTA and CETA, vanished. A distinctive component of JTPA was its congressionally mandated national evaluation. As the 1990s drew to a close, there were numerous employment and training programs funded by the federal government (see Chapter 1 for a summary). In 1999, the final year of JTPA authorization, the Department of Labor had $5.3 billion in budgetary authority for its job training programs. Just under 70 percent of that spending went to three programs: JTPA Dislocated Workers, Job Corps, and JTPA Adult Training Grants (see Krueger and Rouse 2002, Table 10.6).

The Workforce Investment Act (WIA) replaced JTPA in 1998. The goal of WIA is a comprehensive workforce investment system, where all workers, disadvantaged or not, can gain access to information about jobs and life-long skills training, and where employers can find skilled workers. Two features are central to WIA: 1) one-stop centers where all employment and training programs can be accessed in one physical location, and 2) universal access to core employment services, with more restricted and sequential access to intensive services for workers who need more help. It is still the case under WIA that job training is targeted at economically disadvantaged and dislocated workers. In fiscal year 2001, $6.4 billion was spent on public job training in the United States, with 63 percent in a similar set of programs as discussed above: adult and dislocated workers, TAA and NAFTA-TAA training (also dislocated workers), and Job Corps (see Table 1.3 in Chapter 1).

Japan

Japanese labor market policy is tied closely to its overall system of employment practices in the sense that both are enterprise-based with importance attached to long-term employment and seniority related pay. For our focus on training, an essential feature of Japanese employment is investment by firms in skill development. Table 8.1 shows that the Japanese spend very little on labor market measures (more than Korea and the United States as a share of GDP, but less than all the other countries). Expenditures on adult training are even lower than those of the United States. Enterprises, and networks of enterprises, are responsible for employment and training. With respect to training, the firm-based model is built up from a strong foundation of skills established by the educational system. Skills are not just those of literacy and technical competency, but also teamwork. With a homogeneous set of school completers, all with solid basic education, firms focus on specific training. Workers are rotated through positions so that they become broadly trained within the enterprise. There are strong social norms against poaching, and a steep wage-tenure profile keeps turnover low.

As Leigh (1995) summarized, several characteristics are essential parts of the Japanese firm-based training system: homogeneity in basic skills, willingness to learn and teach others, and functioning as part of a team. These characteristics lower training costs. Are they transferable to the United States, where basic academic skills are lower and more heterogeneous? Leigh, based on Hashimoto (1994), concluded yes, given the success of Japanese automobile transplant operations.

For Japan, the overarching question is how to restore the macroeconomy to some reasonably robust state of health. There are also concerns about the labor market. From the 1960s to the early 1990s, low turnover and high levels of specific training were strengths. Labor immobility helped keep unemployment low. As Japan contends with the restructuring needed to address global competitive pressures, increasing labor mobility across firms will be a key issue for the future.

Korea

Korean active labor market policy should be viewed through the lens of recent history, societal attitudes toward higher education, and the government's reputation for program oversight and cost–benefit testing. Recent economic history, the still-developing political system, success in raising basic education levels, and a societal aversion to nonuniversity higher education degrees all provide a backdrop for the government's attempts to impose an extensive system of publicly and privately financed vocational training and education.

Throughout the 1970s and 1980s, Korea experienced remarkable growth stopped only by the regional financial crisis in 1997. This growth period allowed the government to experiment extensively with a variety of vocational education and training programs funded by levies on firms. These efforts included an explicit attempt to duplicate the German dual system of vocational education and training in 1994.

Korea has been remarkably successful in raising the level of basic education: in 1970, 75 percent of Korea had only an elementary education, and by 1990, only 30 percent of the population had a similar level of education. Over the same period of time, the number of students in vocational and academic secondary education jumped from 600,000 to 2 million, and university enrollment increased from 200,000 to 1.6 million. The number of vocational trainees rose dramatically. The country as a whole experienced sizeable increases in labor productivity and wages.

Vocational education in Korea is administered by the Ministry of Education and provided by vocational high schools, junior technical colleges, and open colleges. Education lasts from two to three years with classes in a major field. The breakdown of theory and practice in classes is roughly 70 percent and 30 percent, respectively. The training side of the equation is either administered directly (through the Korea Manpower Agency [KOMA]), or overseen by the Ministry of Labor. The actual provision of vocational training is split between privately financed in-plant institutes, public institutes and government authorized private institutes.

In attempting to implement its employment and training policy through vocational education and training programs, the Korean government had to contend with a negative social attitude towards vocational training. University degrees are prized and accorded much higher status than that accorded to a degree from a vocational school associated with practical training. There is a recognized preference among parents for children to go to university rather than participate in vocational education and training, despite a higher incidence of unemployment for university graduates than for vocational school graduates (Gill, Fluitman, and Dar 2000).

The Korean government in the 1980s, responding to political and societal pressure, increased access to general higher education. As a result, a shortage developed for production workers. Starting in 1990, an attempt was made to address this particular skill shortage by setting a goal of a 1:1 ratio of vocational to general secondary school enrollment by 1995. By the late 1990s, some additional students had been induced to enroll in vocational secondary schools; however shortages remained for skilled production workers in various industries (KRIVET 1999).

In 1994, to increase the relevance and flexibility of training in a changing technological environment, and to facilitate communication between the education and training parts of the system, a "2+1" program, patterned after the German dual system, was implemented. The "2+1" label indicates two years of education followed by one year of training with a firm. Implementation of the "2+1" system has been left to the discretion of technical training schools since 1999. The program has not been successful at generating large numbers of appropriately skilled workers. While it is difficult to pinpoint the precise reasons (to date) for the disappointing results, there are some broad outlines. In Germany, labor and industry enjoy a cooperative relationship—a collaboration that increases the chances for designing and implementing relatively effective training policies. Current and historical Korean industrial and labor relations cannot be similarly characterized. More generally, the close cooperation between government, business, and labor in financing and administering the "dual" system in Germany does not exist in Korea. In addition, Korea exhibits a distinct societal preference for nonvocational higher education, whereas the tradition of vocational training in Germany is well established. The weaknesses of Korea's "2+1" system reveal the importance of having a solid infrastructure foundation of vocational training and social partner cooperation from which to build an apprenticeship program.

Summary

Table 8.7 summarizes the key features of the country training programs profiled in this section. All countries maintain an array of active labor market policies, with the exception of Japan, where the government's role is notably secondary to private firms. All countries face the need for systems that can respond to the diversity of known and emerging skill needs. Most countries focus on the unemployed and at-risk (of unemployment) youth, although many countries are moving to

Table 8.7 Key Features of Publicly Funded Job Training Programs, by Country

	2000 spending (% GDP)[a]	Administrative structure	Main target groups	Issues for the future
Canada[b]	0.18	Centralized historically, with movement toward decentralization since 1996. Federal funding, with shared federal/provincial implementation authority.	Unemployed; displaced workers	Reorientation from basic & classroom training toward training in private sector with work experience.
Germany[c]	0.35	Highly centralized and established vocational education and training system, with explicit coordination of social partners. Firms and federal government share costs.	Youth entering job market; unemployed	Making the system more flexible & responsive to emerging skill needs
Hungary[d]	0.07	Retraining programs within overall context of a centralized national coordination of vocational training funding and evaluation, with decentralized provision by local governments and enterprises.	General unemployed	Addressing transition economy problems of high unemployment & low labor demand with limited public budgets
Japan[d]	0.03	Training system is private and enterprise-based. Firms and networks of firms provide training within context of long-term employment system. Low levels of public funding, within this system, for core workers at risk of displacement.	Core workers at risk of displacement	Revamping the delivery of training as long-term employment continues to decline in influence.
Korea[d]	0.09	Centralized with national government coordinating funding, provision and curricula of formal vocational education.	Youth entering job market; workers needing skill upgrading	Delivering large number of skilled workers to growing economy

Sweden[d]	0.31	Large-scale training and retraining system. Single agency with local offices. Until early 1990s, standardized training (w/ std. teaching methods & materials) in gov. training centers. Recent (late 1990s) shift to a more decentralized structure using firm-based training.	Unemployed and employed workers	Making the established system more flexible & responsive to emerging skill needs
United Kingdom	0.05	Decentralized, with central funding authority at national level, training devolving to localities. Curriculum decided by local providers & local councils (business leaders, political leaders, labor). Local units receive Whitehall funding, and use subcontracts (especially for classroom training) to private providers (proprietary schools)	Unemployed workers; out-of-school youth	Strengthening services for youth; maintaining decentralized but easy-to-navigate system
United States	0.05	Decentralized, with central funding authority at federal level, training devolving to states/localities. Curriculum decided by local providers & local councils (business leaders, political leaders, labor). State/local units receive federal funding, and use subcontracts (especially for classroom training) to private providers (proprietary schools, community colleges). One-stop centers for delivery of services	Displaced workers; out-of-school youth; unemployed; economically disadvantaged	Targeting appropriate services for heterogeneous groups; obtaining sufficient funding

[a] Labor market training includes support of apprenticeship and related forms of general youth training.
[b] Provisional data.
[c] Does not include training for employed adults.
[d] Data do not include youth training.

improve training access for employed workers. In almost all countries, the trend in administration is toward decentralization of training provision.

The countries in our select sample represent a variety of training systems, in a diverse set of political systems. There are some commonalities in motivations, goals, and principles. The common motivations are to supply adequate numbers of skilled workers to insure global competitiveness while providing programs to lower unemployment. More advanced industrialized countries share a common goal of addressing the needs of economically disadvantaged workers. We see the following common principles:

1) Build flexibility into any training system to allow for rapid curricula changes in response to market signals.

2) Be able to adequately evaluate and certify any occupation or sub-occupation training program on a countrywide basis to maintain training standards and to encourage mobility.

3) Maintain close links at the local level between workers, training providers, and firms to assure the supply of skilled workers appropriate to the demands of local business.

4) Provide for the specific training needs of different worker groups in society (i.e., unemployed adults, low-skilled adults, youth and the disabled). Targeted groups are heterogeneous, making it unlikely that a "one size fits all" approach will be effective in improving worker welfare and in yielding positive cost–benefit analyses.

5) Maintain a high level of consensus between government, business, and labor and be clear about the responsibilities of each group.

6) Fund at a level that is adequate and sustainable given the current (nearly global) constraints on government activity.

One challenge presented by those principles is that while a given subset may be followed, it is very difficult to adhere to all simultaneously. For example, if the training system is designed to be flexible and react quickly to market signals (principle 1), it may not be possible to adequately evaluate and/or certify changing curricula (2) and maintain the quick reaction ability. If an effort is made to adequately address the training needs for all groups in society (4), such a system could be prohibitively expensive in the long run (6) and may not even work given the heterogeneity of needs. Maintaining a high level of consensus among major groups (5) implies a great deal of bureaucratic inertia and makes it difficult to react quickly to changing market conditions (1). If strong links are maintained at the local level (3), any country-wide training certification system (2) might not address a given region's requirements.

DISPLACED WORKER PROGRAMS

Starting with the 1960s' fears of automation, displaced worker programs have been a mainstay of labor market policy within the OECD. The United States is a particularly strong example of the central role of displaced worker programs in federal training efforts. Displaced workers, however, have some characteristics different from the other main target group for publicly funded training, the economically disadvantaged. Displaced workers are often older, experienced, and established workers, whose needs are related to abrupt structural economic change rather than to lifetime low skill. As Leigh (1992) highlighted, displaced workers want jobs, not training. For the most part, job search assistance produces favorable cost–benefit evidence, in large part because it is low-cost, and for many displaced workers, rusty job search skills are a real barrier to reemployment. Two key difficulties for training are the design of effective programs for these (often) experienced workers, and allocating sufficient funds. Evidence from various JTPA demonstrations, conducted over the 1980s, reveals mixed evidence on the benefits of training, with the best training being intensive and skills-based, not longer term. Yet for some workers, more expensive and longer-term classroom training yields earnings gains, but only where training is relatively rigorous at the vocational and academic community college level (see Jacobson, LaLonde, and Sullivan 2001).

For these workers, Leigh (1992) concludes that a training system needs to separate from the educational system and be permanent and institutionalized. One key advantage of a separate training system is its open-entry/open-exit flexibility, allowing intensive short-term skills-based courses with employer ties.

Canada's Industrial Adjustment Service (IAS) is a federally funded agency specializing in job development. Its goal is to bring together local labor and business interests to find job opportunities for displaced workers. IAS offers assistance to firms in advance of mass layoff, and helps negotiate an agreement on an adjustment plan. According to Leigh (1995), the basic thrust of IAS is to place unemployed workers in jobs that are never publicly announced, but rather filled by word-of-mouth. The emphasis is on prompt local placement rather than retraining, relocation, or counseling. Workers who cannot be placed are referred to the CEC system for relocation or retraining assistance.

An essential characteristic of this IAS assistance is its local component. People with experience in local business, from either a labor or management perspective, are involved in making the placements. ". . . [T]he basic philosophy of the IAS [is] that displaced workers are to be assisted individually by persons who know them personally" Leigh (1995, p. 151).

For Swedish displaced workers, a key aspect of the AMU training system is its open admission and individualized study plans. The curriculum is organized in a modular system, providing flexibility in scheduling. Trainees receive a diploma upon completion that conveys clear information about curriculum and skills. Training centers are organized to mimic work environments rather than schools.

For Germany, the focus is on avoiding layoffs (with the exception of restructuring in the former East Germany, where the main policy response was unemployment insurance after massive layoffs). The German employment adjustment process is based on codetermination, or structured decision making, among the social partners. With layoffs costly (due to collective bargaining agreements and statutory employment protection) firms face incentives to use other options. Two important options are UI compensation for reduced work hours and early retirement. Evans-Klock et al. (1998) notes that redeployment within the enterprise is possibly facilitated by the broad-based job skill training that is a result of the apprenticeship system. If layoffs are used, the General Dismissal Protection Act requires a selection of workers for layoff to be socially justified, based on criteria such as age and income.

The Japanese have a two-tier system. For core, or permanent, employees (approximately one-quarter to one-half of the workforce), the Japanese response is based in the enterprise or in networks of enterprises. The state pays part of retraining and relocation costs when firms take these steps to avoid layoffs. More generally, there is public funding for enterprise-based training that targets workers at risk of displacement. Japanese firms retain flexibility in employment levels through the hiring and layoffs of temporary, or contingent, employees. For these workers, there is little or no employment security. With no secure link to an enterprise, there is little access to training when laid off.

CONCLUSION

Looking across our selective sample, we find striking the evidence in favor of a "virtuous" cycle between basic education, literacy, skill, and training. A strong foundation in basic education, especially literacy, is associated with greater access to training, not only through improved access to employment, but also through occupations with greater training content.

This link has three implications. The first is that training, in the main, belongs in the private sector, where it is closely tied to basic skill. The second implication of the schooling–training association is that strengthening schooling is an indirect, if slow, method for strengthening training. The third implication follows from the first two: whereas individuals in the "virtuous cycle" are well served by the current system, there is a "vicious" cycle for the individuals who are not well-served by the educational system. That "vicious" cycle consists of skill deficits, continued underinvestment in skills, low earnings, and declining employment (see Betcherman, McMullen, and Davidman 1998). Workers who face this cycle present heterogeneous needs. The literacy, education, and training needs of out-of-school youth are very different from the needs of established workers who lose their footing in employment (the displaced). Another group faces the complications of work and family (single parents, usually mothers). For these individuals and other workers tenuously connected to the labor market, publicly funded training offers a crucial second chance to recover from "falling through the cracks" of the private training system. The failure of the basic educational system followed by employer-provided training to provide skills to these workers stands as a "market failure" justification for publicly funded training.

Our view is that increased awareness of how ALMP/training programs work in other countries can improve (or at least inform) the way the United States addresses the issue of publicly funded training. Some of the lessons put forth in Haveman and Saks (1985) bear repeating. They emphasize the comprehensive and stable institutional structure for (most) Western European employment and training systems. This structure includes 1) a single primary agency established by the national government but often independent, 2) a network of local offices emphasizing outreach to employers and employees, 3) participation in policy development and implementation by employers groups and trade unions, and 4) expenditures for the development of a professional staff of placement, counseling, and training personnel.

More recently, Martin and Grubb (2001) offer four features crucial to the design of effective public training programs: 1) targeting on participants, 2) relatively small scale programs, 3) programs should produce a qualification or certificate that is recognized by the market, and 4) a strong on-the-job component to establish links to employers. These features are on exhibit in the programs of a number of countries.

It seems clear that successful programs involve the private sector, particularly from the perspective of offering a curriculum of relevant classes teaching marketable skills. Integration is key. Skills training needs to be integrated with jobs, remedial skill training integrated with occupational skill training, private sector demands integrated with public sponsorship, and employee supply with employer demand. With an integrated approach, training can be tailored to the needs of local employers. To do this, the training system needs up-to-date, comprehensive labor market information.

It is commonplace for literature in this area to conclude by noting that evaluations find programs to have modest or mixed results at best. Even modest gains can make the economically disadvantaged less poor and raise, albeit modestly, the employment prospects of the unemployed. Expecting otherwise may be unrealistic, given traditional U.S. politics and programs. In his review of government-sponsored training programs and their evaluations, LaLonde (1995) writes, "The best summary of the evidence about the impact of past programs is that we got what we paid for. Public sector investments in training are exceedingly modest compared to the magnitude of the skill deficiencies that policymakers are trying to address. Not surprisingly, modest investments usually yield modest gains . . ." (p. 149).

Notes

We appreciate the comments and suggestions of Gerard Pfann and Christopher O'Leary. Financial support was provided by the Social Sciences Division and Academic Senate Committee on Research, University of California, Santa Cruz.

1. Workers increasingly need problem-solving skills and skills that cross jobs as teamwork and quality control replace simpler and more hierachical production processes. See Lynch (1994) for a discussion.
2. The OECD countries promoted that goal in 1994 in the OECD Jobs Strategy, when they agreed to move labor market policy toward active programs (see OECD 1994). That goal has not been uniformly met within the OECD.
3. The reauthorization of Trade Adjustment Assistance (TAA), contained in the Trade Act of 2002, included a program of refundable tax credits, payable in advance, to cover 65 percent of the cost of health insurance for TAA eligible workers.
4. This observation is related to the received wisdom that countries with greater spending on active labor market policies tend to have lower unemployment (see Layard, Nickell, and Jackman 1991 and Forslund and Krueger 1994).
5. See OECD (2000). Although the IALS offers a wealth of information on literacy skills and training, information is not currently available for Korea and Japan.
6. The distinction between all education and training and job-related training is not available for Sweden in the IALS.
7. Unfortunately, the information reported in Table 4 is available only for a limited subset of our sample.
8. For more on this point, see OECD (2000).
9. The existence of established ongoing programs, with substitutes, may be a concern for European training programs. In this situation, the risk of program disruption is higher, complicating the interpretation of the program effect. See Heckman, LaLonde, and Smith (1999).
10. Interested readers are directed to the detailed discussion of the evaluation of active labor market programs in Heckman, LaLonde, and Smith (1999).
11. New Techniques for the Evaluation of European Labour Market Policies is a research project bringing together eight research institutions from seven European Union countries. The Center for Economic Policy Research (CEPR) is coordinating the study. For information, visit http://www.cepr.org/research/Networks/LERTN/Summary.htm.

12. Given the overall institutional background of U.S. training, its evaluation context has limitations for inference to other countries. There are questions of external validity, or the extent to which estimated program effects can be generalized to different locations. Social attitudes, government institutions, the business cycle, and skill demands all differ across countries. In addition, many U.S. evaluations are of small demonstration or pilot programs. Scaling these programs up to more universal participation could influence community perceptions and/or combine with institutions and other forms of social interaction in ways that influence program success (see Friedlander, Greenberg, and Robins 2000).

13. An important follow-up question to a finding of employment gains is the nature of employment displacement for nonparticipants. See Davidson and Woodbury (1993) for an insightful discussion.

14. A central point in Kluve and Schmidt (2002) is that Europe needs to catch up to the U.S. "evaluation culture."

15. The comparable figures for the United States in 1990 was 19 percent.

16. See Forslund and Krueger (1994, Figure 3). They report a weighted average percentage wage effect of −0.8 that is not statistically significantly different from zero.

17. See Soskice (1994) for an analysis of the incentives faced by the various actors in the German system, and for citations to the larger research literature on the German system.

18. Firm-based training is much less common for workers over age 24 in Germany (see Lynch 1994).

19. In practice, employers do not have much input in how vocational education is structured and what classes are offered.

20. This issue has an interesting parallel in the United Kingdom, where a system of "unit certification" is being implemented to bring coherence to a decentralized flexible training system (Reuling 2000).

21. Prior to 1988, much training of adult workers was the responsibility of industry employers, through a system of industry-specific Industrial Training Boards.

22. The Learning and Skill Council is part of a reorganized Department for Education and Skills.

23. In July 2002, an Advanced Modern Apprenticeship program with Swan Hunter, a Tyneside shipbuilder, was extended to workers in their thirties.

24. See O'Leary, Kolodziejczyk, and Lazar (1998) for evidence of creaming in retraining programs in Hungary.

References

Betcherman, Gordon, Kathryn McMullen, and Katie Davidman. 1998. *Training for the New Economy: A Synthesis Report.* Canadian Policy Research Network.

Burghardt, John. 2001. *Does Job Corps Work? Summary of the National Job Corps Study.* Princeton, NJ: Mathematica Policy Research, Inc. Princeton, NJ.

Casey, Bernard and Gert Bruche. 1985. "Active Labor Market Policy: An International Overview." *Industrial Relations* 24(1): 37–61.

Crowley-Bainton, Theresa. 1997. *United Kingdom: Encouraging Employer Investment.* International Labour Organization, December. http://www.ilo.org/public/english/employment/skills/training/publ/uk.htm.

Davidson, Carl, and Stephen A. Woodbury. 1993. "The Displacement Effect of Reemployment Bonus Programs." *Journal of Labor Economics* 11(4): 575–605.

Evans-Klock, Christine, Peggy Kelly, Peter Richards, and Corinne Vargha. 1998. "Worker Displacement: Public Policy and Labour–Management Initiatives in Selected OECD Countries." International Labour Organization, Employment and Training Department, Employment and Training Papers 24.

Forslund, Anders, and Alan B. Krueger. 1994. "An Evaluation of the Swedish Active Labor Market Policy: New and Received Wisdom." NBER working paper no. 4802. Cambridge, MA: National Bureau of Economic Research.

Friedlander, Daniel, David H. Greenberg, and Philip K. Robins. 2000. "Methodologies for Determining the Effectiveness of Training Programs." In *Improving the Odds: Increasing the Effectiveness of Publicly Funded Training,* Burt S. Barnow and Christopher T. King, eds. Washington, DC: The Urban Institute Press, pp. 261–292.

Gill, Indermit S., Fred Fluitman, and Amit Dar. 2000. *Vocational Education & Training Reform: Matching Skills To Markets And Budgets.* Washington, DC: World Bank/Oxford University Press.

Gunderson, Morley, and W. Craig Riddell. 2001. "Training in Canada." In *Labor Market Policies in Canada and Latin America: Challenges of the New Millennium,* Albert Berry, ed. Boston: Kluwer Academic Publishers, pp. 243–265.

Hashimoto, Masanori. 1994. "Employment-Based Training in Japanese Firms in Japan and in the United States: Experiences of Automobile Manufacturers." In *Training and the Private Sector: International Comparisons,* Lisa M. Lynch, ed. Chicago: University of Chicago Press, pp. 109–148.

Haveman, Robert H., and Daniel H. Saks. 1985. "Transatlantic Lessons for Employment and Training Policy." *Industrial Relations* 24(1): 20–36.

Heckman, James J., Robert J. LaLonde, and Jeffrey A. Smith. 1999. "The Economics and Econometrics of Active Labor Market Programs." In *Handbook of Labor Economics*, Orley Ashenfelter and David Card, eds. Volume 3A. Amsterdam: Elsevier, pp. 1865–2097.

Jacobson, Louis S., Robert J. LaLonde, and Daniel G. Sullivan. 2001. "The Returns to Community College Schooling for Displaced Workers." Working paper. Chicago: Harris School of Public Policy, University of Chicago, January.

Kluve, Jochen, and Christoph M. Schmidt. 2002. "Active Policy Evaluation: Problems, Methods and Results." Economic Policy: A European Forum 35(October): 409–448.

Korean Research Institute for Vocational Education and Training (KRIVET). 1999. "Reform and Innovation for Technical and Vocational Education in the Republic of Korea." Second International Congress on Technical and Vocational Education. Seoul, Korea.

Krueger, Alan B., and Cecilia E. Rouse. 2002. "Putting Students and Workers First? Education and Labor Policy in the 1990s." In *American Economic Policy in the 1990s*, Jeffrey Frankel and Peter Orszag, eds. Cambridge, MA: MIT Press, pp. 663–728.

LaLonde, Robert J. 1995. "The Promise of Public Sector-Sponsored Training Programs." *Journal of Economic Perspectives* 9(2): 149–168.

Layard, Richard, Stephen Nickell, and Richard Jackman. 1991. *Unemployment: Macroeconomic Performance and the Labor Market.* Oxford: Oxford University Press.

Leigh, Duane E. 1992. "Retraining Displaced Workers: What Can Developing Countries Learn from OECD Nations?" Policy Research Working Paper 946. Population and Human Resources Department, The World Bank, August.

———. 1995. *Assisting Workers Displaced by Structural Change: An International Perspective.* Kalamazoo: W.E. Upjohn Institute for Employment Research.

Lynch, Lisa M. 1994. "Introduction." In *Training and the Private Sector: International Comparisons*, Lisa M. Lynch, ed. Chicago: University of Chicago Press, pp. 1–24.

Martin, John P., and David Grubb. 2001. "What Works and for Whom: A Review of OECD Countries' Experiences with Active Labour Market Policies." OECD working paper, Office of Labour Market Policy Evaluation, September.

Organisation for Economic Co-operation and Development (OECD). 1994. *The OECD Jobs Study—Facts, Analysis, Strategies*. Paris: OECD.

————. 1999. *Employment Outlook*. Paris: OECD.

————. 2000. *Literacy in the Information Age: Final Report of the International Adult Literacy Survey*. Paris: OECD.

————. 2001. *Employment Outlook*. Paris: OECD.

O'Connell, Philip J. 1999. *Adults In Training: An International Comparison of Continuing Education and Training*. Paris: OECD.

O'Leary, Christopher J., Piotr Kolodziejczyk, and Gyorgy Lazar. 1998. "The Net Impact of Active Labour Programmes in Hungary and Poland." *International Labour Review* 137(3): 321–347.

Oulton, Nicholas, and Hilary Steedman. 1994. "The British System of Youth Training: A Comparison with Germany." In *Training and the Private Sector: International Comparisons*, Lisa M. Lynch, ed. Chicago: University of Chicago Press, pp. 61–76.

Park, Norm, Bob Power, W. Craig Riddell, and Ging Wong. 1996. "An Assessment of the Impact of Government-Sponsored Training." *The Canadian Journal of Economics* 29 (Special Issue: Part 1): S93–S98.

Reuling, Jochen. 2000. "Qualifications, Unitisation and Credits—The German Debate." Presentation at "Meeting the Needs of Learners" QCA International Research Seminar, London, February.

Soskice, David. 1994. "Reconciling Markets and Institutions: The German Apprenticeship System." In *Training and the Private Sector: International Comparisons*, Lisa M. Lynch, ed. Chicago: University of Chicago Press, pp. 25–60.

UNEVCO. 1998. *Cooperation with the World of Work in Technical and Vocational Education*. Berlin: UNEVCO.

9

Public Job Training

Experience and Prospects

Christopher J. O'Leary
Robert A. Straits
Stephen A. Wandner

Federal job training policy in the United States has been a case of learning by doing. New and proposed policy represents a synthesis of lessons learned from previous programs. The United States is currently operating under the fourth major federal administrative structure since the 1960s. It can be argued that despite the inevitable political wrangling over employment policy, each incarnation has brought improvements born from lessons of previous arrangements.

Although the Great Depression witnessed some public works programs, including on-the-job training, focused and federally funded job skill training policy did not begin in the United States until 1962, with the passage of the Manpower Development Training Act (MDTA). Initially, training authorized under MDTA was viewed as motivated by an antipoverty agenda. MDTA's structure called for the federal government to administer the program directly to local service providers serving specific target groups. MDTA expired in 1969, largely due to the federally oriented administrative structure, which circumvented state and local authority—an arrangement deemed politically unacceptable.

While most workforce development programs have evolved, incorporating lessons learned from previous initiatives, the Job Corps program, designed to offer disadvantaged youth a one-year residential workforce development program, has continued virtually unchanged since it was established by the Economic Opportunity Act in 1964. Today, the Job Corps program continues to operate within its original structure, serving an estimated 60,000 youth per year, with an annual budget of approximately $1 billion. Job Corps provides remedial academic instruction, job training, and other supportive services, in an environment that encourages participation and successful program completion. Relative to other similar programs for youth, Job Corps participants achieve significant earnings gains.

Following MDTA, the next major workforce development program was the Comprehensive Employment and Training Act (CETA) of 1973. CETA introduced the private industry council (PIC) as a local advisory board. CETA job training was targeted toward the economically disadvantaged, welfare recipients, and disadvantaged youth. Evaluations of programs authorized by CETA found no measurable employment or earnings impacts for men; conversely, impacts for women were positive and significant. CETA evaluations also found on-the-job training usually to be more effective than classroom training in terms of job placement and cost per placement. CETA also included the last federal public service employment (PSE) program. The improper enrollment and spending practices documented for PSE under CETA spelled the end for the program.

CETA was succeeded by the Job Training Partnership Act (JTPA) of 1982. The new workforce development agenda under JTPA limited training choices to skills in demand by local employers. The program was performance-driven through a system of standards for participant reemployment rates and earnings. The JTPA-targeted population for job training included dislocated workers and economically disadvantaged welfare recipients. JTPA training had positive net benefits for both men and women. The net benefit to society for both genders was just over $500 per participant.

The experience of the past 40 years has taught us that women often benefit from job training, while men sometimes benefit. The most effective job training programs for youth have been costly and of long duration.

The Workforce Investment Act (WIA) of 1998 devolved authority from the federal government to the states, and increased customer choice in selecting job training. It increased the private sector presence on local workforce investment boards, institutionalized one-stop centers, revised performance monitoring practices, and emphasized job placement services over skill training. The most pioneering addition to workforce development service delivery adopted under WIA is the introduction of training vouchers as Individual Training Accounts

(ITAs). A review of vouchers and ITAs is provided in this summary chapter. Under WIA, requirements for performance measurement and reporting were greatly simplified. Additionally, WIA required establishment of Eligible Training Provider (ETP) lists, and thereby the idea of accountability and competition among training providers. These systemic service delivery changes authorized under WIA represent a new approach to workforce development service delivery. However, WIA was given modest funding compared to previous federal employment and training programs.

In the next two sections of this final chapter, we briefly review the two sides of the market for job training under WIA: the choice environment for job training participants, and the regulatory environment governing job training providers. The fourth section offers speculation on the shape of future federal workforce development policy. A final section provides a summary and concluding remarks.

CHOICE OF JOB TRAINING UNDER WIA

Vouchers are WIA's key structural innovation. A voucher is a "subsidy that grants limited purchasing power to an individual to choose among a restricted set of goods and services" (Steuerle 2000, p. 4). Vouchers are one of many ways that the government can provide services. Alternative delivery mechanisms include direct government delivery, contracting out government services, and use of competitive public suppliers, providing loans or cash payment (Steuerle 2000, pp. 12–17).

Vouchers are viewed as a mechanism for making government more effective and efficient by making use of the market mechanism. Vouchers introduce multitraining provider competition in contrast to the usual way government services are provided. They have been found to be useful in a wide variety of contexts (Osborne and Gaebler 1992).

Under MDTA, CETA, and JTPA, classroom training was mostly provided as slots in classes through contracts with training providers. Since the private sector has been providing training with government funding, privatization per se was not a major aim of WIA. Instead, vouchers were introduced to increase customer choice, with the hope that it would lead to better employment outcomes.

To introduce job training vouchers under WIA, a variety of practical implementation issues had to be resolved. As documented in Chapters 4 through 6 of this book, identifying the best institutional arrangements for job training vouchers under WIA involved a review of vouchers in other contexts, local demonstrations of voucher methods, and a random trial evaluation of alternative voucher designs.

Voucher Designs

To use vouchers wisely when shopping for training services, prospective training participants must have enough information to make an educated choice among alternatives. In particular, a voucher recipient must be able to appraise the quality and effectiveness of prospective training providers, while at the same time know whether the training will match their own skills and abilities (Barnow 2000, p. 227). To help improve the choice environment, WIA Eligible Training Providers (ETP) are required to be preapproved by the local workforce development board. Part of the approval process requires posting on the Internet descriptions of available training and employment success information for recent participants.

In competitive job training markets, a "free choice" model is viewed as theoretically ideal. It permits unrestricted expression of customer preferences. However, in practical terms it may be wanting. This model presumes that customers free to express their will could make choices superior to those possible in consultation with training counselors. A critical assumption is that consumers have accurate and adequate information both about which occupations they are suited for and which training providers are best. Customers would need to know which occupations were in demand, and what wages they could expect when they completed training. Knowledge about which occupations offered the best long-term career paths would also be useful. For the free choice model to be superior, customers would need to make informed and wise decisions.

When configuring vouchers, individuals receiving public training could be given more or less freedom to choose services compared to the unlimited flexibility presented by the free choice model. Frontline staff in one-stop centers could provide more or less information and guidance about how to use vouchers. Three models for providing public training vouchers emerged following the continuum of the degree of freedom, information, and guidance (Barnow and Trutko 1999; Perez-Johnson and Decker 2001; D'Amico et al. 2002).

Informed choice represents the middle ground of the voucher structure spectrum. It is the closest to the intent of WIA legislation and is the model most widely adopted by local workforce development boards due to its low risk nature. This model has four main characteristics. First, assessment and counseling specialists check if available training is appropriate given customer skills and aptitudes. The specialists then check local labor market information (LMI) to ensure adequate occupational demand. Next, training vendors are screened for value by success of participants and training cost. Then there is joint decision making between the counselor and the participant, with the frontline staff acting as a guide or information broker. Finally, the voucher offer is limited in its cash value and time availability, with a definite expiration date set.

Free choice is one extreme of the voucher spectrum and gives the individual training recipient the most flexibility and responsibility. Indeed, the role of frontline staff is usually restricted and limited in this model. Customers judged to require training are offered vouchers, and they can make use of them with no further guidance from staff. Voucher recipients are able to make use of LMI, ETP performance information, and self-assessment tools available at the One-Stop Career Center. They can use the voucher for training for any occupation that is not restricted by law, and they can use the voucher to purchase training from any provider on the ETP list.

Directed choice is somewhat similar to informed choice and falls at the opposite end of the scale compared to the free choice model. Assessment, LMI, and ETP information are provided, but frontline workers play a stronger role. Rather than simply providing guidance, frontline staff use their professional judgment about what program and training provider to select. Staff use their knowledge about training programs, training providers, occupational demand and wages, the skills and aptitudes of customers, and the prospect of successful training completion. The model can be used to guide customers to more cost-effective training choices or to restrict choices that are less likely to be cost effective.

Effectiveness of Training Vouchers before WIA

A review of the prior use of vouchers for public training programs for disadvantaged and dislocated workers did not yield a success story. Barnow (2000, p. 234) wrote "there is little evidence that vouchers for these workers are effective and that they are a better alternative than other service delivery mechanisms." The U.S. Department of Labor (USDOL) reviewed voucher-like programs for low-wage workers under the Seattle-Denver Income Maintenance Experiments of the 1970s and the evaluation of the Trade Adjustment Assistance program of the late 1980s, and found neither to have a positive impact. "They offered non-directive counseling and a wide range of educational opportunities" (Barnow 2000, p. 236). The inadequate informational aspects of customer choice were seen as a deficiency.

Although WIA represents the first federal policy initiating the use of vouchers, voucher implementation began before WIA's enactment. Some individual localities experimented with vouchers on their own. For example, the Atlanta Regional Commission first used vouchers in 1991 as the means to provide training services to about 13,000 Eastern Airlines workers when the company went bankrupt. Vouchers were an expedient forced by the massive size of the dislocation and limitations on staff available. Atlanta's experience saw many voucher recipients making poor training choices, selecting training for occupations with low wages and poor career development prospects. In response, the Atlanta Commission began to build its own vendor list and monitor vendor performance, long before the enactment of WIA (D'Amico et al. 2002, pp. II-2–3).

Just before WIA implementation, USDOL performed a formal evaluation of vouchers under JTPA in nine demonstration sites. Eight sites had the informed choice voucher design, while the other site used the free choice model. In all sites, the vouchers were a limited-time offer (usually two years or less) with a limited dollar value (between $2,000 and $10,000). Voucher payment by the workforce development agency was not always contingent upon job placement of the training participant; however, it was usually contingent upon training completion. Eligible training providers were usually prescreened based on past performance (Barnow 2000).

USDOL began examining the operation of vouchers in the mid 1990s as policy interest grew. Anticipating enactment of ITAs as part of the new workforce development legislation, USDOL implemented a Career Management Account (CMA) demonstration. This project was conducted from 1995 to 1997 in 13 sites (Public Policy Associates 1999). An average of 335 offers was made per site. All vouchers were targeted to dislocated workers. The average voucher value was $3,292, with a maximum of $8,500. Participants were permitted free choice in using their vouchers, but preferred being provided with information by frontline staff to guide their decisions (D'Amico et al. 2001).

A number of CMA demonstration sites continued using vouchers after the demonstration ended in 1995. Metropolitan Portland, Oregon, initiated an Individual Learning Account (ILA) approach after CMA under which customers made regular contributions to an account that can be used to pay for training or education, with contributions matched by employers and social service agencies. The Baltimore Office of Employment Development continued the voucher approach after CMA ended, making case managers into coaches who helped customers make informed choices and were empowered to make decisions about customers with special needs (D'Amico et al. 2002, pp. II-2–II-3).

Early Evidence from WIA

To gain a better understanding of the new service delivery design adopted under WIA, and to jump start the use of ITAs and ETPs, USDOL contracted to have a study of the early implementation of WIA (D'Amico et al. 2001). Under WIA, ITAs are required for all types of training except on-the-job and customized training. ITAs are not required in a limited number of circumstances, such as situations where there are insufficient numbers of providers or a particular provider is exemplary for a particular subgroup with multiple barriers to employment.

Localities usually set policy for job training delivery, including criteria for training providers to be placed on ETP lists. While most localities do have ETP lists, usually these lists are paper rather than Internet-based. In some cases, states have created automated ETP lists, such that training providers can enter their own initial and subsequent applications directly into the system. Local WIBs also determine eligibility and registration procedures and set priorities for selection of ITA recipients.

Local WIA training funds have usually been a residual budget item. That is, the amount left after all other WIA services have been provided. Setting performance levels was not difficult in the first year (program year 2000) because training providers who were already eligible for Pell grants were not required to submit performance information. It was expected that this process would be much more difficult when training providers have to apply for subsequent eligibility. Conditions for subsequent eligibility were still being developed.

States have developed fairly similar procedures for establishing whether an individual was appropriate for training. Individuals determined eligible developed an employment goal, completed a confirming assessment, and searched for alternative funding for training programs. Local sites generally have also set minimum basic education skills needed before undergoing training.

WIA training delivery arrangements were slow to develop, with some still incomplete at the end of 2000. Localities have implemented procedures for administering ITAs. Ongoing case management is proving difficult, because with ITAs, it is hard to get direct feedback and reports from training providers. Consequently, local sites are trying to monitor performance both for themselves and for ITA recipients, by developing consumer report card systems and by conducting site visits or hiring independent monitors of training providers.

To accelerate and guide the local implementation of ITAs under WIA, in March 2000, USDOL selected and funded 13 sites (6 workforce investment areas and 7 states) for early implementation through an ITA/ETP Demonstration Project (D'Amico et al. 2002). Twelve of these demonstration sites mainly used the informed choice model, though some flexibility was practiced. Only 1 site predominately used the free choice model.

The study found that training declined significantly from JTPA levels during early WIA implementation. The drop in training enrollments probably happened for several reasons. The new WIA obligation to provide core and intensive employment services and the time lags associated with satisfying new standards for designating service providers as eligible are prime candidates. Given the announced "work first" emphasis of WIA, cautious local administrators may also have tried to first assure adequate funding for core and intensive services before committing funding to training services. The ongoing WIA obligation to provide core and intensive employment services could have permanently depressed training enrollments; however, training enrollments rose somewhat in program year 2001. Possible causes for this rebound were rising unemployment and USDOL's effort to dispel the original interpretation that WIA was strictly a work-first program. The characteristics of training participants under WIA remained largely unchanged from JTPA, with participants being mostly low wage adult and dislocated workers.

All sites had dollar caps on the ITA amount, varying between $1,700 and $10,000. Given WIA performance measures, sites had an interest in having their ITA recipients complete training and find subsequent employment. Frontline staff maintained contact with ITA recipients during their training and tried to help solve problems. Although the level of staff contact varied, all sites contacted recipients at least once a month. Among training vendors, proprietary schools were more proactive in helping trainees complete training and had strong programs for helping them find jobs after completion. Community colleges were less proactive, although they provided counseling and placement services.

Sites had developed ETP lists and consumer reports systems. The ETP lists were based on initial eligibility in all states except Texas. States made it easy for training vendors to appear on the list. Only two states required vendors to meet performance requirements for initial eligibility. Most states also tried to automate the ETP lists and the ETP list application process to make completion of applications easier for vendors. States expected great difficulty in keeping vendors participating in WIA training after they implemented their subsequent eligibility requirements. States had implemented consumer report systems, but half of them only included WIA vendors on the ETP list.

TRAINING PROVIDERS UNDER WIA

Institutional classroom job training under JTPA was provided by a combination of community colleges, nonprofit, and for-profit training institutions. Under WIA, new policy has emerged to place increased emphasis on and encouragement of the key role played by community colleges.

While continuing to maintain their role in supporting academic students planning to transfer to four-year colleges, community colleges in the 1990s moved strongly into the job training market. This role expanded along with labor demand during the 1990s, when employers struggled to fill job openings for skilled workers. Community colleges increasingly developed alliances with industries to provide customized training for incumbent workers, and thereby became a principal source of training for employers. This expanded job training mission of community colleges in the 1990s was not in response to governmental funding, but rather a consequence of large increases in formal training provided for employers in 1980s and the projected continued future increase (Carnevale and Derochers 1997).

Nearly all of America's 1,300 community colleges offer workforce training and educational courses. They increasingly serve their communities directly and through the workforce development system.[1] A national survey of 10 percent of community colleges and 2,500 businesses found that 95 percent of businesses that contract out training for their workers preferred using community colleges. The community college system is also interested in expanding and improving its capability to provide workforce education and customized training (McCabe 1997, pp. 30–32).

Community colleges are the primary providers of training under the workforce development system. Coordination between workforce development agencies and community colleges tends to be close, but the relationship varies a great deal. In most cases, community colleges provide much of the training in local areas. Under JTPA, however, training programs offered by community colleges tended to differ greatly from training programs offered by other providers. The latter tend to be shorter in duration and less intensive than the former. Thus, there was little outright duplication between the two (Grubb 1996, pp. 114–118).

While community colleges are the most important providers of workforce development training, this training is a small part of the business of community colleges. States and local educational institutions frequently provide more of their state workforce development funds than the workforce development agency. For example, in Texas in FY 2000, the Texas Higher Education Coordinating Board provided 40 percent of all state funds for workforce development, while the Texas Workforce Commission provided only one-sixth of the state funds. Similarly, Washington State estimated that community and vocational technical education contributed 25 percent to workforce development funding, while the WIA provided only 7 percent (O'Shea and King 2001).

In recent years there has been close coordination of policy between the U.S. Departments of Education and Labor to coordinate the 2003 reauthorization of both WIA and the Perkins Act. The goal of this effort is to accommodate "community colleges as engines for workforce development in this country [by] examining ways to enhance the community colleges' growing role in workforce development [and reconsidering federal policies that] . . . inadvertently discourage community college activity in workforce development" (D'Amico 2002, p. 22).

An evaluation of the operations in 13 workforce development areas found a wide variety of training providers (D'Amico et al. 2002). Community colleges, available in all sites, offered a wide variety of courses at low cost, a certificate or a degree, and relatively inflexible time schedules. Community college courses also tended to be longer and less suited to the needs of WIA recipients than proprietary schools. Nontraditional students from the WIA system also found it difficult to negotiate community colleges because they tend to be so large.

Proprietary schools, by contrast, are more expensive and have fewer course offerings. They tend to be smaller in size and specialize in particular areas. They may specialize in serving a particular population and use particular pedagogical methods to suit that group. However, proprietary schools tend to be more flexible and are more likely to offer open entry/open exit programs. They also tend to have shorter, more intensive courses that were judged to be more appropriate for WIA participants in many cases.

Nonprofit or community-based schools tended to specialize in providing training to economically disadvantaged workers under JTPA. Interviews of local board and one-stop center staff indicated concern that these organizations would not be successful under WIA because their economic base likely would be eroded with the provision of greater choice among training providers. Concern was particularly related to their ability to compete for the broader WIA clientele, and their financial situation, which may not let them weather the ups and downs of the flow of trainees.

Choice in using ITAs is limited by the number and variety of training vendors. This choice is related to the degree of urbanization of a local area. In 2000, there were numerous job training vendors among urban sites (number of vendors): Baltimore, Maryland (70 to 80), Macomb-St. Clair, Michigan (349), and Indianapolis, Indiana (240). By contrast, the largely rural area of Nebraska had only 100 vendors statewide. This contrast in range of choice may or may not widen as vendors move from provisional to regular eligibility status on ETP lists. In Texas, for example, the only early WIA implementation state among the 13 studied, the drop-off from provisional to regular ETP reduced the list of eligible vendors from 8,000 to 1,000. Due to the performance reporting requirements, community colleges were unwilling to participate in the system and therefore represent a large percentage of this decline. The number of vendors in Texas, however, returned to earlier numbers a year later, with aggressive recruitment of vendors who had initially dropped out of the system. For a more exhaustive description of the Texas example, refer to Chapter 5 of this book.

Screening for regular ETP status was expected to primarily affect community colleges that are concerned about the high cost of collecting reporting performance data. Those colleges view ITAs under WIA as a small share of their student body. They were also concerned that their open enrollment policies would hinder their performance reports. Proprietary schools, being smaller and more selective in their admissions, did not share these concerns.

ITAs did not have a significant effect on the prices of training, despite the increase in competition under WIA. Prices remained somewhat lower among community colleges and higher for training by proprietary schools.

JOB TRAINING IN FUTURE WORKFORCE DEVELOPMENT SYSTEMS

Previous federal workforce programs targeted particular groups facing serious barriers to employment: unskilled and economically disadvantaged adults and youth. The WIA of 1998 reflects a change in emphasis toward universal access. Specifically, the purpose of WIA is to provide for workforce investment activities designed to increase the employment, retention, earnings, and occupational skill attainment of all job seekers, regardless of their background characteristics. Congress envisioned state and local workforce investment systems seeking to improve the quality of the workforce, reduce welfare dependency, and enhance the productivity and competitiveness of the nation. This expanded role, however, was not matched with increased funding for workforce development programs authorized under WIA.

The more than 30 years of searching for ways to reduce poverty through employment policy has evolved into an approach that shifts responsibility from the government to the individual and transfers authority from the federal government to the states.

States' initial interpretation of WIA was a work-first approach, with an emphasis on achieving employment. In this framework, jobs were viewed as the best training. If a job is not available, then training was mostly customized to serve employer needs, provide on-the-job training, and offer short-term training in core skills. The latter was selected by participants using vouchers with significant frontline staff guidance.

USDOL subsequently moved away from the work-first philosophy. Learning from the gaps in the work-first approach, current WIA administrators recognize that there is insufficient funding to address the myriad of workforce development needs. Consequently, policy is designed to leverage resources at the local level and induce cooperation among programs in One-Stop Career Centers. The concept of a physical one-stop center for career development services located in each major labor market is evolving. Coordinating multiple funding streams and administrative reporting lines are remaining hurdles to clear.

For example, there is no requirement that providers of Temporary Assistance to Needy Families (TANF) services be housed in one-stop centers, but the emphasis of TANF is on independence through work and the funding has been more substantial than WIA. A future of autonomous programs is not optimal but is likely to persist at least over the short term. The political environment of labor market policy in which strategic decisions cannot be made independent of centralized planning has persisted over 30 years and will change only gradually. On the other hand, at the customer level, there has been a significant evolution from classroom training based primarily on institutional arrangements towards individual vouchers approved for job skill training in occupations with local employer demand.

Job matching that once required the intervention of a placement specialist is now often provided through self-help employment centers or Internet-connected state and national job banks accessible from any computer. Such technology supports the devolution of responsibility from federal to state and local levels. Furthermore, it helps to accommodate the funding limitations, need for continuous training for most jobs, and the dynamics of today's labor market.

Career planning once involved simply finding a well-paying job. However, the days have passed when high school graduation was quickly followed by stable and high-paid employment until retirement at a local manufacturing plant. Young people today can expect many job changes during a lifetime career process of choosing and experiencing different occupations. Earlier days saw job training emphasize manufacturing occupations such as welding or assembly. Today, training is dominated by service occupations in health care, food service, retail, and customer service.

In the 1960s, training was provided in either classrooms or on-the-job settings. Now, training often uses computer-based instructional modules that permit individually customized programs addressing either the soft or hard skills needed for jobs available locally.

To address skill deficiencies, federal workforce policy previously focused on unskilled and low-skilled workers. In recent years, this has evolved into a focus on the low and medium skilled. This part of the workforce development strategy gives equal weight to the needs of private sector employers. WIA also reflects this shift in emphasis by requiring that a majority of seats on workforce development boards be held by private sector employer representatives.

Historically, federal job training funds were allocated to programs serving specific categories of customers. Now, federal funds are used to leverage state and local funds so as to ensure universal access to all job seekers. The federal role has changed from one of centralized control to that of a technical advisor and guidance provider/performance overseer.

Some would assert that the federal government has general responsibility to promote national workforce development and a particular responsibility to help those most in need. However, federal legislation has continuously moved away from the strong federal involvement in local affairs exercised under MDTA in the 1960s. Federal policy has shifted to one which solicits active participation from local employers to help eradicate poverty through independence. This change reflects a federal view that local employers' best know their own training needs and government resources are most effective as a supplement to private human resource investments.

What follows WIA, namely WIA reauthorization, will be influenced greatly by the state of the economy. There is value to the general marketplace for services offered by one-stop centers; however, a renewed sense of mission to assist the most vulnerable members of our communities, such as at-risk youth and individuals with disabilities, is necessary. We should build upon the past to address the current issues that we face. Some of the lessons learned include recognizing the value in programs targeted toward individuals with special needs. For example, job placement assistance for some individuals with disabilities and "crisis" counseling for individuals faced with the emotions of a job loss can not be satisfied in a one-size-fits-all environment.

A career education system that serves all age groups needs to be incorporated into our educational system. Elements that have proven successful, such as mentoring, job shadowing, and teachers who take a personal interest in the future success of their students, must be emphasized. A prerequisite is the ability to identify potential problems early and ensure adequate resources for appropriate long-term training and employment assistance services.

The future is likely to witness a gradual phasing-in of some components and a refinement of others. If school systems are modified in a way that ensures no child falls behind, it should involve promoting "healthy behaviors" and commitment to community values for all students. This will also mean that both technical and workplace behavior skills are developed simultaneously, and that there is an alignment of career aspirations and educational outcomes with economic opportunities. The workforce system will need to be tied closely with formal education—kindergarten through twelfth grade and beyond. The recognition of symbiotic relationships between education, economic development, government, and the private sector are critical; in other words, good labor market information, good counseling, and a true "community" commitment.

The days of credentials and Internet-based training are just beginning. If all sectors are to be involved, then a common language of standards needs to be agreed upon. There is a need for a strong federal presence in attaining the elusive goal of common definitions, reporting, and outcome measurements. It would be a major accomplishment to have simplicity and clarity in measurements and accountability. Technical assistance provided at the federal level could further benefit the local program operator by facilitating the integration of performance measurement and results-based management.

"Training" as a share of total employment and training expenditure was never as prominent, as the titles of MDTA, CETA, and JTPA implied. Large proportions of appropriations were spent on eligibility determination, counseling and assessment, supportive services, management information systems (MIS), administration and reporting, work experience, and, in the days of CETA, public service employment. In fact, it could be argued that even some of the programs classified as training really do not meet such criteria. For example, rather than providing structured training, on-the-job-training often acts more as an inducement for employers to hire the unemployed.

Soft skills training, such as self-esteem building, grooming, and interview techniques is often an essential part of a participant's "employability plan," but these types of programs are often not viewed as skills training. Human capital development needs to focus on a continuum ranging from the unskilled to the professionals. Employers of entry-level employees expect the soft skills to be present and assume they are included in any basic training program. Employers should also know that even their highly skilled employees in technical and professional occupations require periodic training to maintain a competitive edge.

It is important to recognize the emerging new classifications of jobs, as well as the changes in necessary skills required at traditional jobs, as we look at training for jobs in technology, bio-genetics, robotics, alternative energy sources, virtual assistance, and precision farming. It is predicted that 60 percent of the new jobs will require skills possessed by only 20 percent of the young people entering the labor market unless there are changes in the way our education and training systems operate in the future. The system should be driven by good information about the job skills in demand, and it should involve flexible training methods that can accommodate worker career cycles.

Refinement of LMI, which provides individuals knowledge about the requisite skills for jobs, is critical. The dynamic nature of labor markets means that the need for LMI does not end with early exposure, but continues throughout the working life. Labor shortages should drive training, as well as vocational and technical education. Our systems will need to be agile and responsive to changes in skill shortages, skill surpluses, demographic changes, local economic conditions, and globalization. LMI will need to be timely, effective, and user-friendly.

Jobs requiring specialized skills training will increase dramatically over next decade. The standardization of credentials, particularly at the local level and supported by local businesses, will be important. Where skills based credentials have become a reality, it is the result of employers demanding it. Colleges offer a form of credentials, but the percentage of jobs requiring a college degree will remain relatively constant. It is the technical, vocational, and soft skills areas where standardization and criteria need to develop more fully.

The federal role in employment and training needs to evolve into one of providing information on "best practices," supporting pilot programs, and working toward standardizing the definitions and reporting systems for both finance and management of federal and state funded programs. Ideally, at the federal level, a simplified process would be developed and a clearing house of information would be constructed.

SUMMARY AND CONCLUSIONS

- Individual Training Accounts (ITAs): Experience to date with ITAs has largely been restricted to informed choice models. Little has been learned about how alternative approaches might work. The ITA Experiment will shed light on how free choice and directed choice models compare.

- Eligible Training Provider lists (ETPs): States have created mostly paper ETP lists that include large numbers of training providers with initial eligibility. Much work still needs to be done to automate the lists. States have resisted the next step of determining subsequent eligibility based on performance, fearing a sharp reduction in eligible providers as was experienced in the state of Texas.

- USDOL training programs are a small part of workforce development training in the United States. WIA ITA requirements relating to the ETP lists and WIA consumer reports need to be rethought, given the limited leverage WIA training programs have with training providers. USDOL probably can not successfully require the collection of data that is not required by other agencies that fund education and training programs.

- ITA recipients will have imperfect information when they make training choices, regardless of what happens to WIA consumer reports. Federal, state, and local policy makers should decide what the proper model for ITA choice is along the continuum from free choice to directed choice.

- Community colleges are the primary source of training under WIA. They are well suited to provide a wide variety of more intensive training courses to WIA participants. Community colleges have been resistant to collecting the data needed to create the WIA consumer reports, both because of their fear of the results and because of the cost and effort to collect this data. The majority of community college students prepare for matriculation to colleges and universities, while WIA performance measures emphasize job placement, employment, and earnings. The performance measurement methodology should be modified to recognize the dual role of community colleges.

- Nonprofit and community-based training providers focus on serving the disadvantaged. They also tend to be small and have limited financing. These agencies fear that they will not be able to compete with other training providers after the introduction of ITAs.

- For-profit training providers seem to have entered the WIA training market in large numbers. They seem to have the easiest time collecting WIA consumer report data and reaching the WIA outcome results.

Following the history of learning from previous policies and administrative workforce development structures, future workforce development service delivery faces challenges stemming from WIA. Future policy must confront the coordination of multiple funding streams. Policy will also have to renew the priority of one-stop centers to serve the most vulnerable populations. Furthermore, new policy must promote the integration of educational and workforce development systems. To facilitate this, a common language and set of definitions must be developed. For the evolution of existing workforce development policy to occur, new legislation must recognize the emerging new classifications of jobs as well as corresponding required job skills. As the complexity of employer skill requirements continues to increase, the publicly funded workforce development system must keep pace if it is to remain relevant in the 21st century.

Notes

This chapter reflects the opinions of the authors and does not reflect the policy or positions of either the W.E. Upjohn Institute for Employment Research or the U.S. Department of Labor.

1. The continuing education program of Montgomery College in Montgomery County, Maryland, is called Workforce Development and Continuing Education. Its June–August 2000 course catalog offers a wide variety of courses in areas such as Certification and Licensure, Computer, Professional and Workforce Development, and Technical Trades. These programs served 26,000 people in the prior year.

References

Barnow, Burt. 2000. "Vouchers for Federal Targeted Training Programs." In *Vouchers and the Provision of Public Services*, C. Eugene Steuerle, Van Doorn Ooms, George E. Peterson, and Robert D. Reischauer, eds. Washington, DC: Brookings Institution, pp. 224–250.

Barnow, Burt, and John Trutko. 1999. "Vouchers Under JTPA: Lessons Learned for Implementation of the Workforce Investment Act." Unpublished paper. Washington, DC: U.S. Department of Labor.

Carnevale, Anthony P., and Donna M. Desrochers. 1997. "The Role of Community Colleges in the New Economy." *Community College Journal* April/May: 26–33.

D'Amico, Carole. 2002. "Q&A with Carole D'Amico, Assistant Secretary of Education, Office of Vocational and Adult Education." *Community College Journal* June/July: 22–23.

D'Amico, Ronald, Deborah Kogan, Suzanne Kreutzer, Andrew Wiegand, Alberta Baker, Gardner Carrick, Carole McCarthy. 2001. *A Report on Early State and Local Progress Toward WIA Implementation: Final Interim Report.* Research and Evaluation Monograph Series 01-I. Washington, DC: U.S. Department of Labor.

D'Amico, Ronald, Alexandria Martinez, Jeffrey Salzman, Robin Wagner. 2002. *An Evaluation of the Individual Training Account/Eligible Training Provider Demonstration: Final Interim Report.* Research and Evaluation Monograph Series 02-A. Washington, DC: U.S. Department of Labor, Employment and Training Administration.

Grubb, W. Norton. 1996. *Working in the Middle: Strengthening Education and Training for the Mid-Skilled Labor Force.* San Francisco: Jossey-Bass Publishers.

McCabe, Robert H., ed. 1997. *The American Community College: Nexus for Workforce Development.* Mission Viejo, CA: League for Innovation in the Community College.

Osborne, David, and Ted Gaebler. 1992. *Reinventing Government: How the Entrepreneurial Spirit is Transforming the Public Sector.* Reading, MA: Addison-Wesley.

O'Shea, Daniel, and Christopher T. King. 2001. *The Workforce Investment Act of 1998: Restructuring Workforce Development Initiatives in States and Localities.* Rockefeller Report No. 12. Albany, NY: Rockefeller Institute of Government.

Perez-Johnson, Irma, and Paul Decker. 2001. "Customer Choice or Business as Usual? Promoting Innovation in the Design of WIA Training Program through the Individual Training Account Experiment." Unpublished paper. Princeton, NJ: Mathematica Policy Research.

Public Policy Associates. 1999. *Dislocated Worker Program Report: Career Management Account Demonstration*. Washington: DC: U.S. Department of Labor, Employment and Training Administration.

Steuerle, C. Eugene. 2000. "Common Issues for Voucher Programs." In *Vouchers and the Provision of Public Services*, C. Eugene Steuerle, Van Doorn Ooms, George E. Peterson, and Robert D. Reischauer, eds. Washington, DC: Brookings Institution, pp. 3–39.

Appendix A
Job Training Data

Jonathan A. Simonetta

This appendix provides a longitudinal overview of federally funded job training based on data compiled by the U.S. Department of Labor (USDOL). Summary data are given for historical expenditures on the four main federal job training programs that operated successively since the 1960s. In chronological order these programs are: Manpower Development Training Act (MDTA), Comprehensive Employment and Training Act (CETA), Job Training Partnership Act (JTPA), and Workforce Investment Act (WIA). Descriptive statistics on the demographic characteristics of participants in the later two programs are also provided. For these programs data was originally collected by systems for the JTPA Standardized Program Information Report (JTPA/SPIR) and the WIA Standardized Record Data (WIASRD). The JTPA/SPIR data spans program years (PYs) 1993 through 1999, and the WIASRD data provides an overview of job training activity during PY 2000 and 2001. The review of job training data is presented in five parts. The first briefly describes the data reporting system in place for the CETA program, and then summarizes the JTPA/SPIR and WIASRD data systems. The second presents a 40-year historical perspective on national funding levels for the four major federal job training programs. Part three delves deeper into the JTPA/SPIR data system, and tells the training story under JTPA for dislocated workers (Title III) and disadvantaged adults (Title II-A) from PYs 1993–1999. The fourth part of this appendix compares the JTPA/SPIR system to the WIA/WIASRD system. The final part presents the most recent training picture based on PY 2001 WIASRD data.

TRAINING PROGRAM DATA SYSTEMS

The Continuous Longitudinal Manpower Survey (CLMS) contains quarterly information for a randomly selected sample of persons who participated in CETA programs. CLMS data were compiled from CETA program records, interviews with participants, and Social Security earnings records. Participants were initially interviewed soon after CETA enrollment. Information was solicited about themselves, their families, their work experience during the previous year, and their recent level and sources of income—including whether income was received as public assistance. Up to three follow-up interviews were conducted with each participant, with questions asked about experiences in job training, other CETA programs, any other services, recent employment, and their postprogram use of public assistance.

The CLMS data files include information about program eligibility and termination, participation in employment and training and other program activities, employment or unemployment spells, wage and job search information, and labor market entry and exit decisions. In an evaluation of CETA conducted by Westat Inc., a participant sample was drawn from the CLMS and a comparison group was selected from the Current Population Survey (CPS) using characteristics matching methods. Net program impacts were then estimated controlling for differences across the two groups in observable characteristics (gender, race, educational attainment, age, years of labor market experience). USDOL has archived the CLMS and other data gathered by Westat Inc. for the evaluation of CETA program activity during the years 1975–1980.

Following the passage of JTPA in 1982, the CLMS survey was replaced. The new system was called the Job Training Longitudinal Survey (JTLS), which later became known as the Job Training Quarterly Survey (JTQS). The JTQS provided a nationally representative sample of terminees from the different categories of the JTPA program participants. The JTQS collected information on participant characteristics, program participation, and program outcomes.

Beginning in PY 1993, USDOL departed from the sample survey methodologies found in JTQS and CLMS and began to keep individual records on all program participants and their outcomes in a new system called the JTPA/SPIR. It was the major reporting system that USDOL used to obtain information about the individuals served, services provided, and outcomes obtained under Title II-A (disadvantaged adults), Title II-C (disadvantaged youth), and Title III (dislocated workers) of JTPA.[1]

The JTPA/SPIR includes one record for each person terminated from the program during the program year and the last quarter of the previous program year. In addition to individual level files, the participant data is aggregated to both the service delivery area (SDA) and state levels for each title of JTPA. The SPIR provides information about individuals across the categories of JTPA participants. The SPIR data is organized into five parts:

1) identification/characteristics of applicant,

2) characteristics of participant,

3) activity and service record,

4) program terminations and other outcomes, and

5) follow-up information.

WIASRD is the major reporting system that USDOL now uses to gather information about the individuals served, services provided, and outcomes attained under Title I-B of the Workforce Investment Act (WIA). The PY 2000 and 2001 WIASRD file contains information on individuals who exited the program during PY 2000 (July 1, 2000 – June 30, 2001) and PY 2001 (July 1, 2001 – June 30, 2002). It includes information on individuals served by local WIA funds, statewide WIA funds, or National Emergency Grants (NEGs). Individuals served only by some particular state-funded programs are not included. One record exists for each person leaving the program during a given PY. The data file is composed of following three sections:

1) individual information,

2) activity and services information record, and

3) program outcomes for adults, dislocated workers, older and younger youth.

FEDERAL JOB TRAINING EXPENDITURES IN HISTORICAL PERSPECTIVE

Table A.1 presents a summary of federal government expenditure on job training programs in the United States over the past 40 years. The expenditure figures are expressed in millions of dollars. The GDP figures are listed in billions of constant 1996 dollars. GDP is included in the summary to put the training expenditure into perspective. The unemployment rate is included as a benchmark for the condition of the labor market. It is noteworthy that the federal budget for training programs peaked in both real and money terms in 1979, a year when unemployment stood at the relatively modest level of 5.8 percent of the labor force.[2]

TRAINING UNDER THE JOB TRAINING PARTNERSHIP ACT (JTPA) PYs 1993–1999

Sample percentages for demographic characteristics of JTPA participants in Title II-A (disadvantaged adults) programs are reported in Table A.2 and values for Title III (dislocated workers) participants are reported in Table A.3. These tables are based on the SPIR data for program years 1993–1999. The tables show the shares of JTPA participants by gender and race, the type of training they received, the occupational categories of training, and the occupational categories of jobs they entered after leaving JTPA program participation. Also listed is the overall rate at which participants entered employment after leaving the program.

COMPARING JTPA AND WIA

JTPA and WIA both maintained data on program participation and service delivery through the JTPA/SPIR and WIASRD systems, respectively. Unfortunately, a direct comparison of most WIA data to JTPA data is not possible because the two systems track different performance measures, and the two programs were targeted to different groups.

WIA measures performance of all participants using administrative data while JTPA used sample surveys, with varying response rates, to track performance. JTPA focused heavily on the training of disadvantaged individuals, while WIA has offered universal accessibility of services, increased self-service, and an increased emphasis on work-first. While job training was at the heart of JTPA, under WIA it is not a real option for job-seekers in some states until after a period of self-directed job search. In general, participants and the services they receive are too different to permit direct comparison between the two programs.

The one case where a fair direct comparison of JTPA and WIA may be possible is for dislocated workers. Dislocated workers are defined identically under both JTPA and WIA. Table A.4 compares the JTPA/SPIR data from PY 1999 to the WIA/WIASRD data from PY 2000.[3]

A RECENT PICTURE OF TRAINING: WIASRD FOR PY 2001

Tables A.5 and A.6 summarize the basic demographic characteristics, types of training, occupation of training, reemployment rates, occupation of reemployment, and the credential rate for those who received training services for WIA adults and dislocated workers for PY 2001. In addition to showing job training participation rates, these tables also show rates of participation in WIA core only employment services, and combined core and intensive reemployment services.

SUMMARY

This appendix provides a brief description of the extent of federal job training funding over the past 40 years. It describes the characteristics of participants in job training for disadvantaged adults and dislocated workers under the previous Job Training Partnership Act and the current Workforce Investment Act. The summaries are based on USDOL data from SPIR and WIASRD. The tables in this appendix summarize the age, gender, and race of those who participated in training, the type of training services they received, and the degree of labor market success they enjoyed after program participation. This brief summary provides only a glimpse of the rich data maintained by USDOL on federally funded employment training programs. Some investigations that more fully exploit the data's potential are summarized by chapter authors in this volume.

Notes

1. Information on the JTPA/SPIR system, as well as the WIA/WIASRD system, was obtained from the documentation and data compiled by SPR Associates and provided under contract to USDOL.
2. USDOL has CLMS micro-data for the years 1975–1980, SPIR micro-data from 1993–1999, and WIASRD micro data from 2000–2002 available for purchase through the Employment Research Data Center at the W.E. Upjohn Institute for Employment Research (www.upjohninstitute.org/erdc/index.htm). Unfortunately, micro training data before 1975 (pre-CLMS), and between 1981 and 1992 (JTQS) have been lost. The Employment Research Data Center adds new and archived data as they become available.
3. The exiter figures are raw counts inclusive of all states. All other categories are represented as percentages. Ethnicity figures do not add up to 100% due to the exclusion of Native Americans and Pacific Islanders from the analysis (<0.1% representation). Training figures are represented as a percentage of exiters.

Table A.1 Worker Training in a Historical Perspective

Publicly funded training program	Program year	ETA[a] full-time equivalent staffing (FTE)	Annual rate of growth in real gross domestic product (%)	Unemployment rate (%)	Training budget in current dollars (millions)	Training budget in constant 1996 dollars (millions)
MDTA[b]	1963	—	4.4	5.7	70	302
MDTA	1964	—	5.8	5.2	130	554
MDTA	1965	—	6.4	4.5	396	1,685
MDTA	1966	—	6.5	3.8	399	1,637
MDTA	1967	—	2.5	3.8	390	1,550
MDTA	1968	—	4.8	3.6	398	1,526
MDTA	1969	—	3.1	3.5	407	1,494
MDTA	1970	2,725	0.2	4.9	1,451	5,055
MDTA	1971	4,283	3.4	5.9	1,516	5,021
MDTA	1972	4,052	5.3	5.6	1,682	5,314
MDTA/ CETA	1973	3,853	5.8	4.9	1,549	4,679
CETA	1974	3,520	−0.5	5.6	2,265	6,389
CETA	1975	3,432	−0.2	8.5	2,852	7,316
CETA	1976	3,240	5.3	7.7	2,916	6,977
CETA	1977	3,294	4.6	7.1	5,889	13,072
CETA	1978	3,831	5.6	6.1	3,440	7,150
CETA	1979	3,567	3.2	5.8	6,890	13,278
CETA	1980	3,185	−0.2	7.1	6,508	11,555
CETA	1981	3,247	2.5	7.6	7,245	11,734
CETA	1982	2,525	−1.9	9.7	3,023	4,583
CETA	1983	1,275	4.5	9.6	4,010	5,818
CETA/ JTPA	1984	1,251	7.2	7.5	6,546	9,155
JTPA	1985	1,158	4.1	7.2	3,774	5,112
JTPA	1986	1,815	3.5	7.0	3,337	4,449
JTPA	1987	1,811	3.4	6.2	3,685	4,754
JTPA	1988	1,762	4.1	5.5	3,805	4,751
JTPA	1989	1,852	3.5	5.3	3,831	4,605
JTPA	1990	1,753	1.9	5.6	3,983	4,615
JTPA	1991	1,755	−0.2	6.8	4,180	4,670

Publicly funded training program	Program year	ETA[a] full-time equivalent staffing (FTE)	Annual rate of growth in real gross domestic product (%)	Unemployment rate (%)	Training budget in current dollars (millions)	Training budget in constant 1996 dollars (millions)
JTPA	1992	1,730	3.3	7.5	4,029	4,398
JTPA	1993	1,662	2.7	6.9	4,423	4,709
JTPA	1994	1,680	4.0	6.1	5,013	5,221
JTPA	1995	1,520	2.5	5.6	5,455	5,560
JTPA	1996	1,380	3.7	5.4	4,140	4,140
JTPA	1997	1,335	4.5	4.9	4,719	4,640
JTPA	1998	1,378	4.2	4.5	4,982	4,837
JTPA/WIA	1999	1,388	4.5	4.2	5,729	5,490
WIA	2000	1,371	3.7	4.0	5,436	5,133
WIA	2001	1,363	0.5	4.8	5,669	5,249
WIA	2002	1,384	2.2	5.8	5,797	5,261
WIA	2003	1,385	3.1	6.0	5,574	4,960

NOTE: — = data unavailable.

[a] The Employment and Training Administration (ETA) of USDOL oversees federally funded training activities. Full-time equivalent (FTE) staffing is the total number of staff hours worked in a year divided by the hours in a usual full-time work week for one ETA staff person. FTE data are only available since 1970.

[b] MDTA = The Manpower Development and Training Act of 1962.

Table A.2 JTPA Title II-A Disadvantaged Adult Terminee Data

	1993	1994	1995	1996	1997	1998	1999
Exiters	226,011	312,480	289,734	265,281	255,324	258,451	194,199
Gender (%)							
Male	36.1	34.0	32.7	32.1	32.0	32.6	34.6
Female	63.9	66.0	67.3	67.9	68.0	67.4	65.4
Ethnicity (%)							
White	52.4	51.5	48.0	45.6	44.4	42.1	42.2
Black	31.0	31.9	33.1	34.0	34.9	35.7	36.3
Hispanic	13.0	13.0	15.2	16.5	16.5	18.0	16.4
Asian	2.2	2.2	2.3	2.4	2.4	2.5	3.0
Training service received (%)							
Basic skills	21.1	23.0	22.7	21.7	19.4	19.0	16.2
Career counseling	29.2	27.7	24.1	22.6	22.4	22.4	20.9
Skills training	56.1	58.3	60.8	62.8	64.6	63.8	62.8
OJT	14.1	13.0	11.4	11.3	10.3	9.9	9.8
Skills training categories (%)							
Managerial	1.5	1.4	1.4	1.5	1.4	1.4	1.4
Technical	15.6	15.0	17.1	16.8	16.3	16.9	18.0
Sales	2.5	2.3	2.1	2.1	2.6	2.3	2.3
Clerical	29.1	30.5	30.2	31.3	30.3	29.5	29.4
Service	20.6	21.8	20.8	20.6	20.6	20.6	19.4
Agriculture	0.7	0.6	0.9	0.6	0.6	0.7	0.7
Production	30.1	28.3	27.5	27.2	28.3	28.5	28.9
Employment categories (%)							
Managerial	1.5	1.5	1.5	1.5	1.5	1.6	1.7
Technical	12.1	12.7	12.9	13.2	13.4	13.5	13.6
Sales	6.0	6.5	6.6	6.7	7.1	7.2	7.4
Clerical	22.2	22.5	23.6	23.1	22.3	22.1	22.2
Service	25.2	25.9	25.3	24.7	23.7	23.5	23.3
Agriculture	1.1	1.1	0.9	0.9	0.9	0.8	0.8
Production	31.9	29.8	29.2	30.0	31.1	32.1	31.1

	1993	1994	1995	1996	1997	1998	1999
Entered employment rate of skills-training terminees (%)							
Received training	63.8	64.5	66.0	68.1	72.0	71.9	67.9
All others	58.1	59.3	56.6	59.9	66.4	69.2	68.2

NOTE: The JTPA exiter figures are raw counts inclusive of all states. All other categories are represented as percentages. Ethnicity figures do not add up to 100% due to the exclusion of Native Americans and Pacific Islanders from the analysis (< 0.1% representation).

Table A.3 JTPA Title III Dislocated Workers Terminee Data

	1993	1994	1995	1996	1997	1998	1999
Exiters	164,826	241,433	328,883	371,893	346,445	314,536	247,638
Gender (%)							
Male	55.2	54.7	50.2	47.4	45.9	46.2	46.5
Female	44.8	45.3	49.8	52.6	54.1	53.8	53.5
Ethnicity (%)							
White	73.5	72.2	69.9	67.7	65.0	61.9	62.1
Black	15.1	15.8	17.3	18.1	18.8	18.5	18.7
Hispanic	8.0	8.3	9.1	10.4	11.9	15.0	13.6
Asian	2.7	3.0	2.9	3.0	3.2	3.5	4.4
Training service received (%)							
Basic skills	7.1	10.1	10.1	11	11.5	11.4	6.7
Career counseling	23.3	22.2	18.8	18.3	18.0	16.6	15.4
Skills training	43.2	43.6	44.8	47.9	50.1	51.4	52.7
OJT	6.1	5.9	5.0	4.3	4.2	4.1	4.2
Skills training categories (%)							
Managerial	3.6	4.2	4.4	4.2	4.0	3.6	3.4
Technical	24.7	25.9	25.4	26.2	25.0	25.5	29.6
Sales	2.9	2.6	3.0	2.6	2.6	2.3	2.0
Clerical	24.7	23.7	24.8	27.9	27.3	27.4	28.9
Service	8.2	9.1	8.7	9.2	9.2	8.8	7.8
Agriculture	1.4	1.1	1.2	1.4	1.8	2.1	1.2
Production	34.6	33.5	32.4	28.7	30.1	30.2	27.1
Employment categories (%)							
Managerial	4.4	5.1	5.7	5.7	5.7	5.2	5.3
Technical	16.9	18.9	18.9	19.7	20.1	20.8	22.4
Sales	6.9	6.7	7.5	7.5	7.1	7.1	6.9
Clerical	20.2	19.1	20.8	22.2	22.5	22.6	22.3
Service	9.6	9.8	9.7	10.2	10.3	10.1	9.6
Agriculture	1.1	1.2	0.9	1.0	1.0	0.9	0.8
Production	40.9	39.2	36.5	33.7	33.2	33.4	32.6

	1993	1994	1995	1996	1997	1998	1999
Entered employment rate (%)							
Received training	70.2	56.9	73.0	58.8	73.2	74.7	72.7

NOTE: The exiter figures are raw counts inclusive of all states. All other categories are represented as percentages. Ethnicity figures do not add up to 100% due to the exclusion of Native Americans and Pacific Islanders from the analysis (< 0.1% representation).

Table A.4 Comparing JTPA (FY 1999) and WIA (FY 2000) Participants in Dislocated Worker and Adult Programs

Exiters	SPIR data PY 1999	WIASRD data PY 2000
Dislocated workers	247,638	87,686
Gender (%)		
Male	46.5	45.0
Female	53.5	55.0
Ethnicity (%)		
White	62.1	63.4
Black	18.7	13.4
Hispanic	13.6	17.5
Asian	4.4	4.1
Training service received (%)		
Basic skills	6.7	5.0
OJT	4.2	8.0
Occupational	52.7	47.0
Adults	194,199	108,807
Gender (%)		
Male	34.6	38.2
Female	65.4	61.8
Ethnicity (%)		
White	42.2	44.5
Black	36.3	28.1
Hispanic	16.4	20.8
Asian	3.0	2.3
Training service received (%)		
Basic skills	16.2	4.0
OJT	9.8	11.0
Occupational	63.0	41.0

NOTE: The exiter figures are raw counts inclusive of all states. All other categories are represented as percentages. Ethnicity figures do not add up to 100% due to the exclusion of Native Americans and Pacific Islanders from the analysis (< 0.1% representation). Training figures are represented as a percentage of exiters.

Table A.5 PY 2001 WIA Adults

	All	Core only	Core & intensive	Training
Exiters	172,366	36,918	59,485	75,963
Age (%)				
Under 22	11.3	13.4	9.5	11.7
22–44	67.2	64.4	64.8	70.4
45–54	15.5	16.2	18.4	13.0
55 and over	6.0	6.1	7.3	5.0
Gender (%)				
Male	42.9	45.5	43.6	41.0
Female	57.1	54.5	56.4	59.0
Ethnicity (%)				
Hispanic	20.9	16.8	24.8	19.9
White	43.6	46.9	37.2	47.1
Black	29.8	31.1	31.7	27.7
Asian	2.9	1.9	3.6	2.8
Training type (%)				
Basic skills	5.9			5.9
OJT	12.1			12.1
Occupational	86.6			86.6
ITA established	24.8			54.8
Occupation of training (%)				
Managerial & professional				26.7
Service				20.7
Production				30.6
Sales				19.9
Farming & construction				0.3
Entered employment (%)				
Quarter after program exit	72.2	73.6	69.9	73.5
Employment occupation (%)				
Managerial & professional	19.3	16.3	14.3	23.6
Service occupations	25.2	23.5	27.2	24.8
Production occupations	27.7	28.8	25.2	28.7
Sales and clerical	27.3	30.9	32.6	22.4

(continued)

Table A.5 (continued)

	All	Core only	Core & intensive	Training
Farming & construction	0.5	0.5	0.7	0.5
Entered training related job	76.8			76.8
Training credential rate (%)				
Attained credential				70.2
High school				2.4
College degree				4.7
License or certificate				52.1
Other				11.1

NOTE: The "Core only" WIA exiter number is low because most WIA core partici-pants are not registered in the WIASRD. Training counts are those exiters receiving core, intensive, and training services. All exit percentages include both program com-pleters and dropouts from the WIA program.

Table A.6 PY 2001 WIA Dislocated Workers

	All	Core only	Core & intensive	Training
Exiters	129,969	17,777	46,000	66,192
Age (%)				
Under 22	2.2	2.5	2.0	2.2
22–44	57.7	55.9	54.4	60.5
45–54	28.7	28.9	30.3	27.5
55 and over	11.4	12.6	13.3	9.8
Gender (%)				
Male	50.1	51.2	48.7	50.8
Female	49.9	48.8	59.3	49.2
Ethnicity (%)				
Hispanic	16.6	12.8	21.2	14.3
White	63.0	67.9	58.7	64.6
Black	14.7	14.0	14.0	15.3
Asian	3.8	3.2	4.1	3.7
Training type (%)				
Basic skills				6.2
OJT				7.2
Occupational				91.2
ITA established				56.2
Occupation of training (%)				
Managerial & professional				37.1
Service				8.7
Production				31.2
Sales				22.6
Farming & construction				0.3
Entered employment (%)				
Quarter after program exit	79.6	80.2	79.0	79.8
Employment occupation (%)				
Managerial & professional	26.1	22.8	25.0	27.6
Service occupations	11.4	11.7	12.8	10.3
Production occupations	33.0	34.2	30.9	34.1
Sales and clerical	29.0	30.8	30.7	27.5
Farming & construction	0.6	0.6	0.6	0.5
Entered training related job	72.9			72.9

(continued)

Table A.6 (continued)

	All	Core only	Core & intensive	Training
Training credential rate (%)				
Attained credential				71.1
High school				2.0
College degree				7.7
License or certificate				51.6
Other				

NOTE: Training counts are those receiving core, intensive, and training services. All percentages include both completers and dropouts from the WIA program.

The Authors

Burt S. Barnow is associate director for research and Principal Research Scientist at the Institute for Policy Studies at the Johns Hopkins University.

Ronald D'Amico is vice president and a senior social scientist at Social Policy Research Associates.

Paul T. Decker is the vice president for Human Services Research at Mathematica Policy Research, Inc. in Princeton, New Jersey. He is directing the Evaluation of the Individual Training Account Demonstration for the U.S. Department of Labor and the Evaluation of Teacher Preparation Methods for the U.S. Department of Education.

Janet O. Javar is a manpower analyst in the Division of Research and Demonstrations for the Employment and Training Administration, U.S. Department of Labor. She has conducted and managed research on job training and other workforce development issues.

Christopher T. King is director of the Ray Marshall Center for the Study of Human Resources and Mike Hogg Professor of Urban Policy at the University of Texas at Austin's Lyndon B. Johnson School of Public Affairs.

William L. Koch is a doctoral student in the Ph.D. program in International Economics in the Department of Economics at the University of California, Santa Cruz.

Lori G. Kletzer is a professor of economics at the University of California, Santa Cruz, and a nonresident Senior Fellow at the Institute for International Economics, Washington, DC.

Robert I. Lerman is a professor of economics at the American University. He was the Urban Institute's first senior fellow in labor and social policy, and was director of the Institute's Labor and Social Policy Center from 1995 to 2003.

Signe-Mary McKernan is a senior research associate and economist at the Urban Institute.

Christopher J. O'Leary is a senior economist at the W.E. Upjohn Institute for Employment Research.

Irma L. Perez-Johnson is a senior researcher at Mathematica Policy Research, Inc., with expertise in employment and training programs for displaced workers, welfare recipients, and other disadvantaged populations.

327

Stephanie Riegg is a Ph.D. candidate in economics at the University of California, Los Angeles. Her research interests include labor economics and education policy.

Jeffrey Salzman is a social scientist at Social Policy Research Associates.

Jonathan A. Simonetta is a manpower analyst for the Employment and Training Administration, U.S. Department of Labor.

Jeffrey A. Smith is a professor of economics at the University of Maryland.

Robert A. Straits is business and personnel manager at the W.E. Upjohn Institute for Employment Research, and director of the Employment Management Services division of the Institute.

Stephen A. Wandner is director of Research and Demonstrations for the Employment and Training Administration, U.S. Department of Labor. He has conducted and supervised research on a wide variety of labor issues. He received his Ph.D. in Economics from Indiana University.

"Job Training and Labor Exchange in the United States" Conference Attendees

David Balducchi
Employment and Training Administration, U.S. Department of Labor
Washington, DC

Burt Barnow
Institute for Policy Studies
Johns Hopkins University
Baltimore, Maryland

Timothy Bartik
W.E. Upjohn Institute for Employment Research
Kalamazoo, Michigan

John Beverly III
Office of Adult, Dislocated Workers & Trade Adjustment Assistance
U.S. Department of Labor
Washington, DC

Patty Billen
The Nelson A. Rockefeller Institute of Government
Albany, New York

Mel Brodsky
Bureau of International Labor Affairs, U.S. Department of Labor
Washington, DC

John Colborn
Ford Foundation
New York, New York

Ron D'Amico
Social Policy Research Associates
Oakland, California

Anthony Dais
U.S. Employment Service, U.S. Department of Labor
Washington, DC

Paul Decker
Mathematica Policy Research, Inc.
Princeton, New Jersey

Kelly DeRango
W.E. Upjohn Institute for Employment Research
Kalamazoo, Michigan

John Earle
W.E. Upjohn Institute for Employment Research
Kalamazoo, Michigan

Randall Eberts
W.E. Upjohn Institute for Employment Research
Kalamazoo, Michigan

George Erickcek
W.E. Upjohn Institute for Employment Research
Kalamazoo, Michigan

Pam Frugoli
Employment and Training Administration, U.S. Department of Labor
Washington, DC

Barbara Glover
Human Resources Development Canada
Hull, Quebec

David Grubb
Organisation for Economic Co-operation and Development
Suresnes, France

Kristine Heffel
W.E. Upjohn Institute for Employment Research
Kalamazoo, Michigan

Carolyn Heinrich
University of North Carolina at Chapel Hill
Chapel Hill, North Carolina

Kevin Hollenbeck
W.E. Upjohn Institute for Employment Research
Kalamazoo, Michigan

Harry Holzer
Georgetown Public Policy Institute
Washington, DC

Susan Houseman
W.E. Upjohn Institute for Employment Research
Kalamazoo, Michigan

Wei-Jang Huang
W.E. Upjohn Institute for Employment Research
Kalamazoo, Michigan

H. Allan Hunt
W.E. Upjohn Institute for Employment Research
Kalamazoo, Michigan

Louis Jacobson
Westat Inc.
Rockville, Maryland

Janet Javar
Employment and Training Administration, U.S. Department of Labor
Washington, DC

Martin Jensen
National Governors Association
Washington, DC

Grace Kilbane
U.S. Department of Labor
Washington, DC

Christopher T. King
Ray Marshall Center for the Study of Human Resources
LBJ School of Public Affairs
University of Texas at Austin
Austin, Texas

Carole Kitti
Office of Management and Budget
Washington, DC

Lori Kletzer
University of California, Santa Cruz
Santa Cruz, California

Robert Knight
National Association of Workforce Boards
Washington, DC

William Koch
University of California, Santa Cruz
Santa Cruz, California

Robert I. Lerman
The Urban Institute and American University
Washington, DC

Doug Lippoldt
Organisation for Economic Co-operation and Development
Paris France

Eva Madly
W.E. Upjohn Institute for Employment Research
Kalamazoo, Michigan

Signe-Mary McKernan
The Urban Institute
Washington, DC

Richard P. Nathan
Nelson A. Rockefeller Institute of Government
State University of New York
Albany, New York

Sigurd Nilsen
U.S. General Accounting Office
Washington, DC

Brenda Njiwaji
Michigan Department of Career Development
Detroit, Michigan

Christopher O'Leary
W.E. Upjohn Institute for Employment Research
Kalamazoo, Michigan

Dan O'Shea
Ray Marshall Center
University of Texas
Austin, Texas

John S. Palmer
Michigan Department of Career Development
Lansing, Michigan

Helen Parker
Georgia Department of Labor
Atlanta, Georgia

Alison Pasternak
U.S. Department of Labor
Washington, DC

Irma Perez-Johnson
Mathematica Policy Research, Inc.
Princeton, New Jersey

Gerard Pfann
Maastricht University, IZA, and CEPR
Maastricht, The Netherlands

Miana Plesca
University of Western Ontario
London, Ontario

Jason Preuss
W.E. Upjohn Institute for Employment Research
Kalamazoo, Michigan

Linda Richer
W.E. Upjohn Institute for Employment Research
Kalamazoo, Michigan

Neil Ridley
National Governors Association
Washington, DC

Stephanie Riegg
Urban Institute and UCLA
Beverly Hills, California

Trenda Rusher
Washtenaw County Workforce Development Board
Employment & Training & Community Service Group
Ypsilanti, Michigan

Bob Simoneau
National Association of State Workforce Agencies
Washington, DC

Jeffrey A. Smith
University of Maryland
College Park, Maryland

Ralph E. Smith
Congressional Budget Office
Washington, DC

David Smole
Congressional Research Service
Washington, DC

Robert Straits
W.E. Upjohn Institute for Employment Research
Kalamazoo, Michigan

William A. Tracy
Heldrich Center for Workforce Development
Rutgers Universit
New Brunswick, New Jersey

Lillian Visic-Petrovic
W.E. Upjohn Institute for Employment Research
Kalamazoo, Michigan

Stephen Wandner
Employment and Training Administration, U.S. Department of Labor
Washington, DC

Rich West
Social Policy Research Associates
Oakland, California

Kristin Wolff
Worksystems Inc.
Portland, Oregon

Stephen Woodbury
W.E. Upjohn Institute for Employment Research
Kalamazoo, Michigan

Jim Woods
Employment and Training Administration, U.S. Department of Labor
Washington, DC

Index

The italic letters *f*, *n*, and *t* following a page number indicate that the subject information of the heading is within a figure, note, or table, respectively, on that page.

About the Institute

The W.E. Upjohn Institute for Employment Research is a nonprofit research organization devoted to finding and promoting solutions to employment-related problems at the national, state, and local levels. It is an activity of the W.E. Upjohn Unemployment Trustee Corporation, which was established in 1932 to administer a fund set aside by the late Dr. W.E. Upjohn, founder of The Upjohn Company, to seek ways to counteract the loss of employment income during economic downturns.

The Institute is funded largely by income from the W.E. Upjohn Unemployment Trust, supplemented by outside grants, contracts, and sales of publications. Activities of the Institute comprise the following elements: 1) a research program conducted by a resident staff of professional social scientists; 2) a competitive grant program, which expands and complements the internal research program by providing financial support to researchers outside the Institute; 3) a publications program, which provides the major vehicle for disseminating the research of staff and grantees, as well as other selected works in the field; and 4) an Employment Management Services division, which manages most of the publicly funded employment and training programs in the local area.

The broad objectives of the Institute's research, grant, and publication programs are to 1) promote scholarship and experimentation on issues of public and private employment and unemployment policy, and 2) make knowledge and scholarship relevant and useful to policymakers in their pursuit of solutions to employment and unemployment problems.

Current areas of concentration for these programs include causes, consequences, and measures to alleviate unemployment; social insurance and income maintenance programs; compensation; workforce quality; work arrangements; family labor issues; labor-management relations; and regional economic development and local labor markets.